ADVANCE PRAISE FOR *FALLING FAST*

"Blending personal stories and social science research, Dr. Jones has written a compelling book about emophilia. He carefully defines the concept and the associations of emophilia with other psychological constructs and relationship outcomes. Jones showcases the challenges experienced by and offers hope for individuals navigating emophilia."

—DANA WEISER, Texas Tech University

"Have you ever developed an intense crush for someone you just met and immediately started fantasizing about what your future with this person may look like? Has this happened repeatedly in your life? Did your crushes often involve attractive, smart, and charismatic narcissists who later turned out to be toxic for you? If you check all these boxes, *Falling Fast* is a ground-breaking and eye-opening book about you and other people like you. Dan Jones explains the science behind emophilia with brilliant new ideas, compelling facts, and an engaging writing style. Emophilia is a double-edged sword: the eagerness to find and fall in love with the person of your dreams may be the quickest pathway to marital bliss or it may turn this pathway into a minefield in which your missteps will trigger repeated explosions."

—DARIO MAESTRIPIERI, University of Chicago, and author of *Macachiavellian Intelligence* and *Games Primates Play*

FALLING FAST

THE PERILS AND POSSIBILITIES OF EMOPHILIA

DANIEL N. JONES

OXFORD
UNIVERSITY PRESS

OXFORD
UNIVERSITY PRESS

Oxford University Press is a department of the University of Oxford.
It furthers the University's objective of excellence in research, scholarship,
and education by publishing worldwide. Oxford is a registered trade mark of
Oxford University Press in the UK and in certain other countries.

Published in the United States of America by Oxford University Press
198 Madison Avenue, New York, NY 10016, United States of America.

CIP data is on file at the Library of Congress.

ISBN 9780190612580

DOI: 10.1093/oso/9780190612580.001.0001

Printed by Sheridan Books, Inc., United States of America

The manufacturer's authorized representative in the EU for product safety is
Oxford University Press España S.A. of Parque Empresarial San Fernando de Henares,
Avenida de Castilla, 2 – 28830 Madrid (www.oup.es/en or product.safety@oup.com).
OUP España S.A. also acts as importer into Spain of products made by the manufacturer.

To my wife, Hedy. In our relationship, you gave me a reason to stop my emophilic ways.

CONTENTS

Acknowledgments   viii

1. Introducing Emophilia   1

2. Assessing the Speed of Love   28

3. Are We All Hopeless Romantics? Emophilia
and Cultural Norms of Falling in Love   66

4. The Heart's Wandering Eyes: Emophilia and Infidelity   84

5. Selected for Love: Evolutionary and Developmental Explanations
for Emophilia   108

6. Rose-Colored Glasses and the Emophilic Frame of Mind   124

7. The Appeal of Bad Partners   139

8. Till Death Do We Part: The Dangers of Emophilia   171

9. Emophilia as a Risk Factor for Harming Others   181

10. The Future of Emophilia Research   190

References   210
Index   220

ACKNOWLEDGMENTS

First, I would like to thank Trena White for being my agent at the time and initiating and guiding me through the early processes, I could not have done this without you. Second, I would like to thank the students of the D3cc lab—recruited at both UTEP (Adon, Jessie, Steven, Melissa, and Shelby) and UNR (Edit, Sampada, David, Li-Ling, and Sogol)—your patience with me in writing this book was amazing, especially dealing with hearing the Backstreet Boys blasting from my office. Most importantly, I would like to thank Talaya Flicop; your effort in going through the book systematically with thoughtful and critical edits made the final version far beyond what I thought it could be. I should also mention my daughter, who was not even born when this book was started. Finally, thanks to my family; both my home family (parents and siblings) and my academic family (Del Paulhus—my mentor—and all my labmates). I am lucky to have such a support system.

I

——◆◉◆——

Introducing Emophilia

- *Emophilia describes the tendency to fall in love both quickly and often. It is a stable personality trait on which we all vary*
- *Although emophilia can lead to meaningful love experiences, it is also associated with relationship impulsivity and potential harm*
- *Emophilia does not make love less real, but it changes how relationships are formed and progress*

Have you ever been in love? Such a simple question often results in different life narratives. For some, the answer is "yes," followed by "I still am." Because for some of us, we meet someone, fall in love, and that love lasts for much of our adult lives. For others, the answer may still be yes, but it was in the past and perhaps that lost love is still a source of pain or regret. Still, for others, the answer may still be yes, but twice. Finally, for others, it may be three, four, five times . . . or more. Falling in love repeatedly does happen, and many often believe that people who do so cannot hold down a successful relationship, have mental health issues, or come from a broken family. Many believe that falling in love has to do with who you meet and when. After all, love is about the chemistry between two people. However, as I will argue throughout this book, who you meet and when is only part of the story. The other half deals with an individual difference I call *emophilia.*

Emophilia is an individual difference trait that is defined by how fast and frequently we fall in love. Like many individual differences, it varies naturally in the population and ranges from extremely low to extremely high, with most people falling somewhere in the middle. As I will argue, all people have a threshold that must be reached for the mind to recognize the feeling of love. For some, this threshold is quite low and can be met overnight if the circumstances and potential partner were ideal. For others, this threshold is quite high and may require years (if ever) to be met, even if everything is ideal. Regardless, for all of us, to feel and acknowledge that we are in love, a certain level of emotions must be met, and that level varies across the population.

Although this book often focuses on the higher end of emophilia to demonstrate how critical it is for life outcomes and relationships, it is important to note that there are desirable and undesirable outcomes that can occur at all levels. Not having the capacity to fall in love may lead to less fulfillment and lowered life satisfaction. Similarly, having a high threshold for falling in love means that you may run the risk of falling in love once and never again. In such situations, if that one relationship does not work out, the separation can be more than someone can bear. However, falling in love fast and frequently brings unique trade-offs. Although moving past an ended relationship may be far easier, maintaining a current relationship may be more difficult. Similarly, because people who fall in love fast and frequently feel love much sooner, they see them through a lens of love before they really take the time to screen them as a potential partner. Thus, red flags may be ignored and premature commitments may emerge, leaving the person at risk for harmful outcomes.

Many believe that love is sacred. It may very well be. However, I argue that defining love as something that must last forever, or it is not real, is too narrow of a definition. Robert Sternberg (1986) argued that there were different aspects of love (i.e., intimacy, passion, commitment) that can come together to create "consummate" love. However, all three of these components can emerge rapidly or slowly, depending on the individual and the situation. Thus, love that emerges overnight can be very real and have a very real impact on someone, their life, and their happiness. In fact, there are many examples in popular media that illustrate this point. For example, in the film *Good Will Hunting*, a psychologist-professor discusses how he abandoned his chance to attend baseball's World Series because he saw a woman that "lit up the room." In *City of Angels*, an angel falls from heaven to be with a doctor he met while she was trying to save a patient, knowing very little about her. Though engaging, the trouble with narratives like these is very much the same as with playing the lottery: there are an unimaginable number of misses for every one hit. Thus, for every connection made, many others were merely fleeting fancies or whimsical ideas. Later on down the road, we tend to misremember or minimize the frequency of ephemeral connections and focus on the ones that survived. Although we may not realize it, the truth is that these fleeting moments—times when some of us profess our love within the first week of dating or immediately wonder if we've met the one—can teach us a great deal about emophilia.

Emophilia (formerly referred to as *emotional promiscuity*) describes the tendency to fall in love fast, easily, and often. The term "emotional promiscuity" was not meant to be pejorative, just descriptive. However, the term "promiscuity" carries with it a negative connotation. Thus, my colleague, Dana Weiser, came up with "emophilia" as a better term for the construct. Throughout this book, I will introduce you to this new concept that describes how individuals differ in their tendencies to fall in love fast, easily, and often. It is important to note that emophilia is scored on a spectrum. We all have some of it in us, and people range from very low to very high. To date, there is no diagnostic cutoff. Further, when I refer to "emophilic" individuals or behavior, this is meant as shorthand for "those who are high in emophilia." Emophilia is a trait that we all possess, some more than others. So, in this book when I refer to emophilia and emophilic people, I mean those who are high on the continuum of this trait, unless otherwise noted.

Although many think about love in terms of long-term relationships and lasting commitments, the experience of love, falling in love, and the amount of time it takes to do so differs for many people. Those who are lower in emophilia (i.e., emophilic) tend to fall in love only after years and years of friendship, courtship, and shared experiences, while those who are more emophilic seem to fall in love overnight.

Putting aside the notorious difficulties in defining something as subjective as falling in love, my students, collaborators, and I have studied the differences among individuals in reporting when they feel that they fell in love and how many different people they have fallen in love with. We ask these things to study emophilia in a nonjudgmental manner—after all, neither process of love is superior to the other; they are simply different. In doing this, we have found that someone's willingness to engage in a host of signature behaviors that we can study alongside this idea of "love" provides us with confidence that we are on the right track with our research. These behaviors include vulnerability with a partner, openness to a future together, eagerness to trust, degrees of intimacy, and comfort acknowledging the feeling of love.

For those who fall in love, and not all of us will, we have a moment or a feeling inside that alerts us to the fact that we are indeed in love. For some that feeling comes very quickly, and for others it comes much more slowly. Like any individual difference tendency, there are inherent trade-offs to emophilia. On the one hand, those who are overly guarded with their romantic emotions may rarely (if ever) feel those intimate connections of love in the first place. Thus, if someone is too low in emophilia, they may never experience the rush and pleasure associated with love. However, on the other hand, if someone is too high in emophilia, they may run the risk of problems associated with falling in love over and over. Indeed, love is a wonderful force that can bring out the best in us. It drives us to care for others and teaches us sacrifice and commitment. Love gives us the ability to fantasize about where we will go and what lies ahead.

However, falling in love too quickly can turn a romance novel into a horror film. Individuals who fall in love quickly run the risk of not knowing a person as well as they "feel" they do. This tendency puts a person at risk for exploitation and potential harm (both physical and psychological). Consider the case of the "Tinder Swindler," who went by the pseudo-name: Simon Leviev. He used love and affection to fuel a multimillion-dollar Ponzi scheme. Finding women on Tinder, Simon would flash a lavish lifestyle and a "too good to be true" façade to women. Using carefully crafted manipulation, he would feign affection and a deep commitment in the ultimate service of his selfish goal: extorting money. Individuals who are susceptible to falling in love easily may be at the highest risk for this type of scam. This risk is not because there is anything wrong with those who fall victim to such scams; instead, it is because of the strong emotions they feel upon first connecting, which can be recognized and exploited by manipulative others.

Chrissy and Rick

A year after I moved to Vancouver, I met a woman named Chrissy on a popular dating website. Chrissy was a hairdresser at a salon and was extremely friendly. Although it did not work out between the two of us romantically, Chrissy became a good friend. After only three "chat sessions," she told me, "I feel you were meant to play a big role in my life." Although that felt good to hear, I was alarmed how fast she was falling for a guy she had never met.

Soon after, Chrissy met Rick through the same dating website. Rick worked in a chemistry laboratory at a nearby university. Though Chrissy's friends described her as someone who was shy around strangers, she came out of her shell when meeting new people virtually, meaning Chrissy was very comfortable chatting with Rick online for about four hours before they finally decided to meet. Even before he knocked on the door of her apartment, Chrissy was already fantasizing about the life she might lead with Rick. When he arrived with candy and flowers, Chrissy felt like he was a dream come true. He epitomized everything she had ever wanted, right down to the color of his eyes. Chrissy's affection for traditional courting was lost on other men, but not Rick. She melted at first glance.

Rick and Chrissy never got around to watching the movie they had planned to see. They talked over dinner, coffee, and then wine. Chrissy felt like she had known Rick her whole life. When he leaned over to kiss her, she leaned forward as though the scene had been scripted. They spent the rest of the night in each other's arms discussing what their future would look like.

After four days, Rick and Chrissy were calling each other "boyfriend/girlfriend," and after one week, they moved in together. Many of Chrissy's friends expressed to me that they were concerned about this swift progression. They told me that Chrissy became angry when they brought it up, attributing these concerns to jealousy. Her friends also told me that she began isolating herself. Her free time was devoted to talking to Rick, thinking about Rick, and spending time with Rick. When she did get a moment to call or see a friend, the interaction usually consisted of talking about Rick.

Their relationship was blissful for the first few months. After a while, though, they ran out of things to talk about. In fact, between Chrissy's and Rick's work schedules, little time was left for each other, and the old spark seemed to dim. Soon, she could not remember the last time they held each other and talked or spent all night sharing their dreams. When Chrissy thought about it, Rick seemed to be the last thing on her mind most of the time.

But then, one day, things got interesting again when Chrissy met Jason, a handsome young attorney who lived upstairs from her. When Rick had to work late, as he often did, Chrissy found herself fantasizing about what life would be like with Jason. All her problems with Rick would just disappear, and life would be blissful with Jason.

Situations like the one with Chrissy are more common than we may realize. Emophilia tends to create cycles where friends and family may say, "We heard this before with that other person." Although emophilic people realize that the pattern is repeating, they do believe in earnest that this time will be different.

Emophilia Is Not Good or Bad, but It Does Change Things

Consider the effect of romantic love on trust, biased thinking, vulnerability, and (at times) irrational behaviors. If someone you were in love with developed a drug addiction, you are more likely to report standing by that person than if you did not love them. For most of us, however, we would not dive into a relationship with someone knowing this ahead of time. Instead, we might approach the situation more cautiously. However, individuals high in emophilia often fall in love with a person before truly knowing important things about them. Thus, biased processing takes over too soon, and they tend to dive into a relationship with someone while ignoring potentially serious warning signs. Because they are prone to feeling and responding to the rush of emotional connection, people high in emophilia are also more attracted to personality types that are effective at short-term charm. Further, they engage in biased thinking and irrational decision-making earlier in a relationship than those with lower levels of emophilia. These tendencies lead them to trust partners at much earlier stages of the courtship process before some of their partner's charm has worn off. Further, the rush they feel when they are falling in love reinforces their biases and irrational decisions.

The speed and frequency at which we fall in love is neither a good thing nor a bad thing on its own, but increased speed and frequency of love can come with consequences. Love is beautiful, as anyone who has experienced it will tell you. For thousands of years, humans have ruminated on and celebrated the experience of love. It is one of the greatest gifts to humanity. Most of us will fall in love, perhaps even a couple of times. However, the unguarded may find themselves, under certain circumstances, feeling the temptation to emotionally bond with someone outside of a primary relationship. Thus, because emophilia leads to developing emotions for someone that we have known for a shorter period, that someone could be outside of a relationship as well.

Differences in emophilia can affect not only how individuals initiate relationships but how they react to relationship dissolution. We have all known that someone who just cannot manage to stay single. Well, there are several reasons for this phenomenon. The individual may fear being alone or struggle with anxious attachment. However, another explanation is that the person is high in emophilia and finds themselves rushing into the arms of a new love. Thus, following relationship dissolution, someone high in emophilia may find themselves falling in love faster with someone new because they are no longer committed to someone, and a new relationship holds excitement. In contrast, someone who is low in emophilia may take *even longer* to fall in love again, which can come with its own burdens, including increased loneliness. Thus, there are some personal circumstances that affect how high vs. low emophilic individuals behave. Further, one's environment may also play a critical role in how fast and often someone may fall in love in different situations. These things are natural. In fact, this point is key to truly understanding emophilia.

Emophilia and Mental Health

In the early days of my examining emophilia, many people said to me that it was just "borderline personality" or "anxious attachment." Although I will discuss these alternative constructs later, I want to say a quick word about this now. Emophilia is not a pathology. Colloquially, I have heard some refer to this type of behavior as "daddy issues." Emophilia is not a mental disturbance, manic depression, or insecurity. Nor is emophilia the result of physical, emotional, mental, or sexual abuse. Further, emophilia varies among all genders, sexualities, and cultures I have surveyed. So, this is not some isolated phenomenon idiosyncratic to a particular demographic or descriptive of people who are "damaged." Thus, I assert that emophilic people are not "crazy"— and really, we should do away with that word when it comes to mental health, anyway. Although, there are some diagnosable mental disorders (e.g., borderline personality disorder) or abusive/traumatic experiences (e.g., rape; incest) that can create behaviors that *look* like emophilia. In fact, they may even create identical-looking behaviors (e.g., moving in with someone days after meeting at a bar; running away to a new city with someone after meeting for one night), but the difference is that emophilia is not caused by these traumatic events or mental imbalances. It is simply an individual difference variable that we all possess to a greater or lesser extent. Thus, one's level of emophilia (which we will refer to as an "EP score," short for EmoPhilia) does not predict any severe psychopathology.

Although emophilia itself is not psychopathology, some of the choices emophilic individuals make may indeed cause harm or trauma because they are emotionally exposing themselves to a wider variety of romantic partners. Further, they may harm others because of their romantic impulses, although such harm is often unintentional. In sum, emophilia itself is not something from which a person derives suffering, and I do not consider emophilia to be a pejorative term or a harmful trait.

Emophilia Is an Individual Difference

Notwithstanding, just as it is with any individual difference that is stable over time—extremes in either direction can lead to problems.

For example, extreme extraverts have trouble with sensation seeking, meaning that they often take too many risks. They are uncomfortable with being alone for any period and have difficulties stemming from hyperactive, reward-seeking behavior. On the other side of the spectrum, extreme introverts have issues with interpersonal relationships, feel uncomfortable in social situations (especially new situations), and have a hard time engaging with others. Similarly, individuals who are extremely agreeable often fail to be assertive. They might get taken advantage of because they do not want to rock the boat. However, individuals who are extremely disagreeable frequently get into fights and disagreements. They are also prone to betraying the trust of others, which can lead to reputational concerns down the line.

The Nature of Emophilia

Love at first sight is a popular idea (Sprecher & Metts, 1989). Individuals high in romantic beliefs often fantasize about a chance encounter with a stranger that turns into a lifelong romance. Indeed, we find that art, movies, and music reflect such ruminations. However, when these fantasies are acted out repeatedly, they no longer reflect mere romantic beliefs, they reflect emophilia. Emophilic individuals often engage in what is called "hindsight bias." Hindsight bias is a process that leaves individuals believing that they "knew it all along" when it comes to an important phenomenon. For those high in emophilia, reflecting on what they know *right now* about their partner biases how they feel about the past and biases how they think they will feel in the future. In other words, emophilic individuals in love often assume that they "knew it all along" and that they loved their partner from the start. At the very least, most report that they knew "something was special" about this person from the moment they met. Although it is a romantic notion, it is often inaccurate. Instead, the individual's current knowledge and feelings are likely biasing retrospective memories of past knowledge and feelings.

An example comes from one of my good friends in El Paso. He told me that the night he met his wife, he said to one of his buddies, "I think I met the woman I am going to marry." Indeed, he introduced himself, asked her to dance, and the rest (as they say) is history, and they have been married over 15 years. However, I should have asked him if he ever previously reported that to his friends about other women with whom it did not work out. Thus, I do not rule out that there are cases of what we might call "love at first sight." However, if this process repeats, and there are many failures along the way or numerous relationships that occur, then it is probably a case of serial romance or emophilia.

Cognitive Biases and Emophilia

Because emophilia lends itself to hindsight bias, it can alter perceptions of budding relationships, even vicariously. The columnist Dan Savage once noted in his writings that individuals who engage in romantic hindsight bias really do a disservice to people who are in the early stages of a relationship. This disservice stems from the fact that people who are in the beginning stages of courtship may say to themselves, "Well, gee, I'm just not sure, this must not be *the* one." The people who are on the fence feel like they are "wasting" their time because they aren't feeling butterflies immediately. However, the truth is that the people who say they knew it all along probably did not either.

The perceived pressure to judge a relationship right away based on a rush of emotions may encourage those who are emophilic to rely too heavily on those emotions and abandon self-reflection. They may also engage in reckless behaviors in the name of romantic love, behaviors they may not engage in normally. Similarly, emophilic individuals may try to *convince themselves* that they feel things they might not feel or prioritize those relationships where they feel a "rush" of excitement. However, first impressions are often misleading, and those who are most charming and engaging during first encounters are often toxic for long-term relationships. Thus, people who feel that they should "dive in" if they are feeling the arousal of love may be doing so into the "shallow" end of the pool. In sum, hearing from others that you will "know" when you meet the right person may negatively influence others, especially those high in emophilia.

That said, it is not my intention to have the term "emophilia" used as a weapon against people. It is simply a descriptive term to help articulate a phenomenon in which I have been interested. I would hate to hear that term used to tear someone down or criticize a person or group of people. It is meant to help us describe a certain disposition toward relationships and love. In fact, as I will show throughout the book, emophilia has positive and negative aspects to it, and most people fall somewhere in the happy middle.

Emophilia Is Not Just "Love at First Sight"

But what if someone really did fall in love at first sight? Is that emophilia? If it happened just once, then the answer is likely no. As we will discuss later in the book, emophilia requires *two* fundamental components: *speed* and *frequency*. Naturally, these two things go together—the faster you do something (generally speaking), the more often you will do it. Further, the more often you do something, the faster you generally do it. However, in defining emophilia, you cannot have one without the other. Emophilia is not just "falling hard" for someone. Although the rush of love and excitement comes sooner and more frequently to those high in emophilia, the strength of the actual love is likely similar to other people's experiences of love. It is just that less emophilic individuals take more time to reach that level of rush and excitement. One way to think of it is how two cars reach a speed of 100 miles per hour. A Lamborghini, for example, will reach that speed much faster and more often (if law and traffic permit). A fuel-efficient economy sedan, such as a Prius, can also reach 100 miles per hour. But it will take a longer stretch of road, require flat or downhill roads, and more time.

For example, someone could have fallen in love five times in their life, but the love for each romantic partner took 10 years to develop. Conversely, someone may fall in love overnight and find that the love they feel lasts a lifetime. Thus, those who fall in love overnight, but stay in love until death, are not emophilic. They fell in love fast, fell in love hard, but not frequently. Further, emophilia is not the same as polyamory. Individuals who are polyamorous do indeed fall in love with more than one person at the same time. Although it is possible to be both polyamorous and emophilic, they are not the same thing. For example, polyamorous individuals may fall in love with two people and maintain a relationship with both. However, if those two people are the only two people with whom they ever fell in love, or the love they felt took years to develop, then that would not be aligned with emophilia.

I recall one story my friend told me of a man who was driving his car on I-10 in Tucson, Arizona. He passed a woman he thought was incredibly attractive. He scribbled his name and number on a scrap of paper he had somewhere in his car, crumpled it up, and threw it into her car through an open window. Sure enough, a relationship ensued. Note that I do not recommend this approach to dating. It is not a particularly "safe" way to meet people (I imagine highway patrol would agree with me). Not to mention how scary that might be for some women thinking they have a highway stalker. However, it nevertheless resulted in a marriage. From what I heard, that couple has been married over 12 years.

Emophilia Is "Real" Love, It Just Happens Faster

Despite these important links and behavioral outcomes, emophilia remains an understudied topic in the field of relationship research. Yet, the experience of love, or the time that it takes to feel "in love," does indeed vary from person to person. Sexual intimacy is a parallel I use when discussing emophilia. Although some people are ready to share physical intimacy with attractive others right away, other people require more time. I argue the same is true of love. The difference is that we are not talking about physical intimacy; we are talking about emotional intimacy.

To describe what I am talking about with emotional intimacy, I will turn to my favorite movie of all time: *Chasing Amy* (written and directed by Kevin Smith). At one point in the film, the two main characters are having a conversation about virginity. The character Holden takes a more traditional or "standard" definition of virginity, arguing that virginity is lost through "penetration." Alyssa, a self-described "experimental girl" responds by asking, "Physical penetration or emotional?" Holden is confused by what is meant by "emotional penetration." She goes on to describe how she fell in love "hard" with one of her friends in high school. Holden then retorts quickly, "*Physical* penetration." Although the conversation moves on from that topic, it does raise an interesting point. Most would not define virginity loss through "emotional penetration."

Although it is an interesting question to consider what happens when you fall in love for the first time and whether that experience is unique, a more central question is what happens when the process is repeated. Stephanie Madsen and W. Andrew Collins (2011) assessed the frequency and quality of relationship involvement of a sample of adolescents ages 15–17.5. They then tracked these individuals into their 20s. They found that participants who dated more people in mid-adolescence, as well as those who lacked quality in their romantic relationships, tended to have difficulties with negative affect and communication in their later relationships. Thus, falling in love or frequently being "emotionally penetrated" may be a helpful way to look at love when we discuss what it means to be high in emophilia. In particular, the difference between sexual and emotional penetration is helpful in a few important ways.

Emotional penetration may include (a) entertaining (rather than resisting) feelings of romance or infatuation with a person we just met; (b) unguardedly sharing secrets, hopes, dreams, wishes, or fantasies, with someone; and (c) defining oneself through the relationship we have with another person (Aron et al., 1991). Thus, those who are emophilic will embrace emotional penetration quickly. Further, they are more likely to interpret intimate feelings as love. Consequently, individuals high in emophilia are likely to cognitively restructure their world such that they can easily imagine a "new life" with their exciting novel partner. Although feeling excited about a new partner is not synonymous with emophilia, those high in emophilia tend to experience these types of thoughts and emotions often. Further, and importantly, those high in emophilia embrace these exciting thoughts and emotions and base future actions on them.

Psychologist Lisa Diamond (2004) has noted that love and sex are distinct processes that occupy different parts of our brains. Diamond has also noted that emotions like love can evolve in same-sex platonic relationships, such as among heterosexual friends. This evolution of love-like emotions means love can dwell where sex may not be considered. It also creates the possibility that people high in emophilia feel connections to exciting, but nonromantic, relationships more frequently and rapidly as well. Although there is substantially less research on this topic, it is a definite possibility. Because emophilia was designed as a construct to address variations in the frequency and speed of falling in romantic love, future research should explore the speed and frequency of friendship formation.

Most people will draw a parallel between physical desire and emotional intimacy. Someone can feel high levels of sexual arousal for another person but refuse to engage in physical intimacy with them. For example, they may feel too timid or experience fears over possible rejection. They may also feel anxious or feel that sex is sacred and time is needed before it should be shared. Thus, embracing the desire for physical intimacy and acting on it is key.

Cindy Meston and colleagues (1998) have long noted that a high sex drive, or the desire for frequent sex or masturbation, is not synonymous with permissive sexual attitudes or behaviors. Individuals may crave sex all the time or little to none, with one partner (or oneself) or with different partners—desire and number of partners vary separately. Think of it this way: Lindsey is in a committed relationship and has sex or masturbates one to two times per day. She would be considered high in sex drive. However, Michael only has sex twice per month, but every time he has sex, it is with a different partner. Further, there are some who love the sex they have and find it extremely fulfilling, while others may find the sex that they have acceptable, simply having it when they feel the desire. Thus, sexual passion has less bearing than you might think on how fast and often individuals are comfortable having sex with new partners. The same is true of emophilia. Data on over 300 university students from Canada show that emophilia has a stronger correlation with sex *drive* than it does with sexual *behavior*. In fact, once we consider the overlap between sex drive and emophilia, emophilia is no longer related to number of sexual partners. Thus, feeling sexual desire and emophilia are more strongly related to each other than are emophilia and acting on those sexual impulses. In sum, whether the decision is made consciously, unconsciously, or a combination of both, falling in love is still an action that inspires certain behaviors, even if people perceive it to be involuntary.

As we will discuss below, love has some specific biomarkers. For example, it is common for someone's pupils to dilate when they see someone they love. Thus, many people undergo a series of reactions when they start to have romantic feelings for someone. They may experience physiological reactions, such as increased heart rate, sweaty palms, and nervousness when thinking about or being around a particular individual. They may also experience social-cognitive reactions, such as rumination about the person, enjoying spontaneous thoughts about them, or idealizing a life with that person. Finally, there are also specific neurological patterns that emerge when they fall in love.

Sexual vs. Romantic Motives and Power Dynamics

It is almost as though our culture has accepted that sex is something that can be transient or ephemeral, but love *must* be enduring. The truth is that both can be ephemeral, albeit for different reasons. For example, at most colleges and universities it is considered sexual harassment (and rightfully so) when a professor engages in a sexual relationship with a student. In fact, it is generally frowned upon when a professor engages in a sexual relationship with a student, even when that student is not under direct supervision of the professor. Researchers have found that men teaching at colleges and universities are significantly more likely to be divorced than are women or men who teach younger ages (Kanazawa & Still, 2000). Following from Kendrick's evolutionary theory on contrast and exposure, Kanazawa and Still (2000) argue that being consistently surrounded by young women compromises marital satisfaction for some.

Although these desires are seen as inappropriate despite their evolutionary origins, there may be fewer societal sanctions when a professor actually falls in love with a student, especially if the two eventually get married. Throughout my career, I personally knew of several cases when professors divorced their wives and married their graduate student. None of these professors received any censure. When their faculty mates were questioned, most indicated a sentiment of: "It was fate, who are we to stand in the way of love?" Although the power differential is inescapable, it is important to note that within a consensual relationship involving love and commitment, the dynamics of consent and exchange are likely to be less toxic in most cases. Thus, much of the negative outcome would depend on whether this process was repeated.

Although gender likely plays a part in how harshly someone is judged for marrying students, love seems to be universally tolerated more than sex. Yet, the blurring of professional boundaries and psychological impact it has, both professionally and personally, may be just as profound, if not more so, than merely a sexual relationship. Even so, we believe that because it is "love" it is somehow "OK," even if it is a repeat occurrence. For an emophilic professor (for example) who repeatedly falls in love with students, the damaging outcomes may be like that of repeated sexual encounters (perhaps worse, in some cases). Nevertheless, looking at students as potential mates may be something that some emophilic professors would do, whereas other emophilic professors may simply not entertain the possibility. Whether it be for love, sex, or both, there is still a power dynamic, and love may not mean damage and harassment did not take place.

Perhaps one of the key misunderstandings about love comes from our limited understanding of its nature, and how different people come to define it. Love implies an enduring bond. Words like, "forever," "eternal," "sacred," "special," and "lasting" tend to be associated with the notion of romantic love. Even a diamond, a common symbol of one's commitment and love for another, is a *lasting* and durable rock that is incredibly dense and seemingly eternal. However, love is different for different people and can last different lengths of time. Further complicating matters is that, for some, the definition of love may evolve over time. What we may have emphatically and insistently referred to as love at 15 years of age may be scoffed at by our adult self. Regardless of how ardently we believed we were in love then, we may have refined our definition now. For example, the high school classmate who gave us butterflies when they visited our locker, our first kiss, and other such experiences may be defined as love in that moment. But, as adults, we often refine our definition as we learn more about what it means to romantically love. As we grow, get hurt, and learn, we refine our definitions of what we really mean by love. Thus, the parameters and necessary characteristics of love change through life experience, and ultimately, those experiences change what we mean when we say, "love."

How Do I Know if I Am Actually in Love?

So how do we know that we *are* in love? Is there some neurochemical path that we can track? Some telltale markers we can refer to? Behaviors exclusive to love? Most likely, no—or at least, not yet. As it stands, we must let individuals define love for themselves. More than a few people have heard the phrase, "I love you; I am just not *in love* with you." What does that even mean? Well, to delve a little deeper, we may say that the person genuinely cares for, is concerned about, and feels connected with someone, but they do not want the emotional penetration or monogamy that comes with romantic love.

When it comes to defining love, knowing you are in love, and what the very nature of love may be, there are many more questions than there ever will be answers. To quote one of my favorite movies, *The Matrix*: "Being the one is just like being in love. No one needs to tell you, you are in love, you just know it, through and through." I believe the fictional character of the Oracle from the Wachowski sisters (formerly the Wachowski brothers) sci-fi masterpiece is a decent place to start. So, we will proceed on the premise that no one can tell you that you are in love or not in love. Love is a subjective experience. A 15-year-old who insists they are *in love* and feels such powerful feelings should be taken seriously. Maybe, as older adults, we know better (or think we do) because we have lived longer and had similar experiences—experiences we grew out of later.

But, nevertheless, to the 15-year-old, the love is real, the feelings are real, the connection is real, and (should the relationship end) the pain is real. Lisa Diamond has argued that *"romantic love* typically denotes the powerful feelings of emotional infatuation and attachment between intimate partners" (Diamond, 2004, p. 116). Although this definition is somewhat ambiguous, it is also a good starting point when looking for a scientific definition. There are concepts related to love, such as *passion* (e.g., Tennov, 1979) and *companionship* (Hatfield & Sprecher, 1986). There is also what is referred to as "limerence" that describes short-term or fleeting (i.e., immature) types of love. Further, there are combinations of these concepts that may be present (or absent) in a relationship. For example, one may feel a tremendous amount of passion for someone but not a tremendous amount of commitment, or vice versa. Alternatively, both may be present, but intimacy may be lacking. Thus, there are multiple components of love that may or may not be present when someone says, "I'm in love" (e.g., Fisher, 1998; Sternberg, 1986).

It is prudent at this point to pause and be clear, then, what we mean by falling in "love" frequently and often. What we do *not* mean, when we discuss emophilia, is some alternative form of love. Limerence, "crushes," "puppy love," or "infatuation" do not explain the phenomenon of emophilia. Individuals high in emophilia experience the same subjective experience as others,[1] they just experience it faster and more frequently. Thus, the actual phenomenon of love does not seem different for those high in emophilia.

Now, it is worth noting that different forms of love for different people (as discussed above) may also vary across emophilic individuals. So, an emophilic person may report feeling only passion or commitment, or some combination of these aspects, much how a low emophilia person might. Thus, it is *not* the case that an emophilic person is some unique combination or unique experience of love. Instead, I argue that high emophilia individuals feel the same phenomenon with the same sincerity as others.

Love may also be defined through its enduring and evolving nature in the human mind. For example, in 1967, William Kephart argued that true love is best defined as those relationships we have had that we *reflect* upon and indeed acknowledge as being or having been in *love*. In other words, some individuals "delete" or "edit" their list of past loves. For example, "well, I was young, I didn't know what I was doing" may be a typical explanation for what was called love but was later redefined as non-love.

---

[1] I have surveyed individuals who claim that they are in love, and the words they use to describe their love, the emotions they report having, the commitment to the partner they report having, the resolve to make the relationship work, and the overall connection and all the concepts of love seem to be there.

Whatever we call it, however we define it, *love* varies across people. The definitions and necessary conditions vary, too. Given that individuals develop emotional connections, attractions, and bonds at different speeds and across different situations differently, it really is not that absurd of an idea that love may be lasting or ephemeral and, regardless of either, may be sincere.

Does Real Love Have to Last?

In fact, research on sexuality seems to embrace the notion that individual sexual attraction may be lasting or ephemeral, so why is the same not true for love? Research on frequent sexual encounters has been conducted from perspectives based on personality (e.g., Eysenck, 1976), orientation (Simpson & Gangestad, 1991), and attitudes (Hendrick & Hendrick, 1986). Hans Eysenck, for example, found that there were two fundamental personality traits that led to frequent sexual encounters with different people: extraversion and psychoticism (psychoticism's definition is similar to that of psychopathy). Whereas the former trait is associated with social visibility, charm, and social skills, the latter is associated with manipulation, deception, and coercion. Nevertheless, both types of individuals end up having many sexual partners. From the attitude perspective, Susan Hendrick and Clyde Hendrick (1986) were among the first to demonstrate that people differed in their attitudes toward casual sex. Some believe casual sex is acceptable and would personally engage in it, whereas others believe it is not acceptable and avoid it.

In 1991, Jeffrey Simpson and Steve Gangestad developed the Sociosexual Orientation Inventory to assess sexual disposition, or the tendencies to feel comfortable with, fantasize about, crave, and engage in casual sex with multiple partners. Those scoring high on this inventory are referred to as "sociosexually unrestricted." Through the studies conducted with this inventory, and revisions of it, we have discovered that individuals with restricted sociosexuality are less comfortable with casual sex, need to get to know someone more before feeling comfortable having sex, and prefer long-term commitment over short-term sexual encounters. More recently, sociosexuality has been broken into three distinct subcategories, or "facets"—together these three aspects capture sociosexuality: fantasy, attitudes, and behaviors (Penke & Asendorpf, 2008). One can be restricted or unrestricted in any of these areas, but when someone scores low on one facet (e.g., attitudes) they tend to score low on the others (e.g., fantasies). Fantasies have to do with how often someone craves or thinks about sexual interactions with strangers. So, you would not be sociosexually unrestricted in your fantasies if you fantasized about sex with your wife every day. The second facet is attitudes. Individuals with unrestricted attitudes believe that sex without a commitment is OK and that they would not particularly need to know someone well to have sex with an attractive person. Finally, the last facet involves sociosexual behaviors. In this case, someone with unrestricted sociosexual behaviors would actually be having multiple sexual partners in a given year, having sex without commitment, and having frequent "one-night stands."

In general, "unrestricted sociosexuality" is a term used to describe comfort with and frequency with which one wants casual sex. I will also describe the research on sociosexuality (i.e., "sexual permissiveness") to provide a parallel to emophilia. Further, I will demonstrate that emophilia is distinct from more well-known psychological orientations toward romantic relationships, such as insecure attachment (in particular, anxious attachment).

Emophilia, a trait found in ordinary people, may start to unravel some of the questions about emotional infidelity that have barely started to be asked, let alone answered. However, like any psychological trait, there are always trade-offs with respect to life outcome benefits and downsides. Extreme scores (either too high or too low) often lead to problematic outcomes, and most people fall somewhere in the middle. Most of this book focuses on the outcomes associated with high levels of emophilia, however, it is important to note that low levels of emophilia carry with them some unique outcomes as well, such as being lonely, picky, and prone to dissatisfaction in dating. Thus, individuals who are emotionally restricted may struggle with relationship issues as well. Individuals who are emotionally restricted (if they choose to enter a relationship at all) may also choose relationships for overly practical reasons, and these relationships may lack passion. Thus, these individuals may never get to feel the excitement associated with love.

Further, individuals who are emotionally restricted may not feel connections with others at all, leading to a sense of loneliness. Further, such individuals may take years of courtship to ever feel comfortable opening up to someone. Perhaps more problematic is that when such individuals do fall in love, they find it very difficult to find that same love with anyone else ever again.

It should be noted that there are two closely related constructs that I will be exploring throughout the book as a compliment alongside emophilia: anxious attachment and sociosexuality (or sexual permissiveness; see Hendrick & Hendrick, 1987).

Sexual permissiveness. Often referred to in psychology as "sociosexuality," individuals who are sexually permissive are comfortable with engaging in casual sex (Simpson & Gangestad, 1991). Such individuals require little time to pass between meeting someone and feeling comfortable having sex with that person. They are also willing and likely to engage in sexual contact with many different partners. Sociosexuality is very similar to emophilia, except such individuals are focused on the sexual or physical aspects of a relationship, whereas individuals high in emophilia are focused on the romantic or emotional aspects of a relationship.

Anxious attachment. Anxious attachment is similar to emophilia in that these individuals will latch onto a romantic partner (Hazan & Shaver, 1987). However, unlike emophilic individuals, the process is more of a "need" rather than a "want." Anxiously attached individuals are neurotic, vulnerable, and desperate to be loved and stay loved. They fear that partners will abandon them. As a result of this insecurity, such individuals will engage in various behaviors (crying, self-harm, aggression, manipulation, even threatening suicide) to keep a partner from leaving. Their inability to be convinced that a partner will remain with them often has the ironic effect of ruining their relationships.

However, anxious attachment is actually only *one* type of insecure attachment style. Avoidant attachment is another type when individuals are convinced that others are unreliable and will eventually disappoint them, leave them, or abandon them. They are not comfortable relying on others for anything and are not comfortable with others relying on them. They would rather stay independent and focus instead on taking care of themselves.

Avoidantly attached people generally disappear or break-up, or at the very least, begin to disengage from a relationship at the first hint of a problem or rejection. It is important to note that both anxious and avoidant attachment are associated with poor relationship outcomes. Anxiously attached individuals tend to see others as trustworthy and reliable but do not see themselves in a positive light (i.e., low self-esteem). Individuals with avoidant attachment, although insecure, tend to see themselves as reliable but others as unreliable. Finally, it should be noted that one can have a mixture of these two types and be both anxious and avoidant, which is sometimes referred to as "anxious-ambivalent" attachment.

As we will see in later chapters, it is important to define these constructs early because I will be discussing these related concepts alongside emophilia to help the reader better understand what emophilia is and what it is not. As I will mention later as well, emophilia is not an attachment style nor is it redundant with sociosexuality. Emophilia tends to correlate with anxious attachment in a modest way, as it does with sociosexuality. However (as you will see), emophilia predicts unique outcomes, behaviors, and consequences that other traits do not.

Spotting an Emophilic Person

While writing this book, I asked many people to tell me about those they know who might be high in emophilia. Most people initially described to me someone who did something quite unusual and risky with their personal lives. As I probed deeper, I began to realize most people were simply telling me the "craziest" stories they knew. In fact, they usually couched the story with, "This woman was insane, she brought her boyfriend of three days to Christmas with her, and he was doing cocaine in the bathroom!"

While bringing a cocaine-addicted boyfriend of three days to a family holiday party is certainly unusual, it does not necessarily mean that this woman was high in emophilia. Certain diagnosable pathologies, such as bipolar disorder, borderline personality, severe attachment issues, or depression, may all drive individuals to engage in a torrid and risky romantic affair with a questionable partner. Further, individuals without pathology may simply make poor choices in relationships, such as individuals who have low self-esteem.

I would encourage readers to remember that most behaviors have multiple contributing factors. Over 80 years ago, Kurt Lewin argued that human behavior is a function of the person, the environment, and an interaction between the two. Lewin is one of my favorite historical figures in psychology. Not only was he a brilliant scholar, but he also treated all individuals (regardless of things like student status, race, gender) as equals in his lab despite prejudicial attitudes of the time. His groundbreaking work on field theory provided a road map for person*environment interactions that has had a great impact on psychology. Much like physics or chemistry, Lewin argued that the fundamental equation for understanding human behavior was the following: Behavior = Person, Environment, Person*Environment. Now, the tricky part, of course, is measuring the person, their environment, and that interaction. Nevertheless, the critical message from Lewin was that there are many reasons, both situational and dispositional, as to why someone would engage in a certain behavior.

Take criminal behavior. Not everyone who steals from others is a psychopath. We tend to throw labels around quite readily in colloquial speech, and *psychopath* is popularly leveled against someone we may not like (Hare, 1996). For example, someone may have stolen from you because they were desperate. The person may have stolen because they feel society owes them and that the injustice of the world needs to be paid back. They may also simply have impulse control problems and feel bad about it after they do it. The person may be a paranoid schizophrenic and believed that what they stole was their property that was unfairly taken from them in a former life. Finally, a psychopath, on the other hand, who cares little about things like the law, honesty, or harming others may steal just because. Look at all these different explanations! Thus, it is difficult to know what is driving someone's behavior without proper scientific and clinical training, and even then, clinicians can be wrong in their diagnoses.

So, what types of people *do* qualify as being highly emophilic? First, if a person is clearly insecure, disturbed, narcissistic, or pathological, and shows the same behaviors, that person may not necessarily be high in emophilia—there might be situational or developmental factors influencing their behavior. Although a person can be both pathological and highly emophilic, one can (and often does) exist in the absence of the other. Thus, emophilia *can* coexist within an individual along with psychopathology, but emophilia is not *caused* by psychopathology. Thus, there is little correlation between emophilia and any form of psychopathology. However, emophilia may interact with other psychological constructs to predict unique behaviors. For example, in the case of anxious attachment, high levels of both emophilia and anxious attachment may produce individuals who are torn between clinging to a romantic partner for security and feeling a rush of romantic passion that comes from a new love interest. Thus, the want and need processes of such individuals may create unique psychological and relationship outcomes.

So what telltale signs *are* there for someone who is high in emophilia when there is no other explanation for their behavior? As we will see throughout the book, some of the thoughts, attitudes, and behaviors associated with emophilia are similar to what we would expect from anyone in love. They see partners in an unrealistically positive light, they feel a rush in thinking about a person with whom they are in love, and they feel trustful of and vulnerability to a person. However, these things happen much sooner than is typical, and they repeat with similar sincerity when compared to previous times. Thus, emophilia should predict reinforcement, excitement, or dopaminergic processes, such as the following:

- *Ruminations of love and a future life with someone they just met*
- *Loving the idea of falling in love, and craving that initial rush of excitement*
- *Feeling a tremendous amount of trust, vulnerability, and commitment toward someone they just met*
- *Feeling "validated" or "reinforced" when in the presence of a potential love interest or partner*

However, as we will see throughout the book, other thoughts, attitudes, and behaviors are uniquely associated with emophilia because of their propensity for speed and frequency vis-à-vis falling in love. The mechanisms that drive the desire to be with someone may have consequences or associated behaviors, such as those associated with tunnel vision, unrealistic optimism, and emotional impulsivity. For example:

- *Temptations to engage in emotional infidelity and feeling romantic connections outside of a primary relationship*
- *Feeling attracted to exciting partners rather than nurturing ones*
- *Providing promises concerning a partner (e.g., "I will always be there for you") when it is unrealistic to do so*
- *Sacrificing for a potential partner without a standing commitment*
- *Repeating processes of relationships with optimism despite past experiences*

Emophilic individuals open themselves up emotionally and (sometimes) physically to new partners with unrelenting optimism and trust. Consequently, they generally ignore warning signs of a potential partner, such as having a concerning past or engaging in potentially dangerous behaviors. Friends and loved ones may warn or even admonish an emophilic individual, perhaps repeatedly asking, "Are you sure this is a good idea?" Especially in cases where there are clear red flags associated with the relationship or potential partner. These admonitions may be increasingly harsh because the emophilic individual may be bright or competent in other ways.

Even when individuals high in emophilia do find a wonderful partner and have a happy relationship, they often tend to have difficulty staying faithful. Although emophilic individuals can be faithful, it presents unique challenges because the temptations are greater because their threshold for interpersonal bonds and excitement is easier to reach. Because emophilic individuals are sensitive and receptive to making emotional connections with others, feeling bonds quickly upon initial encounters, they may get swept into the undertow of a passionate affair without really intending to. Thus, they will find themselves with a bit of a wandering eye.

Because those high in emophilia are drawn to the excitement of meeting someone new and trust potential partners at face value, emophilic individuals are frequently attracted to the overconfident or manipulative. Because the rush and excitement of new encounters is what draws them in, they are often less attracted to the "boring" type.

Instead, they are usually drawn to individuals who are whimsical, unrealistic, and extreme in their plans, passions, and activities. They might find themselves drawn to partners who will "pack everything right now and move to Paris!" They are drawn to fantasies and ideas that partners are going to become famous rock stars or actors, and they will travel the world together. They tend to buy into daydreams that these individuals can "make it work" if they stick together. So, they might find themselves moving to Hawaii with an aspiring professional surfer, with no real way to survive, no savings, and generally no backup plan. As we will see later in the book, individuals high in emophilia are attracted to those who are initially charming and exciting, making them vulnerable to risky decisions. It is important to note that someone too low in emophilia may also endure a great sacrifice to be with their romantic partner as well. As mentioned, they have a very high threshold for falling in love and may recognize that finding another love is unlikely. The difference is that someone high in emophilia will make that sacrifice knowing less about their love interest when compared to the person low in emophilia.

Because of their rapidly evolving feelings, those high in emophilia make premature promises that often are unrealistic at any stage of a relationship. For example, "*I will always be here for you*" is generally an untenable statement, especially in the early stages of a relationship. However, emophilic people may utter those words to a new love interest. They do not mean to be "manipulative" or deceitful. They probably really do want to believe that they will always be there, and in that moment, they sincerely mean it. However, they tend to "bite off more than they can chew" when it comes to relationships. They find themselves letting romantic partners "move in" with them or borrow money that is never paid back. Further, they find themselves in over their heads, even in terms of promises. As the passion fades, the promises and commitments pile up, and these individuals might feel trapped. It is important to note that individuals who fall in love, regardless of emophilia levels, may end up trapped in a suboptimal situation. Because of the rapid development of emotional connection, however, those high in emophilia sacrifice sooner and deeper than others. Consequently, they find themselves at higher and repeated risk for overinvestment and premature commitment.

Finally, and this is probably the most telltale sign: the person re-peats these processes *over* and *over*. It is not the case that the person is masochistic or wants to be hurt; it is just that they are desperate enough to believe that things will be different this time and convince themselves of it. As we will discuss shortly, Emophilia is a two-factor process: one must fall in love *easily* and *often*. In the following chapters, we will explore how to assess emophilia and how it is found in everyday cultures.

2

———•○•○•———

Assessing the Speed of Love

- *Emophilia can be reliably and validly measured using the Emophilia Scale (EP Scale), which is distinct from related constructs such as anxious attachment, fear of being single, and sociosexuality*
- *The EP Scale captures both components of the construct: falling in love quickly and frequently, which are core features*
- *Emophilia, using the EP Scale, is associated with impulsive romantic behavior and critical life outcomes. These outcomes include early relationship commitment, multiple engagements, and pregnancies with different partners, all of which are driven by reward-seeking and want-based desires*

Patterns that we observe in our day-to-day lives may lead us to believe someone is "emophilic." However, there are multiple causes for human behavior, and without a proper assessment, much of our observations are at risk for hindsight bias. For example, someone may ruminate about a potential partner after a stellar first date, or we may observe that our friend seemingly never stays single and jumps from relationship to relationship. Although these behaviors would certainly be consistent with the explanation that these individuals are emophilic, they could also be the result of other psychological processes. For example, anxious attachment creates rumination about potential partners, and fear of being alone may predict jumping into a new relationship. Thus, proper assessment is necessary to distinguish emophilia from related psychological concepts.

However, there are additional reasons why both the concept and assessment of emophilia are important. First, the idea that people high in emophilia can make decisions that affect them for the rest of their lives should not be surprising. Further, it follows that the byproducts of emophilia can be major life changes, which include (but are not limited to) unintended pregnancies, tumultuous relationships, psychological or physical harm, and even death. However, before the study of emophilia, there was no way to measure these tendencies at a dispositional level, nor has there been an acknowledgment that a dispositional tendency such as emophilia even exists. Take for example an experience from my own life, in 2012, when I briefly took a job at the University of Nebraska, Lincoln.

I met a woman, Tammy, who was a single mom. Tammy and I got to know each other through neighbors, and we hung out a few times. Over coffee one night, Tammy told me a bit about her relationships. Shortly after her divorce, she began a relationship with a music teacher. She told me that he was incredibly handsome and talented but not quite reliable. She was certain that he was seeing other women in addition to her, although she pleaded for fidelity. He eventually left Lincoln, and she focused her attention on my neighbor, Tony. Tony had told me several times that Tammy seemed very much in love with him, buying him gifts every month to celebrate "one more month" of dating. When they reached month six, she presented him with an offer: Let's have a baby.

Tony was taken aback. She already had a child with her ex-husband, and although they were dating, Tony was reluctant to make serious long-term plans with her, let alone have a baby with her. Nevertheless, she insisted that she really wanted to have Tony's baby. She added that if something happened to the relationship, she would be happy to raise the child no matter what, and he would not be called upon to parent if he really resisted the idea later.

When I had coffee with Tammy one night, she confirmed that these facts were true and that she just loved Tony so much that "it all made sense." In addition, she told me that her primary motivation was to bond with him and have a part of him in her life, always. She also admitted that she understood that Tony was a bit full of himself and very immature. She realized that he would probably never settle down, but she said she "owed it to herself to try and reel him in." When I was packing my house to leave Lincoln for a new job at the University of Texas at El Paso, Tammy knocked on my door and handed me her phone. It was a picture of a home pregnancy test with *two* lines across the meter (two lines = pregnant, one line = not pregnant), with a large grin on her face. She told me that she would be happy no matter what the outcome and that if Tony "ever grew up," she would welcome him in her life, even if he left now.

Although I fell out of touch with Tammy, I kept in touch with Tony after leaving Lincoln. He told me that he had broken it off with Tammy awhile back but wanted to stay friends with her. Most recently, he said that she has not returned his calls and has told their mutual friends that she is "through with his childish ways." Although they live in the same city, I doubt Tony has met his own child.

There's much that can be said about this situation, but is it emophilia at play? How do we measure and assess this? This chapter will examine behavioral cues that are most likely the result of emophilia and the best current assessment tool—a questionnaire that I call the "Emophilia Scale" (EP Scale; i.e., Jones, 2011) that has been used across a variety of settings and populations to study how variations in scores explain variations in various emophilia-related behaviors. I will discuss the theory behind the scale, how to take it, and what your score means. I will also discuss the implications that different scores have for both research and real life, including several other measures of personality and relationship orientation that may help individuals distinguish emophilia from other related, but nonidentical, concepts.

Measuring Emophilia

Like most studies in personality psychology and individual differences, the easiest way to assess someone's traits is to simply ask them questions related to the trait and examine their responses. The best tools are questionnaires that are continually revised and updated as new perspectives are made available but also maintain a demonstrated record of being a valid predictor. As my mentor, Del Paulhus (an emeritus psychology professor at the University of British Columbia), always told me, a questionnaire is only as good as its items!

Test construction is not an easy task. Samuel Messick, who was a seminal figure in the theory and approach to the validity and validation of psychometric scales in psychology, always argued that a scale itself is not validated; it is only validated for particular uses. In fact, scale development in psychology takes a long time.

My initial interest in research on emophilia started in 2008. Shortly after, I began working on an emophilia scale, which was a questionnaire to assess emophilia by self-reporting. I tried to write items that captured what it meant to fall in love easily and often. There were many cases where items did not correlate well with other items or items were too similarly worded to different concepts. I went through *many* versions of the scale. Having the patience to go through trial and error, especially when developing a scale for a construct no one has ever studied, is critical. I tried and tested version after version until I finally arrived at *10 items* that seemed to hang together, make sense, form a good structure, and assess the concept I was after. These 10 items (e.g., "I fall in love easily," "I feel romantic connections right away") became the Emophilia Scale (EP Scale).

I published this scale in 2011 in the *Handbook of Sexuality-Related Measures* along with a brief description of it and, recently, an updated version of the chapter in 2019. To take the EP Scale with feedback relative to your age, gender, and other demographics, go to the following link www.darktriad.co and fill out the survey entitled: "How fast do you fall in love?" . . . Or answer the following items:

The Emophilia Scale

1	2	3	4	5
Strongly Disagree	Disagree	Neither Agree nor Disagree	Agree	Strongly Agree

Rate your agreement using the above guidelines

1. I fall in love easily.
2. For me, romantic feelings take a long time to develop.
3. I feel romantic connections right away.
4. I love the feeling of falling in love.
5. I am not the type of person who falls in love.
6. I often feel romantic connections to more than one person at a time.
7. I have been in love with more than one person at the same time.
8. I fall in love frequently.
9. I tend to jump into relationships.
10. During your entire life, how many people have you fallen in love with?

1 = none 2 = one 3 = 2 4 = 3 5 = 4 or more

Scoring: *Reverse items 2 and 5, then add all items together.*

Now, to score your results, you need to reverse your responses to questions 2 and 5. This means the *stronger* you agreed with those questions, the less emophilic you are. So, recode your responses in the following way: replace a 5 for a 1, a 4 for a 2, and so on. Then average or sum your questions together. A 50 is the absolute *maximum* score, and a 10 is the absolute *minimum* score.

Where Do I Fall? Am I High or Low in EP?

The best way to answer this is to go to our lab website and take our emophilia survey ("How fast do you fall in love?") and for feedback at the website www.darktriad.co.

Regardless of how you score, it is critical to understand that emophilia is not broken into categories or reflects a clinical diagnosis. Nevertheless, I understand that people generally want to know where they score compared to others. Figure 2.1 highlights thousands of individuals who have taken the EP Scale. As you can see, the scale goes from 10 to 50 when added together (1–5 when averaged).

Most people fall in the middle range, or about 30.00. Thus, the mean score on the EP Scale across almost 4,000 adults is 29.77. The median

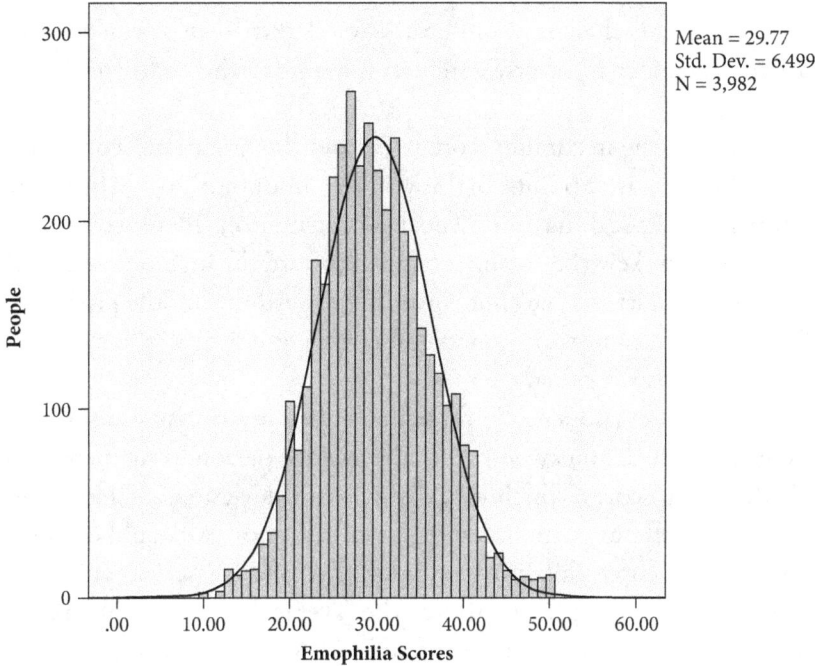

FIGURE 2.1 A histogram and distribution curve of emophilia scores across a large sample.

score (29.00) is close to the mean. When we split the sample by men and women, men tend to be slightly higher than are women—30.92 for men and 28.68 for women. However, their medians were almost identical, as were their standard deviations (meaning that the distribution of scores is almost identical). The modes were interesting. The most common score for men was 32.00 and the most common score for women was 26.00.

In a large sample of Mexican American and Mexican National vs. White American respondents, we found no significant differences in race, ethnicity, or culture. Further, we do not find any differences between people who are gay or straight. Thus, the scale seems to do a good job of capturing the same thing across at least some different populations.

Getting back to how to "score" yourself on emophilia, first take the EP Scale (and be *honest!*). As mentioned, you can either take the scale on paper in this chapter or online at www.darktriad.co. If you do it on paper, remember to reverse code items 2 and 5. Then add your score together.

Naturally, the maximum score is 50, and the minimum score is 10. Thus, the range is 40 points. In this way, the "midpoint" would be 30. As it turns out, the scale has quite a normal distribution. There are not a lot of issues with skew (i.e., being too much toward the high or low end of the scale) or kurtosis (i.e., not clustering toward the middle properly). Further, the mean (29.77), median (29.00), and mode (27.00) are all fairly close to each other.

Again, there is no "cutoff" for being high or low on the scale, we can gauge how much you *deviate* from the average person using these simple deviation scores, which we call "standard deviations." Simply put, if we broke all our participants into a distribution, we could estimate how many people fall into the middle group. These individuals— give or take—are representative of the "average" score, or the middle of the distribution, which accounts for 64% of all scores. One standard deviation above the mean, which in a normal population is just over 36, shows us people who are high in our measure. In the case of emophilia, having a score between 37.00 and 43.00 makes you about "1 standard deviation above the mean" of the sample we tested, which would make you *high* on the EP Scale. Similarly, having a score between 17 and 23 makes you about "1 standard deviation below the mean" of the sample we tested, thus, you would be *low* on the EP Scale. From there, you can calculate more extreme scores, such as 2 and 3 standard deviations above or below the mean. For example, scoring 3 standard deviations above the mean (in this case, 49.5) is considered "extremely high" and represents someone who has a lot of the trait. Same thing with someone 3 standard deviations below the mean. Thus, we would consider anyone with a score of 49/50 on the scale to be "extremely high" in emophilia or 10–12/50 to be extremely low.

In sum, because the mean is about 30, and the standard deviation is about 6.50, it means that if your score falls within the range of about 23 to about 37, this means you are likely typical or average on emophilia compared to the general population. Scores that exceed 36 start to get into the "high" range on the EP Scale. Similarly, scores that dip below 24 start to get into the "low" range.

Despite how you scored, the Emophilia Scale is *not* a diagnostic tool. Which means that it does not diagnose emophilia, and this lack of diagnostic capability simply means that we cannot categorize or determine if someone has or does not have emophilia. Further, because I do not consider emophilia to be a mental *disorder*, it would be inappropriate to label a person as "having" emophilia. Rather, it is more appropriate to say that individuals higher in emophilia engage in certain behaviors more often than those who are low in emophilia. Thus, like most personality assessments, emophilia is measured on a continuum (i.e., on a numerical range of scores from highest to lowest). Another way of thinking about the Emophilia Scale is as a guide to understanding a person's (e.g., patient, client, co-worker) emophilia levels, keeping in mind that there are no accepted "thresholds" or "diagnostic criteria" that exist.

It is important to note that throughout this book I may refer to individuals high in emophilia as "emophilic" to abbreviate the statement "individuals who are high in emophilia" or "individuals with higher scores on the Emophilia Scale." However, this term should not be misinterpreted as diagnostic language or categorical thinking. Finally, although emophilia can lead to different approaches toward interpersonal relationships, being very low or very high can create both interpersonal problems and blessings, albeit different ones. Further, depending on your situation, emophilia may be an advantage or disadvantage, much like all personality traits in everyday populations.

In summary, individuals who fall in love extremely fast and often *and* individuals who have never (and might never) fall in love would be the two extreme ends of the Emophilia Scale. Thus, for some, what they experience as "love" will be experienced quickly and repeatedly, but for others what they experience as "love" may happen once, if ever. However, this statement also raises the question of whether love is experienced differently for those who are high in emophilia.

Is the Experience of Emophilic Love Different?

When considering if someone is high in emophilia or not, it is critical to honestly gauge the level of intimacy and passion the individual is experiencing, commensurate to how much they really know about the focus of their romantic attention. Researcher Robert Sternberg (1986) argued that there are three primary components to consummate (full) love: intimacy, passion, and commitment. Passion is certainly something that most individuals feel at the start of a relationship. However, research shows that, over time, passion tends to wane and intimacy and commitment tend to increase. However, emophilic individuals feel intense levels of intimacy right away when meeting someone, which encourages premature commitment. Thus, it is likely that emophilic individuals do feel "consummate" love, they just feel it right away. In fact, individuals high on the Emophilia Scale may be no different than anyone else once they experience consummate love. Although I am sure there are other individual difference variables and circumstances that predict whether a couple experiences a consummate relationship, and to what degree, emophilia is not one of them.

Further, emophilia is *not* uniquely associated with any specific style of love. According to relationship researchers, individuals approach love from different angles (see Hendrick et al., 1998). Some see love as a game that has winners and losers and needs to be played out via manipulation (*Ludus*). Others see love through sacrifice and give of themselves entirely so their partner can be happy (*Agape*). Still others will engage in calm and pragmatic forms of love, where they make rational decisions about who to love and how (*Pragma*). There are some who are swept away with love, feel the rush of love all at once, and are obsessed with the thought of their partner (*Mania*). There are some who feel love in a very romantic and passionate way (i.e., *Eros*). Finally, there are those who feel that love, for them, is a continuous friendship (i.e., *Storge*). Although emophilia correlates significantly with Ludus, this overlap is wiped away when we consider the overlap between sociosexuality and Ludus. In other words, emophilia has merely a "spurious" relationship with Ludus because it also has a correlation with sociosexuality. Thus, it is not the case that emophilic individuals are any more or less "romantic" "practical," or any of these love styles, in their relationships with others. Whatever love is for them, and however they define it and engage in it, they just do it quickly and often.

Closely and Not-so-Closely Related Concepts to Emophilia

Before launching into a full discussion on emophilia for the rest of the book, it is necessary to pause and articulate why this is worth studying. Not in the "interest" sense, but in the sense of originality. Whenever a new concept, idea, or scale is introduced to the field of psychology, it is met with quite a skeptical eye, and for good reason. In psychology, there are at least *10,000* scales out there to assess traits. Further, there are hundreds of constructs that have been published, discussed, validated, and used to study human behavior. Thus, I had to grapple with questions such as, "Is it possible that emophilia is redundant with something already out there?," or, "Am I just reinventing the wheel?" Well, as mentioned in Chapter 1, an obvious place to start would be attachment styles and sociosexuality, given that emophilia theoretically overlaps with these two constructs and scores on the Emophilia Scale shares correlations with scales assessing sociosexuality and attachment styles. As I mentioned earlier, we tend to fall in love with those whom we have sex with, and we tend to have sex with those whom we love. Further, the people whom we want in our lives may also be people we need, and people we need we tend to want. Although these correlations are far from perfect, it would be reasonable to think that individuals who are permissive or unrestricted with their sexual activity would be permissive with their desire for love. Further, it is reasonable to assume that those who cling to romantic partners for meaning may also have a heightened sense of romantic attraction to others as well.

Like those high in emophilia, anxiously attached individuals have many romantic interests (Tracy et al., 2003), fall in love faster when they find someone (Hazan & Shaver, 1987), and feel uncomfortable *without* a romantic partner. However, unlike those high in emophilia, they cling to romantic partners for their own sense of security. Anxious attachment and anxious-ambivalent attachment articulate traits that are *needs* based. These individuals feel it necessary to be in a relationship. However, unlike those high in emophilia, they may not even like the relationship or the partner, but they feel like they need them. Thus, it is critical to examine sociosexuality and anxious attachment alongside emophilia to dispel any doubt that they may represent emophilia with a different name. From there we will discuss one other key construct that may be redundant with emophilia as well: romanticism, or what has been referred to as romantic beliefs (Sprecher & Metts, 1989).

Insecure attachment. The roots of insecure attachment date back to the 1940s with the Neo-Freudian Karen Horney (1945), who theorized that there were typically three consistent patterns children had when it came to dealing with anxiety: passive, aggressive, and withdrawn. In 1969, John Bowlby built on these ideas to argue that there were three types of parents: (a) those who met the child's needs and were warm, loving, and consistent; (b) those who were inconsistent with affection and meeting the child's needs; and (c) those who were aloof, cold, or unresponsive. According to Bowlby (1969/1982), these different parenting dispositions led to three types of children: (a) securely attached (i.e., those who felt comfortable relying on the parent and trusted that their needs would be met), (b) anxiously attached (i.e., those who were hypersensitive to abandonment and screamed, cried, or got aggressive for attention), and (c) avoidantly attached (i.e., those who realized that they had to rely on themselves because their parents were unavailable). Finally, there is the combination of these insecure attachment styles, referred to as *anxious-ambivalent*. This attachment style is marked by intense needs followed by extreme frustration when these needs are not met. Such individuals are hypersensitive to perceived rejection and although they crave closeness, they fear a lack of reciprocation. In sum, attachment styles fit into one of four categories: secure, anxious, avoidant, and anxious-ambivalent.

Although there is only one secure attachment, anxious, avoidant, and anxious-ambivalent are three forms of insecure attachment. Originally, attachment styles were assessed by giving participants a paragraph and asking them to indicate how much each of these paragraphs were descriptive of the self. Although interesting, this type of assessment was unreliable psychometrically. Thus, in 1998, Brennan, Clark, and Shaver developed the Experiences in Close Relationships, or ECR scale, which is a 36-item scale (18 items for anxious attachment, 18 items for avoidant attachment) that assesses attachment styles using self-reported measures that are more robust, psychometrically. This scale has been revised (Fraley et al., 2000), and there is a brief version

(Wei et al., 2007) that is only 12-items long (6 for anxious, 6 for avoidant). It is this short form that I most often use throughout the investigations reported in this book.

Given that, growing up, our primary attachment figure is a parent(s), we tend to adapt to that environment. However, as we get older, our primary attachment figure shifts from parents to a romantic partner. Hazan and Shaver (1987) noted that anxiously attached adults tended to cling to romantic relationships, fell in love quickly, and had high levels of anxiety over fear of their partner ever leaving them. Further, Jessica Tracy and colleagues (2003) published a chapter on dating and attachment styles, finding that anxiously attached individuals accumulate a greater number of romantic interests. In this way, one can see where the perceptions of redundancy between emophilia and anxious attachment may emerge for some.

When I was proposing the idea of emophilia for my dissertation in 2011, one of my potential committee members told me, "I don't buy it, this sounds like anxious attachment." He was not alone in arguing that emophilia sounded too much like an attachment issue. Early on in my publication pursuits for emophilia, I would receive the same comments from peer reviewers, e.g., "I just don't think you have anything new here above anxious attachment." In response, I have included anxious attachment (and avoidant attachment) as control variables in many of my studies to ensure that I was not reinventing the wheel.

One potentially competing construct is fear of being single (FoBS; Spielmann et al., 2013). Although emophilia has not been correlated with FoBS, the bigger concern for redundancy comes from the overlap between FoBS and anxious attachment, which consistently show correlations exceeding .50, which according to most statistical experts is a high correlation. FoBS is associated with not terminating relationships when dissatisfied, no particular ideals in relationships, and pursuing relationships when the other party is less attractive or shows minimal interest. None of these theoretical or empirical associations are related to emophilia. Individuals high in emophilia are likely to move on when the excitement fades in a relationship and have strong ideals when it comes to romantic partners. Finally, as the title would imply FoBS is a "fear-based" process, whereas emophilia is about a rush of emotional connection and excitement.

To be clear, there are significant and positive correlations between assessments of anxious attachment and the Emophilia Scale (.2 to .4 in most studies). According to Jacob Cohen and colleagues (2013) this is a "moderate" sized correlation. Thus, in most cases when studying emophilia, around 15% of the variance is accounted for by overlap with anxious attachment. However, it is important to articulate the key differences between anxious attachment and emophilia to dispel any doubts that may exist that these are two different constructs.

Need vs. want processes. In 2017, my graduate student, Shelby R. Curtis, and I published an article to address the reinforcement processes that go on for these two constructs. Although we will discuss this article in more depth in a different chapter, it is worth pointing out that emophilia is associated with reward-based processes (or want). They get excited at the idea of a romantic connection and feel the rush of romantic love immediately. This rush reinforces them and causes them to repeat the process of falling in love. In contrast, anxious attachment is associated with fear and inhibitory processes. Those high in anxious attachment are fearful of being hurt or abandoned. Further, anxiously attached individuals often do not feel OK about themselves without the external validation of a primary attachment figure. These processes are not present in those high in emophilia. Instead emophilic individuals are excited by romantic connections and are driven by the excitement of the connection with their romantic partner. Thus, there is a reward process associated with the rush of love, and this rewarding rush of excitement is part of the definition of emophilia.

Vigilant to threats. The research on anxious attachment highlights the fact that such individuals are vigilant to potential abandonment and threats to their relationship. Thus, they tend to be highly reactive to their partner's negative affect and tend to be quite jealous. High emophilia individuals, on the other hand, tend to be optimistic about the odds of their relationships surviving and their partners loving them. Further, in a study that will be discussed later, we found that individuals high in emophilia tend to report greater intention to work things out in the face of infidelity, whereas anxiously attached individuals tend to report the opposite.

Researchers in drug abuse and addiction will tell you that a particular individual's reaction to drugs tends to change over time. The pathways that say, "I *want!*" eventually become pathways that say, "I *need!*" Often, people who need something do not even necessarily like what they need; they simply need it. This finding has been articulated by behaviorists who argue that compulsive need may be present even when liking is not (Berridge et al., 2009). The same is true of relationships. Anxiously attached people *need* their partners. However, some may not even like their partners that much, but they feel that they have no sense of self, hope, control, stability, or future without them. Thus, leaving an anxiously attached individual may cause the anxious partner to get desperate to keep you, which can even turn violent. The anxiously attached partner might direct that violence inward or outward (or both), depending on how effective they believe it will be at stopping their partner from leaving. I have found no evidence that emophilic individuals will become violent or aggressive when someone breaks up with them. In fact, we found no evidence that individuals high in emophilia are any more or less likely than others to terminate relationships or have others terminate relationships. This finding is unlike anxiously attached individuals, who are much more likely to have others terminate the relationship.

Individuals high in anxious attachment tend to be extremely jealous and hypervigilant to external relationship threats. They want to merge completely with their partner. They seem to never want to be without them. In fact, I conducted a study asking people how much they would love to hear some of the following things, "I will never leave you," "I am always with you," and "I will love you forever." Even though none of these promises are possible to keep, anxiously attached individuals wanted to hear them anyway. Further, their anxiety emerges when they persistently call or text their partners, show up randomly, or prevent their partners from going places where they may meet those they perceive as competition.

Insecurity as Avoidance: Avoidant Attachment

As mentioned, insecure attachment comes in different forms, which also includes avoidant attachment. Like those high in anxious attachment, avoidantly attached individuals deeply fear rejection. However, to cope, they disengage from intimacy rather than be hurt. Thus, rather than engaging in the frequent attention-seeking behaviors (e.g., constant texting and phone calls) of those high in anxious attachment, they simply prepare to leave. Like those high in anxious attachment, individuals high in avoidant attachment are sensitive to external threats to their relationship and potential loss of their partner, except that they prepare for relationship dissolution instead. When the avoidant individual perceives a relationship challenge or threat, they begin to withdraw physically, mentally, or emotionally from the relationship. Some examples include starting fights, cheating, or engaging in cold or emotionally distant behavior.

Sociosexuality

Since the studies of Kinsey and colleagues in the 1940s (Kinsey et al., 1953), the research community has been familiar with the idea that desire for and comfort with casual sex varies across individuals. Because sex is pleasurable and reinforcing at both the ultimate (i.e., evolutionary) and proximate (i.e., experienced) level, people generally enjoy sexual activity. However, sexual contact is also an intimate act that carries significant consequences. Evolutionarily, sex with the wrong person, or even the right person at the wrong time, can bring social, biological, and evolutionary costs. For some, sexual activity eventuates into repeated contact with a partner, further bonds, and eventually a relationship (Kelley, 1978). For others, however, sex is an act for its own sake and engaging in temporary or even one-time sexual encounters are reinforcing.

However, not everyone is comfortable with casual sex or early sexual encounters, and for such individuals a relationship must be formed before they feel comfortable with sexual contact. This preference or aversion to casual sex, sex outside of relationships, or sex on one occasion forms the basis for what Kinsey and others referred to as sociosexual attitudes. These attitudes, and the associated behaviors and fantasies that correlate with these attitudes, form the sociosexual variation that was formally operationalized by Jeffrey Simpson and Steve Gangestad in 1991 with the publication of their Sociosexual Orientation Inventory (SOI). Individuals who scored higher on the SOI were more unrestricted in their sociosexuality. Individuals with an unrestricted sociosexuality tend to be more comfortable with engaging frequently in casual sex, having sex with more partners, and having sex sooner upon meeting an attractive other. In contrast, those who scored lower on the SOI were more restricted in their sociosexuality and preferred long-term relationships, required commitment prior to sex, desired fewer sexual partners in the future, and were less likely to have sex upon meeting an attractive other. The SOI (Simpson & Gangestad, 1991) remains a popular method for assessing sociosexuality. The SOI is a seven-item scale that asks participants about their sexual behaviors (e.g., "With how many people have you had sex in the past 12 months") and attitudes (e.g., "Sex without love is OK."). Thus, the original SOI breaks into two separate factors: behaviors and attitudes (Webster & Bryan, 2007). However, the SOI has been revised several times. One revision was done by Jenee Jackson and Lee Kirkpatrick in 2007. They added new items to the sociosexual behavior and attitudes scales and generated a "long-term orientation" scale. Their argument was that individuals may pursue both long- and short-term relationships separately, focus on just one, or neither. Thus, their revision of the Multi-Dimensional Sociosexuality Orientation Inventory adds long-term orientation.

Another revision, for example, was in 2008, by Lars Penke and Jens Aspendorpf. They revised the sociosexuality scale to address the confusing nature of how the SOI was scored, given that it includes both attitudes and counted behaviors. They further expanded upon, with new items, a third facet of sociosexuality: fantasies. Thus, they assessed SOI from *three* perspectives: behaviors, attitudes, and desires. This scale is my favorite and the one I typically use throughout the investigations reported within this book.

Defining Emophilia as a Theoretical Concept

As I mentioned earlier in this chapter, there was no known scale for emophilia. In fact, emophilia had never been mentioned in the literature prior to 2009, when I hatched the initial idea. However, also as mentioned, there is quite a steep uphill battle when introducing a new construct to the psychological literature. Further, the battle is not done when one introduces the construct. One must then validate a scale that accurately (within reason) reflects that construct. This is a daunting task partially because *you* may know what you mean when defining the construct, but without a common vocabulary (which, by definition, does not exist with a new construct) and a common metric (which, also, does not exist), it becomes exceedingly tricky to get the ball rolling.

To understand the principles of emophilia, I turned to models of sexual permissiveness. Most people can readily understand what it means when someone says, "he's sexually permissive." Typically, people who are considered sexually permissive enjoy casual sexual contact and are willing to engage in sexual contact sooner and with more people. It is important to note that some use these terms to be pejorative toward others, but there are indeed individual differences when it comes to enjoyment of casual sex, eagerness to engage in it, and how many sexual partners one desires. Thus, if someone is "sexually permissive" we tend to know what types of relationships in which the person engages, and we can articulate a bit about what the person's sexual or romantic life is like. Indeed, there are some personality and life outcome patterns associated with sexual permissiveness.

Defining the construct of emophilia in terms of theory was a bit tricky at first. Most good personality assessments start with *theory*. Thus, I had to answer the question: Theoretically, what components should underlie the trait I am trying to study? In other words, what smaller characteristics come together to make up this broad thing we call a *trait*? Because no previous research existed pertaining to emophilia or individual differences in falling in love, I turned to the above research on sociosexuality and sexual behavior. I figured that there should be parallels between individual approaches toward sex and love with respect to the components that lie beneath. In their popular article, David Buss and David Schmitt (1993) articulated a theory entitled sexual strategies, or SST. This article was focused primarily on making a point about evolutionary adaptations to selective pressures, in particular, sexual selection. Their argument was that, although people vary in their comfort with and willingness to engage in sexual behavior, predictable evolutionary differences[1] also exist *between* men and

---

[1] There are social and cultural differences that drive differences in sexual behavior between men and women as well, which in conjunction with biological influences all influence behavior.

women. It should also be noted that these differences can also be attributed to cultural and social forces as well. Further, there is a dearth of research on individuals who are gender nonconforming and identify differently when it comes to gender. For example, individuals may identify with different gender identities, and such identification may vary along a spectrum. Unfortunately, there has not been enough research on these individual differences, and future research needs to begin to explore this.

Nevertheless, to articulate their point, Buss and Schmitt (1993) demonstrated that, overall, men reported an increased desire for more sexual partners throughout their lifespan. Further, men demonstrated a shorter time from meeting someone to readiness for sexual intercourse when compared to women. Note that despite these gender differences, there was substantial variation within men and women. Some women were indeed willing to engage in sexual intercourse upon first meeting someone.

Nevertheless, SST has two components of sexual permissiveness: speed and frequency of sexual contact. These two components seemed like a good place to start to define emophilia: *speed* and *frequency*. In other words, individuals who vary in emophilia should vary across the two closely related components of falling in love quickly and frequently. These two components are important, because, without one or the other, one is not high in emophilia. For example, a "romantic" may fall in love rapidly but do it just once. Similarly, someone may fall in love with multiple people, but perhaps it took years each time they fell in love. Thus, emophilia is made up of both speed and frequency factors.

To test this idea, I recruited a sample of adults with a roughly even balance of men and women. Although I collected variables related to gender and sexual orientation, they had little impact on the results. I borrowed the questions that Buss and Schmitt asked in their 1993 paper. In their paper, Buss and Schmitt asked, *"If the conditions were right, would you consider having sexual intercourse with someone you viewed as desirable . . . if you had known the person for _____."* Then, they gave participants the following options: *(a) 5 years, (b) 2 years, (c) 1 year, (d) 6 months, (e) 3 months, (f) 1 month, (g) 1 week, (h) 1 day, (i) 1 evening, (j) 1 hour.*

However, I added a twist. I asked how likely participants felt that they would be to *fall in love with that person; commit to a relationship with that person; and have sex with that person*, on a scale of 1 (*Definitely Not*) to 6 (*Definitely Yes*). Thus, my study expanded beyond just about sex. Finally, I assessed attachment (anxious and avoidant) styles, sociosexuality, long-term mating aspirations, and (of course) emophilia using the Emophilia Scale.

The results for sex were what might be expected. Individuals high in unrestricted sociosexuality indicated that—across the whole sample—they would have sex with someone after one hour, one evening, one day, one week, one month, three months, six months, and one year. The correlation began to fade after one year. My explanation for this diminished effect is that *most* people, after knowing an ideal partner for a year, would *probably* feel comfortable having sex with that person. Further, from one hour to one year, differences in sociosexuality were the *strongest* predictor of willingness to have sex. It should be noted that the EP Scale correlated with willingness to have sex as well, but the effect was not as strong as it was for sociosexuality. Finally, wanting a long-term, monogamous relationship (i.e., indicating a strong preference for long-term monogamy) was negatively related to reporting a willingness to have sex after one evening up to one year.

After one year, those wanting long-term and monogamous relationships indicated a strong willingness to have sex with someone. Thus, sex after knowing someone for a year is best predicted by a long-term and monogamous orientation, not a short-term and sexual orientation.

Finally, with respect to committing to a relationship with someone and falling in love with someone, the findings were best explained through emophilia. These findings were almost identical, so I will focus on the likelihood of falling in love. Emophilia was an incredibly strong and consistent predictor of one's likelihood of falling in love with someone from one hour all the way up to one year. However, much like the pattern between sociosexuality and willingness to engage in sexual contact, the effect of emophilia on likelihood of falling in love fades after one year. My explanation is that *most* people are likely to fall in love after one year with someone who is really great, attractive, and perfect. Once again, those who wanted long-term and monogamous relationships were the same with love as they were with sex: they had strong negative feelings about falling in love with someone whom they had known from one hour to one year. After that, individuals who were strongly monogamous and long-term oriented were strongly and positively open to falling in love. Figure 2.2 shows the results for the three big relationship variables: emophilia, anxious attachment, and sociosexuality.

In sum, individuals high in emophilia are significantly more likely to indicate that they would fall in love with someone after one hour when compared to other types of individuals (provided the person that they would fall in love with was seen as "perfect for them"). Figure 2.2 shows that emophilia predicts falling in love after one hour, one day, one week, one month, and three months. However, the effect starts to fade at six months, fades further at one year, and then disappears after one year. This disappearance most likely occurs because people who are not high in emophilia are likely to indicate that six months to five years is a realistic time to get to know and, therefore, fall in love with someone.

I also asked participants an additional question about whether they were in a current relationship and whether they were in love. For those who indicated that they were indeed in love, I asked how long it took

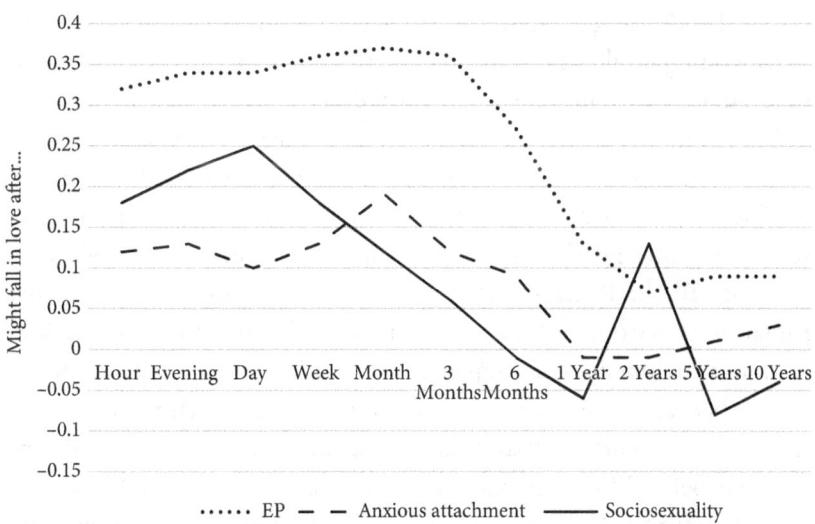

FIGURE 2.2 Likelihood of falling in love across different time periods associated with those who are high in emophilia, anxious attachment, and unrestricted sociosexuality.

to go from first meeting the person to realizing that they were in love. The findings indicated that high emophilia individuals reported significantly less time from meeting to falling in love when compared to all others.

I also asked participants how many people they honestly foresee themselves falling in love with over the next 10 years. The results were surprising. In this case, it was *anxious attachment* that predicted a higher projection of different love interests over time, not emophilia. Further, we asked about their aspirations: With how many partners would they *like* to fall in love over the next 10 years? The results supported the conclusion, this time, that *both* anxious attachment and emophilia were equally strong predictors. Two conclusions can be drawn from these findings. First, individuals high in emophilia are self-deceptive. Even though their history suggests a higher rate of falling in love with different people and a faster time to fall in love, they nevertheless seem to insist that they have either found the one for them or that they will fall in love only once more and that will be it. Anxiously attached people seem to demonstrate a bit more self-insight into their probable romantic future. Perhaps more interesting is that anxiously attached individuals report wishing for more romantic connections in the future. This finding is counterintuitive and requires further exploration: Why would people who want to cling to a single person for value want to fall in love with more people? I still do not have a good answer.

However, one possibility stems from the overlap between anxious attachment and FoBS. Evolutionary theorists have articulated that having "just friends" who are members of the opposite sex can sometimes serve as a buffering effect to the dissolution of someone's primary relationship (Bleske-Rechek & Buss, 2001). Thus, having a desire for more romantic opportunities may be a safety mechanism for those high in anxious attachment, who frequently fear abandonment. If more options are forthcoming, then the person high in anxious attachment does not have to fear *permanent* abandonment because someone else will fill the void left behind by a breakup. This theorizing also highlights a critical difference between emophilia and related constructs such as FoBS and anxious attachment. Those high in emophilia feel love. They want the person with whom they just made a connection to be their one and only. They are not thinking logistically, self-protectively, or about future contingencies. Individuals high in emophilia, as irrational and self-deceptive as it may sound, frequently believe (and want) the person with whom they are in love to be their one and only. Although anxiously attached individuals sometimes think irrationally as well, this irrational thinking centers on fears of rejection, abandonment, and separation. Thus, rather than self-deceptive, they are extremely self-protective. Thus, accumulating future romantic interests is likely to protect against being alone. Much of the process articulated in anxious attachment is true of those who fear being single.

Emophilia and Basic Personality

According to leading researchers in the field of personality psychology, there are at least five key constructs that one must consider when studying basic human personality: extraversion, agreeableness, conscientiousness, neuroticism, and openness to experience (e.g., Costa & McCrae, 1999). Extraversion is a trait associated with outgoing, gregarious, and social behaviors. Agreeableness is a trait associated with kind, warm, and sympathetic social behaviors. Conscientiousness is a trait associated with rule-abiding, achievement-oriented, systematic, and organized behaviors. Neuroticism is associated with emotionally volatile, sensitive, and reactive social behaviors. Finally, openness is a trait associated with creativity, artistic appreciation, and trying new things. These five traits, known as the "Big Five" cover the lion's share of variance when it comes to adult human personality. Each of these constructs have "facet" scores, or subcomponents. Taken together, the facets and constructs of the Big Five do a pretty good job of capturing most of the stable variation we see across different people when it comes to personality. One compelling analogy is colors in the rainbow: red, orange, yellow, green, blue, indigo, and violet (ROY G BIV). Those "primary" colors account for the variety of colors we see in our world. Different combinations, shades, and mixes produce any additional unique colors. The same is true of personality. Thus, when any "new" personality construct appears on the scene, it is usually beneficial to correlate it with the Big Five. This type of correlational study is beneficial for two reasons: (a) to ensure that your scale is not redundant with what is already out there, and (b) to understand how your scale fits within a broader personality context.

We would expect those high in emophilia to have higher levels of extraversion and lower levels of conscientiousness. This assertion stems from the fact that those high in emophilia are easily excited and reinforced by social interaction—a finding associated with extraversion (Eysenck, 1976). Similarly, individuals high in emophilia seem theoretical unable to "apply the brakes," especially with behaviors or emotions that may be counterproductive. In 2017, I published a paper in the journal *Personality and Individual Differences* that demonstrates these patterns. Although, regardless of these patterns, emophilia does not have a large correlation with any of the Big Five traits. This means that emophilic individuals may be high, low, neutral, and so forth on any of these personality dimensions. Although small, emophilia correlated positively with extraversion, neuroticism, and lower in agreeableness and conscientiousness. However, controlling for the overlap between emophilia and anxious attachment leaves only extraversion uniquely associated with emophilia. Anxious attachment, however, correlated highly with levels of neuroticism, and that association persisted regardless of what variables were controlled for or considered. Finally, sociosexuality was associated with low levels of agreeableness and high levels of openness to experience. In sum, emophilia did not have a unique Big Five profile and cannot be explained through general personality patterns.

Emophilia and Self-Esteem

Some may argue that emophilic individuals just don't love themselves and that is why they "throw themselves" at others, right? Wrong! For many years I have been asking my students to tell me about someone they know that they suspect has high levels of emophilia, leaving out any identifying details about the person. In many cases, students speculate that their friend probably has low self-esteem and emotional problems. These assertions are not surprising given that many people assume any form of permissiveness (sexual or emotional) is associated with emotional disturbances. Although insecure attachment (i.e., anxious and avoidant) both have very strong correlations with low self-esteem, emophilia has no significant correlation with self-esteem. Sociosexuality does not correlate with self-esteem either, which replicates previous research. Specifically, researcher and professor David Schmitt conducted a convincing study in 2005 that demonstrated that those who are comfortable with casual sex sooner and more frequently with different partners are not pathological. Naturally, there are cases where someone has endured abuse and turns to sex for psychological validation and comfort or uses sex to hurt themselves or someone else. However, Schmitt's point was that the average person simply varies in sociosexuality, and that variation is often not associated with poor adjustment, mental health problems, or any kind of pathology. In other words, people simply vary in their comfort with casual sex. There does not have to be a problem a person suffers from to make them feel that way. The same is true of emophilia. It is an individual difference variation. Being emophilic does not mean that you are somehow "broken" or "lost" or have significant psychological issues that need to be addressed. However, if emophilia does lead to problems and interferes with the life you want to lead, *then* it is something that may need to be addressed. I have many friends who have high levels of emophilia who go on their merry way living life to its fullest. Thus, if you are happy and fall in love easily and often, then there is little to be distressed over!

Emophilia Is Not Borderline Personality Disorder

One professor at the University of British Columbia insisted that emophilia was nothing more than a unique manifestation of borderline personality disorder (BPD), which is a condition that was best described to me once as "emotional flailing." I would counter that the only thing similar between BPD and those high in emophilia is that they lead people to feel emotions strongly. Individuals high in both traits feel strong rushes of emotions. For example, individuals high in BPD feel intense anger followed by joy followed by sadness. Both traits correlate with anxiously attached individuals who are insecurely attached, impulsive, and handle their emotions poorly. However, those high in or diagnosed with BPD are high in neuroticism and trait anxiety, as well as struggle with their sense of self. At times, they may feel like they do not know who they are.

Is it possible that emophilia is just an unusual manifestation of this familiar personality disorder? As it turns out, no. The correlation between the best assessments of borderline (e.g., Lieb et al., 2004) and emophilia are no higher than the correlation between emophilia and anxious attachment. In fact, taking anxious attachment into account, the association disappears entirely. If anything is redundant, it is anxious attachment and borderline personality. Thus, emophilia cannot be explained by the presence of BPD. Although, it is important to note that someone can be high in any or all these traits.

In fact, BPD and emophilia may *look* similar at times and perhaps even lead people to engage in similar behaviors. However, this overlap is most likely to emerge when the inconsistency and intense emotions found in borderline traits are focused on love and relationships. The difference is that those with BPD enter an "I love you, I hate you" type of cycle that is caused by their erratic and emotional nature, which is not typical for those high in emophilia. Those high in emophilia are often emotionally stable if they lack psychopathology.

Emophilia and Impulsivity: Quick Decisions or Reckless Behavior?

It seemed obvious from the definition of emophilia that it would be correlated with impulsivity. Impulsivity, however, can be assessed in several different ways. One popular method is the Barrett Impulsiveness Scale (BIS; Patton et al., 1995). The BIS breaks impulsivity into three components: nonplanfulness, motor impulsiveness, and inattention (Spinella, 2007). However, this measure has traditionally been used for assessment in populations experiencing pathology and problematic behaviors (e.g., fidgetiness and lack of self-control). Given my focus on everyday personality and relationship-style orientations, I examined impulse-related constructs that reflected everyday personality. This approach assesses impulsivity as *functional* and *dysfunctional* (Dickman, 1990). Whereas the former is associated with fast decisions and confidence, the latter is associated with inhibitory problems and reckless action.

Emophilia is moderately associated with extraversion and has no association with conscientiousness or agreeableness. Thus, emophilic individuals are theoretically linked to high levels of *functional* impulsivity, and indeed we find that those high in emophilia have higher levels of functional impulsivity. To dive deeper into the definition, "functional impulsivity" is defined by fast decision-making, fast-paced thinking, self-assured responding, and confidence (at times, overconfidence) in their judgment and decision-making. They are like a car with a hyperactive gas pedal, speeding through life and the interactions before them. Individuals high in functional impulsivity are sensitive to social rewards and reinforcements in their environment. They are also high in what is known as "sensation seeking." Sensation seeking is a construct that roughly measures how much you seek external stimulation from your environment (Zuckerman, 1971). Skydiving, bungee jumping, rock climbing, and cliff jumping are all examples of activities in which those high in sensation seeking would consistently participate. In contrast, for others (like me, actually), a nice horror movie, pizza, and good company is about all the stimulation needed to have a great night.

"Dysfunctional impulsivity," on the other hand, is linked with poor impulse control. These individuals don't necessarily have a sensitive gas pedal (although they could, functional and dysfunctional impulsivity are only weakly correlated), but they *do* have faulty brakes. When they want something, they simply take it. Those high in dysfunctional impulsivity may not think about the long-term impact or consequences of their actions. If they do, they may not be able to stop themselves from doing something, even if they *know* it will lead to negative outcomes.

Although, as mentioned, functional impulsivity is theoretically associated with emophilia, it turns out that emophilic individuals are high in both types of impulsivities. They have difficulty inhibiting impulses, and they have a heavy gas pedal when it comes to seeking things they want. In contrast, both anxious attachment and sociosexuality are only correlated with dysfunctional impulsivity. In other words, unlike those high in emophilia, they are not heavy on the gas, but they do have faulty brakes. We will discuss these patterns more in Chapter 4.

These findings make sense against the backdrop of much older personality theory dating back to Hans Eysenck (1976), who was one of the pioneers of modern personality psychology. Using Eysenck's personality framework, there are least two components of personality that are linked with impulsiveness and short-term thinking (and relationships): *extraversion* and *psychoticism* (which is a trait made up of two separate personality components: low conscientiousness and low agreeableness). Eysenck found that individuals high in both psychoticism and extraversion reported having numerous relationships. However, he also found that they had different reasons for engaging in these relationships, and they approached relationships differently. Extraverts, for example, were called "Happy Philanderers." This term emerged because they generally had positive and upbeat approaches toward relationships, themselves, and others. This finding makes sense given that extraversion is associated with positive affect, optimistic outlooks, social dispositions, gregariousness, and social engagement. Thus, extraverts reported having many relationships because they *genuinely* enjoyed people and engaging in relationships with others. Those high in psychoticism, however, were different. They were manipulative in their approach toward relationships. They played games with others, saw relationships in terms of conquest and ownership, and engaged in deceptive behaviors to find sexual partners. Thus, high levels of extraversion and low levels of conscientiousness (which is part of psychoticism) predict functional and dysfunctional impulsivity (respectively).

Days to Falling in Love

One key set of factors that emophilia should predict has to do with a set of outcomes that are closely related to the core of the concept (in personality psychology, we call these "criterion-related outcomes"). These types of outcomes help a researcher determine if the core of the construct is predicting what it is supposed to predict. There are a few relationship variables that emophilia should absolutely predict, namely: time to romantic commitment, number of lifetime relationships, and emotional infidelity.

Although infidelity will be covered in a different chapter, it is important to understand that if emophilia fails to predict any of these three things, my assessment or definition (or both) of emophilia may be off. In other words, the Emophilia Scale is not working the way it should, or I am all wrong about some facet of emophilia. Through a variety of studies, I have asked participants to provide me with the amount of time (usually in days) that it took from when they met their partner to when they decided that they were indeed in love. Although this is not an easy question to ask, and there are shades of gray with respect to this type of memory, people are still able to give an approximate number of days. Not surprisingly, across a host of studies, the reported time from meeting to love is substantially shorter among those with higher scores on the Emophilia Scale.

Now, I realize that this could also be hindsight bias on the part of the participants: if this is the case, individuals high in emophilia may *think* they fall in love faster and therefore misremember that amount of time. Although we are trying to follow-up with some studies that track people over time and ask them to report to us when they fall in love, these types of studies are notoriously difficult to conduct.

Life Outcomes

When writing this book, I polled my friends for stories about people whom they have known and who have also behaved in a manner that is representative of emophilia. There is one story I have not forgotten.

My friend knew a woman by the name of Karly who lived in San Antonio, Texas. She had fallen in love with a woman named Stacy. Stacy was a guitar player and singer who planned to leave for Nashville, Tennessee, shortly after they met. Stacy, determined to be a success in the music industry, sold most of her worldly possessions and cancelled her apartment lease. Stacy's band broke up shortly after arriving in Nashville. Thus, when Nashville did not work out, Stacy moved back to San Antonio. However, she had no belongings and no place to live. Karly immediately jumped in and told Stacy that she could live with her. To celebrate, Stacy took Karly to her favorite restaurant on San Antonio's Riverwalk. Right there, in the middle of the crowded walkway, Stacy proposed to Karly. Karly was ecstatic.

The newly engaged couple began planning to buy a house. Stacy started a new job as a real estate agent and applied for a mortgage;

however, she had no savings. Thus, although the mortgage was in Stacy's name, the money for the down payment came from Karly. After moving into the house, Stacy remained enthusiastic about their relationship for a while, but she eventually began to struggle with fidelity. Although Stacy found that she was happy with Karly on most days, other days she concluded that the relationship was not going anywhere, and she didn't feel the same way anymore. After several years of living with Karly and feeling on and off about the relationship, Stacy told Karly she needed to "figure things out." She went to Alaska for two weeks on a cruise with a friend. When she returned, she told Karly that she met someone on the cruise. They had fallen in love and were engaged to be married that summer!

If this wasn't a big enough shock, Stacy then told Karly she had to vacate the premises in a month because her *new* fiancée was on her way to live with her, and Karly was no longer welcome. Because Karly had *gifted* Stacy the down payment and did not marry her, she had no claim to the house! Now, Stacy was not in her heart a dishonest person, so she promised Karly that she would pay her back—but it took five years, one check at a time. Unfortunately, Karly found that it took much longer than that to rebuild her trust in someone who expressed interest in a serious relationship.

In a paper I published in 2015 on emophilia and relationships, which sampled over 800 adults, I examined the life outcomes that participants reported having for their relationships, including metrics such as number of relationships, times engaged to be married, times married, divorces, children, children with different partners, and so on. I also assessed time to first engagement, time to first pregnancy, and time to first marriage.

Massive differences emerged between men and women, so I will discuss men and women separately. Tables 2.1 and 2.2 demonstrate the associations that emerged. When it came to unique associations, there were only a few that emerged for men, but there were more that emerged for women.

For men, I found that emophilia was uniquely associated with total number of relationships (i.e., number of past boyfriends or girlfriends), number of marital engagements, and number of different women they got pregnant. Although emophilia did not predict number of marriages

Table 2.1 Life outcomes associated with four major relationship predictors among men

MEN	EP	Anxious	Avoidant	Sociosexuality
#relationships	+			+
#engagements	+		−	+
#children			−	+
#divorces	+			+
#differentpregnancies	+			+
#marriages		−	−	
Age of first engagement	−			−
Age of first pregnancy	−	−		−
Age of first marriage	−	−		−

Note: + means a positive association, − means a negative association, and a blank cell means no association.

Table 2.2 Life outcomes associated with four major relationship predictors among women

WOMEN	EP	Anxious	Avoidant	Sociosexuality
#relationships	+			+
#engagements	+		−	+
#children	−			
#divorces	+			+
#differentpregnancies	+			+
#marriages	+	−	−	
Age of first engagement	−			
Age of first pregnancy				
Age of first marriage				

Note: + means a positive association, − means a negative association, and a blank cell means no association.

in men, it did predict a younger age for their first marital engagement, first time getting someone pregnant, and first marriage.

For women, like men, I found that emophilia was uniquely associated with total number of relationships (i.e., number of past boyfriends

or girlfriends), number of marital engagements, and number of different men who got them pregnant. However, unlike men, high levels of
emophilia in women predicted more marriages as well. Finally, unlike
men, emophilia did not predict age of first pregnancy or age of first
marriage in women.

Self-Deception and EP

In my research, I have repeatedly found that individuals high in
emophilia will promise the proverbial moon, stars, and the sky to a
romantic partner. The difference, however, between someone high in
emophilia and a "player" is that an emophilic individual *really means
it* at the time. They truly intend, in the moment, to deliver on those
promises. With big declarations, and across most of their relationship-
oriented promises, they are being *self-deceptive*—they are fooling themselves in a way that is not based on reality. This distortion may exist to
shield emophilic folks from a reality they do not want to face or, alternatively, to convince themselves that someone loves them more than is
warranted by observation alone.

The idea of self-deception has been discussed for a long time by the
evolutionary biologist and researcher Robert Trivers. In 2011, Trivers,
along with William von Hippel, made a compelling argument that self-
deceptive enhancement evolved as a means of avoiding lie detection.
Makes sense, if you think about it. Say that I want to convince Maria
that I am trustworthy, when maybe I fear I am not. So, I first convince
myself (i.e., lie to myself) about how trustworthy I am, perhaps even in
good faith. I see myself with rose-colored glasses—as I want to be seen.
Once I truly believe it myself, I tell Maria. In that moment, Maria will
not pick up on any cues of deception, not even subtle or unconscious
ones. My earnest and sincere declarations will be free of guile and ruse,
for the very reason that I, too, believe the misconception.

In psychology, self-deception is quite often studied in the context of
self-enhancement. Professor Del Paulhus found that individuals who
engage in socially desirable behaviors can make themselves look better
along two broad dimensions: self-deceptive enhancement and impression management. Impression management is conscious, intentional,
and (often) planned. Wearing a nice suit for an interview (when you will

never wear that suit at the job again), highlighting (maybe even embellishing) your accomplishments, and being intentionally extra nice are mild forms of impression management. Self-deceptive enhancement is when we convince ourselves of these embellished self-perceptions or we deny negative things about ourselves. Thus, self-deceptive individuals, whether consciously or unconsciously, deny that they have certain bad traits or they exaggerate their abilities to an unrealistic degree. However, unlike impression management or intentional deception, self-deceptive individuals really *believe it*. A self-deceptive person may walk into a room believing they are the smartest, sexiest, or nicest person there when that most likely is not the case. However, there is no prevarication; they typically believe that these assessments are true. I have found that although emophilia has a weak association with self-deceptive enhancement, they are even more likely to self-deceive in ways that pertain to relationship outcomes. Thus, the kind of self-deception in which individuals high in emophilia usually engage is more dependent on their relationship expectations. In other words, they engage in *relational* and *altruistic* self-deception.

Individuals high in emophilia genuinely believe that they will always be there for someone when they make this promise. They further believe that there are no obstacles that could interfere with their relationship or that they can truly help a disturbed partner. Individuals high in emophilia promise things that they simply could not possibly deliver, realistically speaking. For some, it feels euphoric in the moment to let their emotions overrun rational judgment, and for others, it feels euphoric to hear it. In this moment, individuals high in emophilia will promise what they truly want to promise a partner and do not think realistically about the likelihood of delivering on those promises nor the consequences that would befall them or others if they did.

Left at the Alter: Emophilic Individuals and Walking Away from Marital Engagements

There is an old expression that "talk is cheap." Never truer when it comes to an individual high in emophilia promising to be there forever. In a large study I conducted examining the life outcomes of individuals high in emophilia, I found two strikingly different correlations when it came to engagements and marriages. First, individuals high in emophilia reported being engaged significantly more times than those lower in emophilia. On average, someone scoring 1 standard deviation above the mean in emophilia reported a minimum of three marital engagements.

Although these findings are surprising, they highlight exactly what I have been trying to say: promises abound with individuals high in emophilia. Specifically, deciding to be "together forever" for someone high in emophilia does not take very long. In fact, all one needs to propose, or hint at wanting to be proposed to, is a sincere offer and (usually) an engagement ring. Even then, individuals high in emophilia will very often report that their marriage proposal had no ring involved because it literally "just happened." So, the promise of marriage may come easily and quickly for an individual high in emophilia.

However, just because these promises come quickly, does not mean they will be kept. Planning a wedding usually is time-consuming and costly (I did it *once*, and I can sincerely report that it was a ridiculous amount of work). So, individuals high in emophilia may simply promise way more than they can deliver: the feelings to stay the same, the relationship to last, the marriage planned, the expenses paid, the final seal and forms signed—in other words, what it takes to realize that promise. I am not saying those high in emophilia do not get married—they do. In fact, they do at the same rate as most others. However, they typically have more engagements to be married than they do marriages.

I want to reiterate that their behavior is not manipulative. These findings once again illustrate that emophilic individuals mean well. They pour open their heart with sincere and romantic promises and in that moment, they fully intend to marry that person. However, this may have been an impulsive "yes, I will marry you" without really understanding the costs and consequences of marriage because, as discussed, they are not realistically thinking about whether their promises can be kept.

How Should I Break Up with Thee? Let Me Count the Ways!

There are some interesting findings surrounding how people of different attachment styles break up. They fall into three categories: (1) a genuine conversation, (2) the, "it's not you, it's me," discussion, and (3) a disappearing act (Collins & Gillath, 2012). In most cases, securely attached individuals will generally have a conversation with you. They will let you know why they are breaking up with you and generally provide some explanations. "We just are not compatible," "We want different things," and "I think we have drifted apart" are all common reasons for breaking up derived from securely attached individuals.

Anxiously attached individuals will generally throw all the blame on themselves and say that they are just not worthy of your love, they are messed up, and that they simply are not good enough to be with you. It will be the typical "it's not you, it's me" conversation. However, it is important to note that this is only when *they* are doing the breaking up. It is rare because, most of the time, anxiously attached individuals will cling to a relationship for a sense of self-worth and security. The conditions under which anxiously attached individuals make the move to end a relationship are usually when they find someone else or have some other extremely compelling reason why they want to end the relationship. However, if they are on the "ending it" side of things, they will generally berate themselves in the process of ending the relationship.

If their partner attempts to end the relationship, however, as mentioned, anxiously attached individuals may resort to threats, self-harm, harm others, or any measure (no matter how drastic) to keep the partner, even for one more night. However, once the breakup is over, anxiously attached individuals, if their partner ended the relationship, usually have nothing nice to say about their former partner.

Finally, avoidant attached individuals will generally just disappear. You'll be lucky to get a text in a few weeks (in response to your repeated inquiries), but only maybe. However, no one has studied why emophilic individuals break up and how they do it. I examined this question in a large sample of adults. I asked participants how many relationships *they* ended, how many their *partners* ended, and why they broke up. Just as others have found, anxiously attached individuals are broken up with more, and avoidant attached individuals do more breaking up, which fits with previous research. Interestingly, sociosexuality and emophilia had no relationship with either. Thus, they are no more or less likely to break up or be broken up with.

However, I also asked respondents why they broke up with their most recent partner. I surveyed more than 800 adults for this study, and I isolated the top 20% of the sample based on their scores on the Emophilia Scale. Further, to be in the list below, they had to be in the bottom 50% on both anxious attachment and unrestricted sociosexuality. Thus, in this way, we are getting at the emophilic (and *only* emophilic) type of people.

Emophilic reasons for why the relationship ended were the following:

- Lack of love
- Psychological distance
- Incompatibility (e.g., different values)
- Physical distance (e.g., moved away)
- We were very young, and the reasons were foolish (e.g., it wasn't anything serious)
- Possessiveness
- Boredom with the partner
- Grew apart
- Tension/constant fighting
- Cheating

Out of these responses, about half can be attributed to physical distance or love/feelings, with almost a third citing feelings or love as the reason for the relationship ending. Further, only one indicated that it had anything to do with something wrong with their partner (e.g., possessiveness), which, even then, seems to fit an emophilic profile.

So, what about anxiously attached individuals? We isolated the top 20% on anxious attachment (using the Experiences in Close Relationships Scale, or ECR) and reduced the sample by only including those who were additionally in the bottom 50% on emophilia and unrestricted sociosexuality.

The results were as follows:

- Grew apart
- Takes me for granted
- I will not end relationship
- Dishonesty
- Imperfection in partner (e.g., not what I really want)

- Dissatisfaction in relationship or partner
- Infidelity
- Incompatibility
- Didn't love them from the start
- Lack of understanding me (e.g., didn't "get" me)
- Not comfortable with something the partner is doing in their life
- The partner was not interested in taking it further
- They are not worth it
- Not making progress in the relationship

As can be seen through these responses, few indicated that love or feelings were the issue. In fact, one participant indicated that she "didn't love him"—implying that this was not a dynamic thing, rather, the person never loved him from the start. As you can see, the majority have to do with complaints about their partner; in fact, more than half of the responses had to do with the partner not being "interested in taking it further," "lack of understanding," "dissatisfaction," or imperfections (i.e., infidelity, dishonesty, taking for granted) in their partner.

Finally, what about those high in unrestricted sociosexuality? Well, once again we repeated this procedure, isolating the top 20% of those in unrestricted sociosexuality and making sure those folks were in the lower 50% of emophilia and anxious attachment.

Their responses were as follows:

- Commitment-phobia
- Don't know
- Career demands
- He got too clingy
- Boredom
- Incompatibility
- Feeling unappreciated
- Grew apart
- Lack of personal attachment
- They become more destructive than constructive
- Ran its course

These responses are what we might expect. Boredom, noncommitment, and partners being too "clingy" all seem to emerge as common themes. Only one person indicated that love or feelings had anything to do with the breakup.

The Combination of Emophilia and Sociosexuality

Rapid romantic attachment coupled with unrestricted sociosexuality mean that individuals are willing to have sex sooner and get close and trust a lot faster. Thus, such individuals believe that they have found the one and bond with that person quickly. These tendencies lead to a disregard for the consequences that most of us are aware of in short-term sexual encounters. After all, why worry about pregnancy when this is *the one*? The trouble is that people may believe that things will be different this time around, and if they find a partner who seems willing to build a future and a family with them, they jump at the opportunity. When this process repeats itself, it becomes common to have multiple children from different partners.

Recall that I asked participants a series of questions about how many times certain things happened in their life related to relationships (marriages, divorces, children, and so forth). There was one question about how many different people with whom you have become pregnant, or how many people with whom you have gotten pregnant. In predicting this outcome, guided by theory, there was one particularly important interaction that emerged that I did not mention in the paper. There was an interaction between emophilia and unrestricted sociosexuality, such that individuals high in both were significantly more likely to have multiple pregnancies that resulted from different partners.

Summary

In sum, we have defined and operationalized emophilia. The scale used to measure self-reported emophilia scores is the Emophilia Scale. Emophilia is defined as the tendency to fall in love both fast *and* easily. Both are required for someone to be high on emophilia. I have argued that emophilia is not a psychological disorder or a diagnosable condition, although extreme levels of high or low emophilia may interfere with someone's life or goals. Emophilia is not redundant with insecure attachment (i.e., anxious, avoidant, or any combination of the two) and is not synonymous with BPD. Further, emophilia cannot be explained through anxious attachment or unrestricted sociosexuality. Findings indicate that emophilia does not have any unique profile with respect to love styles, personality, or how strongly they feel the love that they feel; they just feel it often and sooner.

Emophilic individuals are, however, self-deceptive, and make numerous unrealistic promises quite soon in a romantic relationship. Emophilic individuals tend to have specific reasons as to why they break up with people; they tend to claim that they do not feel the same way anymore or have fallen out of love. Emophilic individuals fall in love faster upon meeting others and report higher rates of a variety of important life outcomes, especially when it comes to children, relationships, and marital engagements. These outcomes likely occur because emophilia is associated with premature trust, rapid romantic attachment, and a sense that they have truly found "the one" this time. Thus, emophilic individuals really believe that they will "always love" a partner, will always be there for a partner, and that the relationship will last forever. Finally, emophilia interacts with unrestricted sociosexuality in interesting ways that would be predicted by theory. For example, falling in love quickly and being willing to engage in sex quickly upon meeting someone may lead to more pregnancies with more partners.

Now that I have provided a tool for assessing emophilia (Emophilia Scale) for adults, we will use these scores as a potential guide for those who may be dealing with emophilia-related issues. Further, I will explain what behaviors and timelines may be warning signs for emophilia in a friend, family member, romantic partner, or in yourself.

3

Are We All Hopeless Romantics? Emophilia and Cultural Norms of Falling in Love

- *Cultural norms influence how romantic interest is expressed, making emophilia appear prevalent in certain cultures*
- *Some media contain emophilic narratives such as whimsical connections and idealized love*
- *Modern dating also increases the perception of endless romantic options, which may increase emophilic behavior*

An analysis of emophilia wouldn't be complete without examining the cultural determinants of it, so this chapter will cover its sociological and cultural underpinnings. I recall a day when my wife and I took our daughter to the park. As we placed our daughter on the toddler swing and pushed her back and forth, my wife whispered in my ear, "My goodness, look at those two!" Trying not to be too obvious, I glanced over my shoulder and saw two kids, no more than 12 or 13, fumbling over each other with awkward kisses and hugs. My wife, a Taiwanese-born woman, was a little surprised by this public display of affection by two of such a young age. I, a U.S.-born man, was a little less startled. My wife immediately pointed toward the media as a plausible explanation for this type of behavior among young people. We went on to have an interesting discussion about the pervasive impact of media on children's conceptualizations of sexuality and romantic love. Media reflects culture, and media then has a hand in guiding culture in a reflexive process. So, what my wife said is true. Media does impact the way young children want to see their lives, love lives, sex lives, and future partners. However, there are also larger cultural norms at play when it comes to why people in a certain culture may feel that it is acceptable to pair up at 12 or fall in love at a certain age.

Although I openly admit that I am no expert when it comes to all cultural differences, my marriage has opened my eyes to a few major ones, at least between Taiwan and the United States. My wife worked hard, long hours (even before she met me) because she had made peace with the idea that she would probably never be married. According to my wife, in Taiwan, a woman reaching the age of 32 and still being single was a bit of a tolling bell. Although not impossible, the chances of her finding an interested man looking to marry dwindled to almost nonexistence. Considering that, she thought that she might have better chances in the United States. When I met her, she was quite nervous about dating an American man. There were media depictions and socially generated stereotypes that signaled to her that our relationship would be challenging. However, it never occurred to me that meeting her at 32 meant that she was not marriable. Nevertheless, it worked out.

According to David Buss (1989), men across virtually all cultures and countries prefer younger women. Although both Western cultures such as the United States and Eastern cultures such as Taiwan both have music and movies depicting extremely romantic themes, I would personally argue that this type of romantic theme is more centralized in Taiwan than it is in the United States.

Like most research in psychology, I have mostly discussed evidence pertaining to the research on emophilia with a focus on WEIRD cultures (Western, educated, industrialized, rich, and democratic; Henrich et al., 2010). In 1989, sociologists Sprecher and Metts released the Romantic Beliefs Scale that assesses how much an individual endorses concepts of being a "hopeless romantic." They developed their scale using media-centered concepts of extremely romantic notions of love. There are likely hundreds of appropriate examples, especially in the realm of music and film.

Cultural Expressions of Love

In the United States, it is often a norm to avoid contact after a date for two to three days. This strategy is meant to convey a "coolness" and absence of "desperation" to immediately connect and seek another date. Further, contacting someone frequently (i.e., more than one time) throughout the day is often seen as inappropriate, desperate, and can even be classified as "stalkerish" to some. However, these perceptions are far from a cultural universal.

Before I met my wife, I lived in Costa Rica for nearly a year. When I exchanged phone numbers with a woman in a club outside of San Jose, there was clear romantic interest. However, I "played it cool" as per United States culture and texted her once in a while. She responded with multiple texts throughout the day. She expressed extremely romantic sentiments toward me and the potential of us being together. For example, "If my lips cannot kiss you, know that they speak your name." While I was certainly interested, I was uncertain about how to proceed. We met several times, but eventually, the relationship fizzled out.

One likely explanation for the relationship never taking off was that I was not expressing the same strength of romantic interest as she was. I found it disingenuous of me to express such a strong sense of romantic passion when I simply did not feel that way (at least, not yet). However, as I learned later, that is a cultural norm across much of Latin America. They are not being manipulative; it is simply a cultural norm to express romantic feelings passionately and strongly, even if they have not had time to develop. Now, this is not to say she was emophilic or ready to jump into a relationship with me. I found that to be the most interesting part. Because when we hung out, she was not grabbing my hand or attacking me passionately. Instead, we had nice conversations and went on walks. Thus, these romantic expressions were mere expressions of *interest* and should be taken as such. Thus, they do not carry the same expressions of commitment seriousness as they would in the United States.

These cultural norms of passion are even expressed in differences with respect to a sense of personal distance. I remember attending a party in Costa Rica where a young Costa Rican man was chatting with a young American woman. Their conversation began at the beginning of the night. He was positioned all the way to the left of the couch, against its arm. She was seated to his right. A little while later, they had journeyed toward the center of the couch, still talking. Eventually, they gravitated all the way to the left of the couch, with the American woman now leaning back against the arm of the couch and the Costa Rican man facing her on the inside. Again, the Costa Rican man was not being "inappropriate" culturally. The woman was smiling and laughing, seemingly enjoying the conversation. But she kept backing up and he kept leaning forward as per cultural norms, leading them to slide across the couch over the course of the conversation.

When I moved to Vancouver shortly after living in Costa Rica to attend the University of British Columbia (UBC). In Vancouver, near UBC, the population is 70%–80% East Asian descent. Many are foreign nationals who attend UBC. There, dating was a very different situation; it was much slower, much calmer, and much more measured. Because many cultures in East Asia have historically focused on collectivistic values (e.g., China, South Korea) integrating into a person's ingroup often preceded dating. Even then, courtship was a much longer and subtle process. Media depictions of romance in East Asian cultures, such as Taiwan, are more reserved as well. Music videos of love songs often show couples walking on the beach or holding hands. Often the video will end with a small kiss.

On a personal note, I met my wife in El Paso where she moved from Taiwan. For the first four weeks, I genuinely had no idea if she liked me or not. We got to know each other slowly, much like a friendship. Unlike most dates I have had in the United States or Costa Rica, I was genuinely in the dark about her feelings for six to seven dates before her expression of affection finally came through.

Love and affection seem to be cultural universals. Falling in love and the passion behind it is a concept expressed in media across all cultures. However, the norms of how fast and strong we express feelings of romantic interest vary greatly across cultures. In Latin America the norms are to express interest rapidly and passionately, while in East Asia the cultural norms are to be cool and to get to know someone and their friendship network. In the United States, we have a sense of playing it cool also, often waiting a few days to contact someone, even someone we are "head over heels" about. Nevertheless, in studying emophilia across all types of cultures, I have found significant variation, and people across all cultures seem to vary in emophilia.

U.S. Media

With respect to emophilia and the U.S. media, there are dozens of examples that come to mind immediately. I often think of the classic song by The Doors: "Hello, I love you, won't you tell me your name?" The song articulates a powerful attraction to an incredibly beautiful woman who does not return the affection. Another example comes from the movie *Bed of Roses*. In this film, a man falls hopelessly in love with a woman he sees sitting in a window with a sad expression on her face. After meeting this woman one afternoon, his desire for her leads him to send a dozen of her favorite roses every hour, on the hour. His persistence over one afternoon encounter leads to a happily-ever-after romance. Describing the story without the Hollywood touch makes the male protagonist sound more like a stalker than a hopeless romantic, yet it was considered a romantic triumph in the cinematic world. What is it about songs and films like these that draws people to them? Perhaps it is the fantasy of overnight love that reflects star-crossed lovers. Or maybe the presence of *soulmates* is a fantasy embedded in most of us.

One of the best illustrations of this desire for love is a Backstreet Boys song from the 1990s entitled "As Long as You Love Me." The lyrics describe being in love with a particular partner irrespective of her background, behavior, or character. In fact, the only thing the song suggests is required for love is that the partner loves back.

I first heard this song in my high school gymnasium. One of the girls in my class laughed and said, "This song again? God, talk about desperate!" I laughed along with the group, secretly hiding my affinity for the song. Nevertheless, I always found her interpretation interesting. Perhaps desperation is one explanation, but perhaps it is something more. A closer examination of the lyrics reveals an individual who simply cannot get his potential partner "off their mind" and is willing to "risk it all at a glance." That song reflects getting carried away with a feeling of love. This theme is something I have seen consistently in studying emophilia. When people high in emophilia find someone that they connect with, they tend to discount other aspects of the person's history. Whether it be drug addiction, a poor track record of maintaining relationships, a past of infidelity and heartache, or having committed crimes, the individual high in emophilia wants what they want and want it now. So, this song is just a brilliant example of how an individual would get swept away by the rush of falling in love without realistically thinking about how "who she is" or "what she did" may impact the future. This last point is important because one may easily misinterpret this song as simply describing "love at first sight"—which is not the same as emophilia. If it were written from a retrospective account after having been together for a long time, that is one thing. However, there are two key components *besides* falling in love "at a glance" that make this song so perfect for describing emophilia.

The first is the discounting: I don't care what you have done, as long as we are in love. That is a key component of emophilia—being willing to fall for someone who demonstrates all kinds of red flags, or simply falling for someone without knowing what you are getting into. The second is the present tense: the fact that they just met, and thoughts of lifelong romance are percolating immediately.

The concept of falling in love at first sight after one day, or even a weekend, is pervasive not only in modern culture but historically as well. Shakespeare's *Romeo and Juliet* opens with Romeo Montague heartbroken over a rejection by his latest love interest, Rosaline. Upon seeing Juliet Capulet, Romeo is immediately love-struck once more. Although the story of *Romeo and Juliet* was about tragedy, what would have happened if both characters lived? Would Romeo and Juliet have lived happily ever after? Or would Romeo's attention switch, once again, to a new love interest?

When I first began to study the construct of emophilia, I realized that popular culture is replete with examples of it, even in places we never imagined. Take, for example, the popular film *The Little Mermaid*. It depicts a 16-year-old mermaid (very similar to a human in most respects—except for her underwater habitat) who sees a prince sailing a large vessel one night. A terrible hurricane strikes the boat, and the prince falls into the ocean. Smitten by his appearance, the mermaid rescues the prince from drowning. Upon returning to her underwater home the young mermaid is confronted by her father (the Sea King) about her disobedience in rescuing the prince. The young mermaid declares, "Daddy, I love him!" Her father retorts that she must be crazy, given that he is a human and she is a mermaid. What struck me about the film is that the Sea King never brought up the fact that she had never actually *met* the prince, so how could she love him? In fact, most of her dealings were with an unconscious body!

Jasmine Carey coined a psychological term called "need for mystery." Carey suggests that there are some individuals in the world who simply do not want to accept scientific truth—in fact, they *fight* it! Such individuals prefer mystical solutions over practical ones. In this sense, these films and music may appeal to those who believe that there is one, and only one, special person out there for them. Such individuals may be so vehement in their assertions that they actively search for evidence to validate the truth of their partner being a soulmate and reject information that might suggest otherwise.

Although the stereotype is that women enjoy this type of media more than men (e.g., hence the term "chick-flicks"), the actual endorsement of these romantic concepts is higher among men. For example, with respect to Sprecher and Metts's Romantic Beliefs Scale (1989), the two found that *men* endorsed idealistic notions of love more than women. Their explanation was that men, being the more financially and socially privileged of the two, have traditionally had the luxury of choosing to date and marry whomever they felt appropriate. Women, historically more oppressed and socially restricted, needed to think more practically and find a man who would be loyal and provide. Similar findings have been discovered in the evolutionary psychology literature, suggesting men tend to indulge themselves more in the aesthetic "luxuries" of potential romantic partners (such as appearance) than do women, who emphasize certain "necessities" in potential partners (e.g., Li et al., 2002).

Nevertheless, romantic beliefs often *can* be validated if someone has the luxury of painting the rest of the picture. Take for example the opening story of Chrissy and Rick. When Chrissy did not have to deal with the day-to-day boredom and work that a real relationship entails, she could not have been more in love with Rick. In fact, it may have been the psychological distance that kept her desires for him so strong. When individuals are at a distance, it is much easier to paint a picture of how they *will* be. We get to fantasize about how they will respond perfectly to a question or situation. However, when reality meets the relationship, we are confronted with the knowledge of what our partners *do* behave like in most situations. Even the most loving and suited partner will sometimes get it wrong. For an individual who sees the world through rose-colored glasses, the day-to-day lenses they are forced to wear might end up ruining a lot of fantasies.

In the end, it is that initial rush that keeps the individual searching for the perfect partner. Unable to control their passionate impulses, the individual feels as though they are "falling in love" all the time. According to my research, such individuals are highly likely to harbor a disposition of emophilia.

It is critical to point out that the romantic film market about stories of chance encounters leading to "once in a lifetime" romance is a polarizing one. Negative nicknames such as "chick-flicks" and "sappy romance stories" are commonly used to describe these films. Once again, one can see how being too high or too low in emophilia might polarize individuals in their impressions of such media.

Matthew Lombard and Matthew Jones (the second researcher also happens to be my older brother) are both scholars in the field of communications research. They study a topic in media research called "presence." Presence, broadly defined, is a sense of *being there* and *experiencing* what someone in a story is experiencing (e.g., Lombard & Jones, 2015). Presence can occur watching films, listening to music, and reading graphic novels or even short stories. They have argued through numerous publications that individuals project themselves into the media that they are consuming. In this way, individuals who can feel the trials and emotions of a protagonist in a story (whether it be a book, movie, song, or poem) as though they were their own, might be high in this sense of presence. Further, enjoyment of media usually involves some projection of the self into the text. Most people find some common elements between their life and the struggles, successes, or characteristics of a main character in a story. Often, these similarities elicit increased liking or identification with a particular story or film. For individuals at the extreme ends of the emophilia spectrum, an affinity for these romantic tales or stories of chance encounters may elicit strong visceral reactions. For those who fall in love easily, a story about a chance encounter or overnight romance is alluring given that they are either hoping for such experiences or have experienced them before. In contrast, emotionally restricted individuals may find such stories irritating. They seem unrealistic, fabricated, cliché, and (at best) improbable. Further, such individuals may write off such stories as banal attempts to tug at the heartstrings in preposterous scenarios.

Every semester, I give my students musical examples of attachment styles to help them better understand what I mean when I refer to individuals who are high in "secure attachment," "anxious attachment" or "avoidant attachment."

I start off with the Gin Blossoms's "Till I Hear It from You." This song is a great example of secure attachment. Sung in the first person, the song describes how individuals are spreading rumors about their partner, attempting to undermine their relationship, but rather than "take advice from fools," he figures everything is OK unless she says otherwise. For the anxiously attached, I felt that no song better captured the concept of *needing* someone desperately than "How Do I Live Without You?" sung by LeAnn Rimes. The song articulates how the singer could not get through *one night* without their partner, and even worse, if she had to live without her partner, there would be no life or world! In fact, the song's lyrics even speak of no sun being in the sky anymore if the partner left! Those are some drastic feelings and some extreme reactions to a partner leaving. Now, naturally, I realize these assertions are hyperbole, which is meant to illustrate strong emotions associated with the idea of a partner leaving. For this reason, the song is such a beautiful illustration of anxious attachment.

With respect to avoidant attachment, I usually play Carly Simon's "That's the Way I've Always Heard It Should Be." The song describes a very pessimistic young woman reluctantly agreeing to marry a very excited and eager romantic partner. She articulates further how her parents are cold and aloof, how the relationships she sees around her are crumbling, and how most partners simply "cage" their significant others and restrict their freedom. The theme of "I'll be let down" is fairly pronounced.

For emophilia, there are a lot of songs to choose from. In addition to Backstreet Boys's "As Long as You Love Me," there is, Savage Garden's "I Knew I Loved You." The singer indicates that he knew he loved a woman before he ever met her and that he has been waiting forever to meet her. The *best* line from this song that really underscores emophilia completely is the one indicating that he looks into her eyes and sees his future in an instant. Meeting someone and immediately thinking that this person may be your future is a central theme in emophilia.

There are also songs that do not necessarily articulate love at first sight or repeated romance but certainly convey emophilia-type ideas. Not to pick on Savage Garden (I *love* the band!) but their "Truly, Madly, Deeply," is another example of lyrics reflecting an emophilia theme. Being someone's wish, hope, dream, and being "everything" someone needs is a steep order. Further, loving someone more every moment is an unrealistic and untenable statement. Now, I realize that throughout all these songs that I am talking about, hyperbole sells. I am not really suggesting that the lyrics of Savage Garden were written to be literally interpreted as if he wants to lie in a garden on a blanket with his lover forever. Nevertheless, indulging one's passion in a sense of increasing romance, intimacy, and unrealistic drives to be together and provide everything one would ever want in life is an emophilic notion.

It should be noted that these songs sell. Such sales are likely because they are extreme forms of love that are both comforting and powerful. Lukewarm expressions of affection are likely to market poorly and leave people unfulfilled artistically. However, undeniably, these expressions of endless and extreme devotion also speak to people in a way that may reflect fantasies and hopes that many share.

Current Perceptions of Love

How have we changed since ancient times with respect to our conceptualizations of love? In his book *The Natural History of Love*, published in 1959, Morton Hunt articulates how Greek society thoroughly discussed the concept of love from two different angles. As discussed previously, there are different love styles that have emerged from this literature (e.g., Eros, or passionate love; Storge or friendship love; and so on).

Hunt (1959) also talks about how the early Greeks would exalt romantic love and speak of it as though it were a whimsical mistress—full of passion and pain, ups and downs, and should be studied thoroughly like any other topic. I surmise that much of this research went unattended and even ignored during different periods and across different cultures that were not as "free" to discuss such things.

Nevertheless, according to Hunt, it was not until industrialism that the whimsical passions and practices of romantic love were found to fully blossom in cultural norms. It became more culturally acceptable for people to find themselves prey to their emotional lives and inner feelings. However, simultaneous to this social movement was the idea that one must remain earnestly chaste and not give in to carnal pleasures of the flesh. Such sexuality, especially in the absence of love, is often shamed in our culture.

The Pregnancy That Wasn't

I lived in Lincoln, Nebraska, for about six months. During that time, I made a lot of great friends and had a lot of fun. One activity that I especially recall was that of "tanking." The concept was simple enough: they throw you into a big metal tank and you float down a shallow river (maybe three-feet deep max) and talk and drink (naturally, given that you are on a river, it is BOYB). I wound up getting into a conversation with a woman, Alice, who was nice enough to supply the drinks in our tank. Alice and I found ourselves engaged in a long discussion about emophilia, relationships, and sexuality. Alice told me the following story:

She and a young gentleman she had recently met went out on several dates. One night, they found themselves in bed. However, his postcoital reaction was quite different from most of the men she had been with. He immediately recoiled in horror after the sex had ended. He was in a clear panic. Apparently, his religious upbringing and beliefs had become very salient after the sex was over. After that, he was convinced she was pregnant. Apparently, according to her report, he called incessantly every day until she had her period and they were "in the clear." Shame can also lead to approach- or commitment-oriented means of dealing with sexual shame. I recall one teenager growing up who lost her virginity and claimed that it was OK because he was "the one."

Nevertheless, individuals will then often use spontaneous love as a way to rationalize sex. They will argue that fate brought them together or that they now must be together. In the case of Alice, she had *no* intention of having a relationship with this guy, which apparently made matters worse. As a result, that route was cutoff for him to assuage his guilt. Thus, he fixated on a tangible outcome that would (in his mind) be disastrous: pregnancy.

Perhaps an even more appropriate illustration was the experience a friend of mine had in Calgary, Alberta. He had flirted online for a while with a woman, Susan. Susan was nice but found herself in and out of relationships quite frequently. Although they had known each other for many years, they had only been on one date in that time because Susan was otherwise romantically occupied. My friend had long since moved away from Calgary, but he was back on a rare visit. On a whim, he called Susan, and surprisingly she was both single and ready to meet up with him. They wound up in a hotel room together. My friend told me only bits and pieces, but he did tell me that shortly after they had sex, she let out a frustrated groan. When he asked what was wrong, she whispered, "I'm just wondering how we'll make this work." Although they remained friends, he said he had to work hard to dispel the notion that he would move back to Calgary or have a long-distance relationship with her. Fortunately, she understood with no real hurt feelings, but misunderstandings such as these can lead to heartache, disappointment, anger, and perhaps even worse.

In essence, some people are genuinely high in emophilia and really do feel that after a night of passion, they see a mutual future before them. However, others may *seem* high in emophilia but really use love and emotional passion as a cover for shame over their unconscious sexual desires. Such individuals may claim love or try to feel it with all their might, but what they are really after is reducing guilt over a sexual encounter. Further, these feelings can manifest in any gender. Thus, we cannot jump to conclusions about people regardless of their external behavior.

Although a controversial theorist, Sigmund Freud discussed these concepts many years ago. For example, Freud discussed that repression and rationalization (two of Freud's defense mechanisms aimed at protecting the ego from damaging realizations) may unconsciously transfer sexual energy into the idea that destiny brought you to someone and that it was meant to be. Under the guise of "happily ever after" or "together forever," sex does not seem so incredibly shameful to someone prone to feeling that way about sexual encounters. I do not believe the tendency for emophilia has really changed much throughout the decades, but our ability to exercise these passions has evolved tremendously.

For example, back in the "olden days" (before cell phones, internet, and household computers) dating was restricted to those in your locale. It was limited to where you could potentially meet singles. Perhaps it was a little more popular to go to a bar, party, or nightclub to find a potential mate. These days, when I go to the bar with my friends, I see the singles at the bar in a neat row all on their cell phones talking to people not at the bar.

If you wanted a blind date, you were beholden to friends connecting with friends. The only other path to meeting singles in any organized way was restricted to two options: the newspaper (personals ads) or a dating service. For dating services, people would sign up, record a video message, and other singles would decide if they'd be interested in meeting you. In modern society, we have plenty of social media hubs, such as Facebook, Twitter, Snapchat, Instagram, ChatRoulette, and online chat forums just to name a few. Further, we have dating websites, such as Plentyoffish, Match.com, Lavalife, OKCupid, Yahoo personals, Jdate, BBPmeet, cougar, eharmony, Zoosk, badoo, adam4adam, Tinder, and *plenty* more. Finally, we have dating websites aimed at sexual affairs only, such as Ashley Madison, adultfriendfinder, and so forth.

Alpha and Beta Press

Many people have asked me if we are becoming higher in emophilia with each generation. My answer is yes and no. No, I do not believe that there have been any increases in dispositional or genetic proclivities with respect to falling in love faster or easier when compared to previous generations. However, I do believe that through media, social media, cultural shifts, and socialization, we are seeing serial monogamy and ephemeral commitments as more acceptable and exciting. There is a concept in psychology called "press" (Murray, 1938). To explain press, I always make the analogy of fidelity and the temptation to cheat with being a musical rock star. For example, a rock star would objectively have a *lot* of offers for a sexual affair from *many* people. Whether it is from fans, other entertainers, or just everyday folks, a rock star is likely to get offers for sexual encounters. Thus, for a rock star, the temptation to cheat is driven by alpha press. Although some manage to maintain long-term relationships with a romantic partner despite these obstacles, most celebrities seem to struggle with fidelity.

Beta press, on the other hand, is all about perceptions, biases, and distorted reality. Beta press results in an everyday average person feeling unable to be faithful because there are 50,000 singles in their local area on Tinder "looking to hookup." But let's do the math. Even though 50,000 profiles are up and ostensibly looking for love, they probably do not all want the same thing you do. Some are looking for casual sex, others for long-term affairs, and everything in between. So, we can cut down the number right there. A good majority may be unattractive to you, incompatible with you, or may not be willing to meet with you.

In fact, when you really think about it, the perception that all those singles are just a click away is simply biasing you into believing that there is a sea full of fish. In reality, everyone is limited in how many fish they're going to catch. The fish analogy is a good one because even if you could hook multiple fish (i.e., have many relationships), there are only so many you can maintain. So, the virtual world of online dating, which connects us to millions across the globe, may make us repeat familiar counterproductive patterns. Nevertheless, many people (regardless of gender) claim to be interested in a long-term relationship yet report wanting to "keep their options open" or "are not quite looking for a serious commitment yet." In sum, I do not think people are changing drastically. We are not necessarily becoming more cold-hearted or permissive. Instead, I believe that distorted perceptions of potential partner availability have risen with increased global connectivity to the internet.

I also believe that this type of connected environment interacts with individuals who may be sexually permissive or high in emophilia. Online connectivity creates uncertainty about whether we are with the "right one." The availability of so many potential partners creates a never-ending sense that there is someone out there who is better for you. This sense of availability is likely to drive relationship insecurity for those who are insecure or emophilic.

To be sure, there are times when a better partner does come into our lives and decisions must be made. Similarly, a current partner may not be whom we were looking for after all, and it is time to move on. However, it is difficult at times to tell the difference between normal relationship flaws and serious issues. There will always be things we wish were different, issues with our partners that we probably can't correct, or drawbacks to our present situation. However, traditionally, options and alternatives were constrained by physical distance and other logistic limitations. Now, a simple internet search opens a world of new alternatives. However, the perception that there is a never-ending supply of available singles who are attractive, fun, and compatible is misleading at best.

What makes online profiles even more dangerous to modern relationships is that they are designed to paint a picture of fun, sexy, and a world of possibilities. Most online profiles are designed to be eye-catching and paint an exciting world with this person. Indeed, people usually do not put up unflattering or unattractive photos of themselves. They do not highlight their drawbacks or less attractive features in online dating sites. They do not discuss their bad habits such as not doing the laundry or leaving their dirty underwear on the bedroom floor. Consequently, individuals high in emophilia may find themselves more ready to bond with someone after only a few encounters because their minds are wired to rush into a connection with someone.

Marry Me, Divorce Me (Repeat When Necessary)

Few relationship spheres are more tumultuous than those of celebrities. I cannot speak intelligently on the topic because I find myself actively avoiding what celebrities do in their private lives. However, there are high-profile cases in which marriages last months or mere days due to a wide variety of issues, not the least of which may be the ability to indulge in emophilic tendencies. Although I doubt that emophilia is overrepresented in celebrities, celebrities do have the resources, fan base, and social visibility necessary to indulge in whimsical romantic interests (again, alpha press). I will provide two historical examples of people who have certainly engaged in emophilic behaviors. Naturally, I do not know what their motivations were, what their personality is really like, or what their scores on the Emophilia Scale would be. Nevertheless, the publicly available information about their romantic lives certainly lends itself to an emophilia-related interpretation.

Historical Figures

In this section I will provide some examples of historical figures that appear to have demonstrated high levels of emophilia. Naturally, I draw from biographies and historical records and have obviously never met any of these people. So, the causes, motives, and actual nature of their behavior are unknown to me. Nevertheless, I illustrate these behavioral patterns in historical accounts for two reasons. First, it is interesting to see various figures from different classes in society, different backgrounds, and different countries demonstrating behavior indicative of emophilia. This demonstration also supports the idea that emophilia is found across cultures and across history and that it is not just some vagaries of modern generations or social media. It is not the case that "kids these days" are just higher in emophilia than are the generations before them. As I have mentioned, modern websites, online data, chats, cell phones, and instant messenger programs, may have changed the landscape of romantic courtship and provided the perception of more options, but emophilia has likely been with us as an individual difference for as long as love has been around. Modern freedoms notwithstanding, I draw on two historical examples to illustrate that emophilia existed long before modern technology.

Jean-Jacques Rousseau

Few suffered more sexual and emotional outbursts of passion and frenzy than the famous composer, novelist, performer, and all around emophilic man Jean-Jacques Rousseau (1712–1778). Interestingly and anecdotally, Rousseau lost his mother at the age of nine and had issues with searching for a strong mother figure (whom he later found). As we will address later when discussing development, it may be a strong historical example of how the absence of a mother may be associated with a tendency for emophilia. Rousseau was known for falling in love headfirst as early as the age of 12, and kept going. In fact, his main passion (although, he had many passions) was Madame de Warrens, or "Mamma" as he referred to her (yes, I'm serious). She referred to Rousseau as her "little one." Rousseau at one point remarked that he was too wildly in love with her to be intimate with her, although he was anyway.

Given the simultaneous emphasis on chastity and passion, it was not surprising that so many in this era produced spectacularly romantic and passionate works of art across all forms of mediums. As Freud would explain, this behavior is often referred to as "sublimation," or the transference of perceived inappropriate sexual energy into an activity (such as art) that is seen as more appropriate.

Further, given this juxtaposition of passion and principle, love became a common and quite bizarrely used cultural excuse to find someone in bed with someone else. "I couldn't help it; we just fell in love (last night), and we want to spend the rest of our lives together! (Until I meet someone else with whom I want to have sex)." Thus, the rationalization (again, a Freudian term) was clear with all these historical figures who had a passion for engaging in intimacy with an amorous focus. This rationalization can still be found in modern psychology.

Ludwig van Beethoven

According to most accounts, Beethoven (1770–1827) was also quite the serial romantic. According to his biography, Beethoven would give lessons to women and often find himself romantically drawn to them. Given his talent at the piano, this approach likely worked for him. However, Beethoven was also drawn to "forbidden fruit" and found himself in difficult situations that were unrealistic vis-à-vis relationships. Beethoven struggled with differential class issues and often fell for women that would have been impossible to marry. Further, Beethoven found himself in love with women that wound up marrying other men. The clearest example of this was the Countess Anna Brunsvik's daughter, who was referred to as "Josephine." Josephine was married, but Beethoven was in love with her anyway. These patterns of frequent falling in love, coupled with an attraction to women with whom it might seem difficult to have a relationship, reinforces the idea that Beethoven may have been a historical figure with a touch of emophilia.

Summary

Although the modern world and the technology we live with have changed the current landscape of dating and opportunities, I argue that emophilia is a big part of our nature and culture, and there are famous historical examples of people who were likely high in emophilia. Further, emophilic ideas abound in modern media, such as in songs and movies, suggesting that these ideas resonate with many people. However, this type of media is not new and can be found in *Romeo and Juliet* and all the way up to modern bands like the Backstreet Boys.

4

The Heart's Wandering Eyes
Emophilia and Infidelity

- *Emophilia predicts general infidelity and is the best predictor of emotional infidelity*
- *Because emophilia is associated with rapid romantic connections, they experience attraction to past and future partners*
- *Those high in emophilia often promise more than they can deliver in terms of commitment*

Sarah closed her computer and immediately began to feel sad. She was sad because the chat with Gino was over. She also felt guilty knowing that her husband, Michael, was sleeping in the next room beside their son. She just didn't know what to do. She felt like her heart belonged to Gino; always had, and probably always would. Sarah and Gino were college sweethearts. They separated when Sarah got a job in California and Gino stayed in Iowa. Gino did not want to have a long-distance relationship. Sarah met Michael through an online dating site. They built a relationship despite their busy schedules. Sarah felt it was practical to be with Michael. He was an upper-level manager at a top computer company and made his own schedule. He was kind and a great provider.

When Sarah first met Michael, it was an easy process. They had similar interests, similar jobs, and, most importantly, they lived close to each other.

Gino, on the other hand, was an actor. He had tried to move to New York City to launch a stage career but found himself back in Iowa as a drama teacher. In any case, Sarah found herself caring more and more about what Gino was up to. She shared hopes and dreams and stresses with him over chat. In more passionate times, she caught herself thinking, *"Was there ever a way for us to be together again?"* These thoughts disturbed Sarah as much as they excited her. She was even horrified at times by fantasies about Michael dying in a car accident or leaving her, so she could be free to pursue a relationship with Gino once again. Sarah was struck with jealousy when Gino mentioned he had a date, and she was elated when she learned the dates did not work out. She was overjoyed when he would say things like, "You'd never guess how bad this one was." They shared everything over chat and the occasional phone call. Sarah came to plan her days around the chats with Gino and was excited when Michael came home tired and had to sleep early. Sarah looked forward to the chats with Gino more than anything.

Infidelity

When two people enter a romantic relationship, it often comes with the expectation, whether implicit or explicit, of commitment. Although commitment can mean different things to different people, commitment often entails the concept of sexual and romantic fidelity. Fidelity is the expectation that certain activities (i.e., romantic, sexual, emotional) stay within the couple and will not occur with individuals outside of the relationship. Engaging in amorous, sexual, or emotional activity with another person, when the expectation is that those activities and connections stay exclusively within the relationship, is therefore defined as "infidelity." Infidelity has been referred to with a myriad of synonyms such as extradyadic involvement, being unfaithful, or cheating. However, across all these definitions there is some sexual or romantic activity in which someone is engaging that violates commitments to or expectations of fidelity.

Infidelity can be sexual or emotional, but most infidelity typically involves some element of both. Thus, here I define an "affair" as when both romantic and sexual interactions occur forming something of a separate relationship outside of the primary relationship. Some people may even maintain simultaneously serious commitments to two (or more) separate partners and secretly maintain both or all relationships. Others may maintain a primary partner, with one or more "affair partners." For example, a man who maintains a relationship with a wife but has secondary partners may refer to such partners as "mistresses."

However, not all infidelity falls into the category of an affair. A married businessperson, in a committed relationship, who has a one-night stand with someone on a business trip in a foreign country would be considered to have engaged in infidelity. Even though the two have no emotional connection, nor are they likely to ever meet again, this event constitutes infidelity. For example, an old friend of mine once told me of a story where he was waiting in a dentist's office for a visit. A strange man with his arm over his wife's shoulder winked at him as he walked by. My friend went and got the keys for a locked restroom and jingled them as he walked past. The man excused himself and slipped away from his wife into the restroom with my friend. The two engaged in sexual activity. After which, the married man returned to his wife, putting his arm back around her. Most would agree this situation was a case of infidelity, but given the fact that the two barely spoke, not even catching each other's names, few would consider this to have any emotional connection behind it. This sex without love would constitute sexual infidelity. The reverse type of infidelity may also occur (love without sex). Someone may fall in love with someone else yet never sexually or physically even touch that person. In some cases, they may have never even *met* the person, as is the case with online romance. Yet, an emotional connection has been formed, and most would also consider this infidelity, but *emotional* infidelity.

Emotional Infidelity

Emotional infidelity is an understudied and still poorly understood phenomenon (Guitar et al., 2017). It is hard to say when someone has "crossed the line" from friendship to romance, thus marking when emotional infidelity has begun. Pinpointing this first event of emotional infidelity is just as difficult as pinpointing the moment when one falls in love. What we do know is that emotional infidelity (often defined as "falling in love with someone else") is extremely hurtful to one's partner (Sabini & Green, 2004). From an evolutionary perspective, infidelity hurts because it signals one of many threats, which include (but are not limited to) the following: (a) our partner is unhappy with us in some way, (b) there is someone out there attractive enough to lure our partner into infidelity (which has self-esteem implications), (c) our partner, in whom we have invested tremendously, has the capacity for extremely poor judgment, or (d) our partner is about to leave us.

Broadly speaking, infidelity can be purely sexual (e.g., a one-night stand or physical affair with no emotions), purely emotional (e.g., someone with whom we share passions and intimacy, but never have sex), or a mix of both. There has been a tremendous amount of debate over which type of infidelity (sexual vs. emotional) hurts more. For example, Christine Harris (2003) has argued that the difference between the two types of hurt is a false dichotomy (but see Edlund & Sagarin, 2017, for review). We will address these two types of infidelity and the theories surrounding them later in the book. For now, it is important to know that infidelity, in all its forms, tends to hurt tremendously (Shackelford et al., 2000). When it comes to relationship damage, it is often the case that emotional infidelity is often harder to get over because it signals more than just a one-time act of indiscretion. Instead, it signals a persistent emotional longing for another person other than a primary partner. Individuals who are prone to falling in love fast and easily are at higher risk for infidelity because their threshold for developing feelings for someone else is much lower. Thus, given the way individuals high in emophilia are prone to falling in love fast and easily, they are likely to be at higher risk for engaging in infidelity, especially *emotional* infidelity.

Defining and Predicting Infidelity

Infidelity rates vary depending on samples, populations studied, and the infidelity questions asked. In a study I published in 2014 with my friend and colleague, Dana Weiser, we found that 20%–25% of people reported having "been unfaithful" in their current or most recent relationship. However, asking people if they had "been unfaithful" may yield different response rates than asking if they had "kissed someone" or "shared intimate secrets" with someone other than their primary partner. Some may not consider these things "being unfaithful," and, therefore, depending on the questions you ask, you may get higher or lower rates from study to study.

Many clinicians, researchers, and writers have tried hard to examine the causes, consequences, and treatments surrounding infidelity, including the characteristics and behaviors of the betrayed. Excellent books, such as *Treating Infidelity* written by Weeks and colleagues (2003) have described existing research on why individuals find extra-pair lovers, how they engage in these affairs, and how to help both the unfaithful partner and the betrayed partner in these situations. Despite all these investigations, and the volumes of research on infidelity (especially sexual; Buss, 2000), we know much less about the dispositional risks that exist for emotional infidelity. In other words, although external temptations and feeling unfulfilled in a primary relationship are situational risk factors, we still do not know why some individuals in otherwise happy committed relationships find themselves emotionally unfaithful, and some do not.

Perhaps adding to this difficulty is the fact that we do not have a good definition of emotional infidelity in the first place. Almost any behavior (e.g., chatting over coffee) that constitutes emotional infidelity can be seen as completely innocuous depending on the intent and circumstances. Further, seemingly innocuous behaviors (e.g., sending someone a wink emoji in a text) could be an act of emotional infidelity when done with romantic intent and in romantic circumstances. Thus, it is a construct that we all "know it when we feel it," but any one specific behavior may or may not constitute emotional infidelity.

To further illustrate this point, I pose a question: What is the difference between keeping a secret for a good friend that you do not tell your romantic partner and sharing intimate secrets with someone in the form of betrayal? Most may say the element of attraction and feeling "intimate"—but can someone attractive tell you a secret to keep from your partner and it not be infidelity? Emotional infidelity is often defined by asking people if they have committed "it"—aka, emotional infidelity. Now, individuals feeling guilty or prone to guilt may overreport that they have committed an act of emotional infidelity. Further, individuals who have rationalizations for their feelings or behaviors may underreport. However, emotional infidelity is the type of thing that you know you have done even if you cannot pinpoint exactly when you did it or when you crossed the line. Thus, unlike sexual infidelity, you cannot say with clarity, "Ah ha! That's the moment I crossed the line and became emotionally unfaithful!" It is usually a building of feelings, emotions, and intimate exchanges. The general rule of the jungle that I heard from one clinician was that if your partner knew all you are doing and feeling . . . would they be OK with it?

In the end, we are left relying on definitions of emotional infidelity that are vague, such as falling in love with someone else, keeping a secret crush, or engaging in an emotional affair. This vagueness makes identifying actual behaviors that constitute "emotional infidelity" difficult. Thus, it is a challenge to know when and why individuals commit emotional infidelity or with how many people.

Despite these challenges, there is a paper published by Stephen Drigotas and colleagues (1999) that offers a decent approximation of behaviors that may constitute emotional infidelity. Some items include "holding hands" and "sharing personal information such as hopes and dreams." Given the issues above, I would argue that it is insufficient to merely feel something private and special for someone other than your primary partner and not want your partner to know about it. Infidelity is an act, thus a specific behavior had to occur to "commit" infidelity. Thus, I would add that the individual feels these things then acts on them by sharing personal secrets, dreams, hopes, stories, or too much of themselves in general. However, if a person feels romantic love for someone other than their primary partner and walks away, disengages, or stops any personalized contact that could allow the love to grow further, I argue that is not infidelity. Thus, just feeling romantic love for someone is no more infidelity than feeling sexual desire for someone. Typically, one's actions are what really matter.

Definitions notwithstanding, feeling something private and special that you would not want your romantic partner to know about are the first signs that emotional infidelity is occurring. Regardless, when it comes to emotional infidelity, most practitioners will argue that there is some dysfunction or problem with the existing relationship. This problem may stem from dissatisfaction with one's partner or an emotional need for affection that is absent from a primary relationship. To be sure, these are indeed factors in predicting both sexual and emotional infidelity. In fact, anxiously attached individuals will often cite a need for belonging and emotional intimacy as reasons for infidelity (Weeks et al., 2003). However, some individuals are just more likely to be unfaithful, regardless of their satisfaction with their primary partner or their primary relationship.

For example, Barta and Keine (2005) argued that unrestricted sociosexuality (i.e., sexual permissiveness) is a risk factor for infidelity, even in perfectly happy relationships. Their argument, among others, was that individuals who are sociosexually unrestricted simply see more alternatives around them because they are open to one-time affairs whereas sociosexually restricted individuals are not. Although their commitment to their partner may mute these motivations, the desires are nevertheless there. A recent study demonstrates these assertions are supported. For example, there was a study conducted on patrons of Ashley Madison, a website for those in a relationship who are looking to have an affair (Selterman et al., 2023). Although a majority of the sample was cisgendered heterosexual men, the findings were fairly consistent across all demographics. Selterman and colleagues found that the majority of respondents were quite satisfied with their primary relationship. In fact, few reported marital disfunction. Although some had permission from their partner to be on the site, many did not. Nevertheless, few expressed guilt or negative emotions over seeking a sexual, romantic, or affair partner or engaging in infidelity. Thus, those who plan and are fully intending to engage in infidelity are typically not pursuing infidelity out of marital dissatisfaction and experience little guilt.

These results strongly suggest that individual differences play a huge role. A Gallup poll indicates that over 90% of those surveyed consider infidelity immoral (Fincham & May, 2017). Yet, those who are on a website for the explicit purpose of seeking an affair, or at least sexual or romantic connections outside of a primary relationship, feel no guilt over seeking and having these interactions. Thus, traits like disagreeableness and sociosexuality are likely to drive infidelity. However, these traits are particularly likely to drive sexual infidelity. Thus, given that sociosexuality is a strong predictor of sexual infidelity, what about emophilia? Emophilia should also be a strong predictor of infidelity in general, and it is highly likely that emophilia would be a strong predictor of emotional infidelity in particular.

Individuals who have a low threshold for emotional bonds with others, feel romantic connections right away, and fall in love easily may find themselves meeting someone, or thinking about an ex-partner, and wonder what could be or what could have been. Such ruminations, even for a moment, may open the door to a reciprocal exchange. If both parties begin to entertain the idea of a special emotional bond, the emophilia seeds have been planted.

Our first examination of these findings was in the laboratory. Participants were told that we were interested in their love lives. I had them fill out a form that asked for their romantic partner's initials (initials were asked to keep the study anonymous). We then asked for the initials of their best friends, romantic interests, and sexual interests. We also asked about their favorite movies and songs, just to obfuscate the purpose of the study. Then, for eight weeks, every participant logged onto a website (with reminders from both me and my research team) and answered just a few questions about whom they met that week and listed the initials of all their romantic and sexual interests. We went through the dataset and looked for times when the initials of their romantic interests were discrepant from their primary romantic partner.

We found that emophilia was the best predictor of having romantic interests outside of one's relationship. It is important to note that emophilia was the only predictor; sociosexuality, anxious attachment, and other variables had no effect. We also conducted a separate survey on self-reported emotional infidelity. As discussed, we asked about behaviors related to emotional infidelity (e.g., sharing intimate secrets, feeling a close romantic connection). We asked these questions in retrospective and longitudinal fashion. Throughout the study, we kept getting the same answer: emophilia is the best predictor. We since have replicated the link between emotional infidelity and emophilia numerous times.

If nothing else in this book has been clear, the link between emophilia and emotional infidelity is crystal: emophilia is the best predictor of emotional infidelity. Therefore, the next question is "why."

Why does this link exist? Why do emophilic individuals engage in more emotional infidelity? Is it a "need"? Is it "selfishness"? Or can they "not help themselves?" Emophilia does correlate slightly with selfish personalities. In fact, they tend to have a "Ludus" style of love, meaning that they see love as a game to be played. Individuals high in emophilia are not callous or disagreeable, nevertheless, they certainly have high levels of impulsivity, sensation seeking, and hypersensitivity to reinforcement, which are often seen in selfish personality traits. Therefore, they may find themselves so indulgent in their own excitement and wants that they become blind to the people that they are hurting.

So, Which Hurts Worse? Sociosexuality vs. Emophilic Tendencies Toward Infidelity

It should be stated at the outset that there is much still to be learned about non-heterosexual individuals and gender nonconforming individuals in this space. Unfortunately, much of this research fails to address differences among those who are gender nonconforming, nonbinary, and/or transgendered. Further, most of the traditional research focused on forcing people to choose one gender with which to identify: male or female. Thus, we must keep these limitations in mind.

In a widely cited study published in 1992, Buss and colleagues forced male vs. female participants to choose which was more upsetting: sexual or emotional infidelity. Men reported that, hypothetically, they would be more upset over sexual infidelity, and women responded that they would be more upset over emotional infidelity. Their theory behind these findings was that, for men, not guarding a partner's sexual fidelity meant risking raising another man's offspring. This concern was exclusive to men because fertilization occurs in women, thus, women always know that their baby is *theirs*, but men can never truly be sure (at least in ancestral times during our evolution; today, we have DNA tests for that sort of thing).

As a result, men have the exclusive concern of raising another man's child. Women, on the other hand, certain that her offspring is hers, were generally more concerned with abandonment.

Now, these explanations are tenuous because, while, yes, our ancestral environment and evolutionary biology play a big role in adapting our psychological perceptions of different situations, it is not the only driving force. Culture and socialization play a big role, too. Men are raised differently from women and expect women to provide for the house. Further, men were taught *not* to take sexual infidelity lying down. Further, in many societies, women are often raised to be submissive to their husbands and, up until very recently, were not given a whole lot of options for autonomy. Thus, they had to tolerate a lot of sexual infidelity for the sake of survival.

However, What About a Partner's Sexual and Emotional History?

I conducted a study a *long* time ago that examined this dichotomy in past relationships rather than present ones. I never published it, but I found interesting results. Instead of asking people how upset they would be by a romantic partner's infidelity (sexual vs. emotional), I asked how upset they would be if they (ex post facto) discovered a romantic partner's extensive history. Although I get into this later in the book in more depth, we may have had "that talk" with a partner at different phases of a relationship. It generally is bad taste to ask on a first date, "What's your number?" Meaning, of course, how many people that person has had sexual intercourse. Today, people often refer to that number as their "body count."

This question, in and of itself, is off-putting and can be awkward to answer. In fact, the question may not be straightforward. Does oral sex count? What about mutual masturbation? In Kevin Smith's 1994 Sundance award-winning movie, *Clerks*, the characters Dante and Veronica, who are boyfriend and girlfriend, get into a conversation about each other's sexual histories. Although they had been dating for eight months, Dante seems surprised (and pleased) to find out that his girlfriend only had sex with "three different people." However, upon learning that she has given oral sex to 36 people (well, 37 including *him*), Dante is horrified, and Veronica ends up walking away in disgust.

Given my huge affinity for Kevin Smith movies, I conducted a study related to this topic to find out what happens when men and women learn each other's numbers late in a relationship. However, I added a twist: I included a permissive *emotional* past as well as a permissive *sexual* past. As it turned out, neither men nor women reported that they would be terribly thrilled to find out that a current romantic partner had fallen in love repeatedly or that they had dozens of sexual partners in the past. However, women were mostly equal in how much they held men's feet to the fire on either issue. One exception was that anxiously attached women were *quite* concerned over a man's emotional history. Men, conversely, paid slightly less attention to the woman's emotional history. Men reported that they would be much more upset to find that she was extremely experienced, sexually.

This study highlights something I will get into later in the book, which is relevant to a man's ego when it comes to women's sexual history. Men who see sexual contact as a "conquest" or "ego stroke" are especially upset to find out that a woman was sexually active before and often. However, men are not bothered much by an extensive love history, particularly if they view the relationship as only a short-term emotional affair. Thus, men are less bothered to find out a woman had fallen in love a lot in the past. Although the mechanism of this phenomenon is unknown. For example, it could be that men simply stereotype women as "emotional," or it could be that past experiences of love are less ego threatening for men. Regardless, an extensive history of falling in love may be a red flag for future fidelity. This is because emophilia predicts infidelity (even general infidelity) more strongly than does sociosexuality. Thus, men who are truly concerned about a partner's fidelity may be barking up the wrong tree in choosing an emotionally experienced woman over a sociosexually experienced woman.

So, what is more averse in a partner, sexual or emotional permissiveness? Well, in my research my team and I found that for short-term relationships, no one really cares, but this may matter greatly in long-term relationships. I recall a cartoon I once saw that depicted a man and woman in bed together. The first persona said, "I want you to know I've never done this before." The second person said, "I believe you." The first person then responded, "Wow, well, you're the first one."

The second person asks, "The first one you've had sex with?" The first person responds, "No, the first one to believe me."

Knowing Your Partner's Past

Let's assume, for a moment, that you met a new potential partner. You are crazy about this person and really want to start something potentially very special. Then they drop the "bomb" question on you, which is a question that has ruined many great relationships: "How many people have you been with before *me*?" How do you answer? Perhaps your answer will depend on why you think they are asking in the first place. A friend of mine told me that if a potential or current partner ever asks that question, it usually ends the relationship. For her, it symbolizes a sense of ownership and conquest and says something about the partner that she finds unacceptable. For others, they may lie, exaggerate, or dodge the question. In popular media, *American Pie* and *American Pie 2*, made famous the concept of the "Rule of 3." When men give their "body count" you adjust (perhaps divide or subtract) because the number is overreported. This overreporting occurs because it is enhances perceptions of how successful they are with women. For women, you add or multiple by three because it is often underreported. This underreporting is driven by cultural norms surrounding chastity expectations of women. However, some may eagerly answer the question because the number is within cultural parameters of what is perceived as "acceptable" for their demographic category.

Susan Sprecher and her colleagues (1997) found that *most* people, regardless of gender, do not particularly want someone who has had a lot of sexual partners, at least when a long-term relationship is up for consideration. Most people want to believe that sex is something that will be considered "special" between the two of them, and it is hard to consider something special if it has been shared with many other people. Now, I recognize that there are many different attitudes and orientations, so I am only speaking in general. Further, at least among heterosexual couples, men and women diverge in their *reasons* as to why a lot of sexual partners is a turn-off for a potential (or even, current) partner.

As it turns out, women have reasons that are more practical. They focus the concerns over their partner's past on whether he will be *able* to "settle down," maybe start a family, and what kind of husband/father he may become. Research on sexually transmitted infections (STIs) also highlights that women are generally concerned that he may be carrying a disease. However, once these concerns have been assuaged, most women generally do not really worry about sexual history anymore.

Men, on the other hand, appear to have more egoistic reasons as to why they choose women with minimal sexual history. Researchers Roy Baumeister and Kathleen Vohs (2004) argued that many cultures treat a woman's sexuality as something of a commodity. Men are used to investing time, money, energy, or other resources into finding sexual access, and women then engage in sex with a devoted individual. Although it may sound sexist, this has been the way many cultures have taught men to think for many years. Consequently, men are conditioned in many cultures to view sex as valuable only if it is rare. Much like diamonds—beautiful though they may be, we would not pay top dollar for diamonds if they could be found in anyone's backyard.

In a study I published in 2016 in the journal *Sexuality and Culture*, I found that both men and women were generally not interested in partners who had extensive sexual histories and who reported *still* wanting those types of encounters. However, in another condition, the target indicated that they had not had sex in over a year because they do not want that life anymore and were now seeking a romantic commitment. The results were striking. Women were quite open to having a relationship with the individual who changed their ways and wanted a committed relationship. Men? Not even close. Men were *least* likely to choose this type of potential partner. In other words, they were avoidant of a woman who had an extensive past but wants a long-term relationship now.

But what about love? Less attention (both culturally and scientifically) seems to have addressed the question, "With how many people have you fallen in love?" Back when I lived in Tucson, Arizona, I had a friend with whom I would watch a TV show called *Elimidate*. The premise of the show was that three people were courting one person, and each round someone got "eliminated." One episode, there was a woman who bragged about having received marriage proposals over 10 times in her life. I recall looking at my friend and saying, "Gee, does she think that's a good thing?" Certainly, our society has socialized women (and to a much lesser extent, men) to be discrete about their previous relationships. However, it appeared that having over 10 men propose was a badge of honor for this woman. My mind (as an aspiring psychologist) immediately went to question what went so horribly wrong in these relationships that each suitor was on a totally different page than she was when it came to the seriousness of the commitment. Thus, it inspired the question in me: Would anyone be bothered by a partner who was in love 10 times prior?

Nevertheless, the question of one's *emotional* and *romantic* history may end up having more relevant consequences for one's current relationship than the question of one's sexual history. In fact, going back to my argument that women are more open-minded about a partner's sexual history than are men, I asked this same question to men and women (about both sexual and emotional histories). As it turns out, women are more averse to a man who has fallen in love many times than men are with respect to a woman's emotional history. Although, it should be noted that neither men nor women found such a target particularly attractive based on this information alone. This finding once again suggests that men are socialized to focus on sexual reputation with respect to his relationship partner but pay little attention to the emotional past of that same partner. Similarly, other sexist beliefs may attenuate men's concerns such that women are emotional or fickle in their feelings.

The Ego Game

Social psychology has long pointed out that, even among healthy and adaptive adults, we tend to take credit for our successes and tend to dismiss failures and bad events as "bad luck" and "not our fault." (e.g., Miller & Ross, 1975). People in Western cultures like to feel they are special. So, if two people meet at a party and go home together for sex, for ego-related reasons they both may want to feel that the other person does not do this often. However, the same should be true for emotional intimacy. When a person falls for us, it is difficult not to believe that this person is just smitten with us, and that this is the only time something like this has happened before. It is flattering and perhaps exciting (provided you like the person back).

I Just Love You Both

I used to work at the local ShopRite grocery store in my hometown of Oakland, New Jersey. There, I met a lot of different people both at the checkout counter (where I briefly worked as a bagger and a cashier) and those with whom I worked. One woman in particular, Kalie, was someone I wound up talking to a lot. During breaks, I would buy myself a six-pack of muffins and share some with her. We would talk about relationships and other typical topics for 18-year-old high school students. She was briefly dating a guy named Rick. However, Rick was more interested in another woman (Sam), and that woman happened to be interested in a different guy named Kevin (there was a lot of relationship drama for a part-time job). Kevin had a girlfriend at the time, so when Kalie was single, I set her up with one of my best friends in the whole world: Mike. It turned out, however, that Kalie was also quite unpredictable. About three weeks into her relationship with Mike, she started to disclose that her ex-boyfriend recently came back into her life. Upon further inquiry from Mike, she disclosed that she still had feelings for her ex. Although her ex was a recovering crack/cocaine addict, she felt such butterflies around him. She was certainly into Mike as well, which was confusing for Mike. When she said, "I just love you both," Mike figured it was time to end things. I wound up feeling extremely guilty that I subjected my friend to this heartache.

Kalie went on to date a few others before I left my job at ShopRite. It was interesting to find out that the reoccurring theme of her ex coming in and out of her life repeated itself with others. She always seemed earnest in her feelings but kept bouncing back and forth between a new love and an old flame.

Unlike dark personalities, or individuals who are intentionally and overtly manipulative (often referred to as "players"), an individual who is high in emophilia and is unfaithful often feels a lot of guilt about their emotional and sexual indiscretions. Individuals high in emophilia generally do not manipulate on purpose but rationalize that their behavior is somehow OK. Thus, they usually want what they want and are overly optimistic about how things will "work themselves out" eventually. They tend to be slaves to their feelings, even though they may lead to completely catastrophic outcomes and constitute irrational behaviors to an outside observer. They may end up misleading people unintentionally by saying things such as "I will always love you" or "I will always be here for you" when there is no way one could possibly know such things, especially early in a relationship.

Unlike individuals low in emophilia who are unfaithful, high emophilia individuals do not necessarily want to *leave* one partner for another; they find themselves split, like Kalie or Sarah. At this point a discussion on polyamory might be warranted.

Right here, I want to note that more research is needed on emophilia and polyamory. Theoretically all people high in emophilia should experience some level of polyamory. However, not all people who engage in polyamory would be high in emophilia. "Polyamory" is where an individual is in a committed relationship that involves more than two people. For example, three people may be in a polyamorous relationship that involves exclusivity and commitment, just among three people instead of two. However, polyamorous relationships can be committed and lasting. Thus, one could be high or low in emophilia and engage in a polyamorous relationship.

Recall that emophilia is defined by falling in love fast and often. Someone could fall in love with two people after knowing them for 10 years, have a polyamorous relationship with both of them, and remain in those relationships for a long time. That would not be emophilia as per my definition.

Individuals high in emophilia often have difficulty choosing among relationship options. This difficulty with indecisiveness stems from never wanting to sever ties or "shut the door" on an old flame because they feel like they never know what the future holds. Thus, they end up accumulating romantic interests, and they often do not get people "out of their system." Further, an individual high in emophilia may consider a relationship over, but a random phone call, a chance encounter, or an accidental reunion with an ex can reignite amorous feelings and thoughts of "what might have been."

A useful analogy for understanding romantic relapse with those high in emophilia comes from addictive drugs. For some, love might be understood this way as well. For example, among nicotine addicts, especially adolescents and those who started smoking early, there are things called "retrograde cravings." In the early days of quitting smoking, the receptors of the brain that process nicotine are *screaming* for nicotine. As the residual nicotine leaves your system you are craving a cigarette immensely. People can become irritable, depressed, or downright desperate in response to these painful cravings. Once this stage passes, one must get passed social cues. Old bars, someone's house, hanging out with friends, or a particular location may spark mental cravings for a cigarette, even though the nicotine has passed through the individual's system. If the person can pass these steps, there is a final step of retrograde cravings. These can happen 6, 8, or even 10 years after someone has officially quit smoking. This is where a strong stressor often gets combined with availability and reward cues (such as a fight with one's spouse right outside an old 7-Eleven where you used to by a pack with an old friend walking by with a smoke). The individual feels a strong psycho-physiological push to start smoking again.

Aside from giving you a lesson on nicotine addiction, this analogy is actually a great way to understand how individuals high in emophilia feel when it comes to their ex-partners. Individuals high in emophilia feel a "withdrawal" from a romantic partner initially. After a period, they may have gotten that person out of their system, but the residual memories remain. There may be social cues pushing the person to get back with their ex, such as seeing "joint" friends or going to an old spot where they used to date. Even (yes) bumping into each other in a coffee shop or a bar may create not only awkwardness but also a sense of missing each other. Like smoking, most people feel like if they get past this stage, they are all but "in the clear." However, in one survey we did, we found that emophilic individuals are likely to have had intrusive thoughts about a long-lost lover in the past year than are those low in emophilia Thus, emophilic individuals may have retrograde cravings when a perfect storm arises for an old flame.

Emotional Needs Driving Emophilia-Based Infidelity? Probably Not

Emophilia is based on "want," not "need." Individuals high in emophilia are not *necessarily* clingy. They simply have a sensitivity to the rush of love and fall in love faster and more often than others. Going back to the definition in Chapter 1, high emophilia individuals tend to simply have a lower threshold for acknowledging that they are "in love" than others. Further, we also found that high emophilia individuals feel as though they have less conscious control over whom they fall in love with and when. When you combine these perspectives, it becomes very clear why individuals high in emophilia are prone to emotional infidelity.

Self-Deception

Individuals high in emophilia are also self-deceptive, as we will talk about a bit later in the book. Self-deceptive, as the name dictates, means that they "deceive themselves." However, this definition may be a bit misleading because it implies intentional action, such as trying to rationalize behavior or telling themselves things that they actively know are not true. In actuality, it is the opposite. By self-deceptive, we mean that emophilic individuals engage in a motivated, biased, and unconscious way of thinking. By unconscious, I mean that the actual "thinking" part is outside the awareness of the individual. Because individuals high in emophilia often have typical levels of agreeableness, they often look to others to justify or rationalize their behaviors that are often egregiously contradictory and difficult to understand.

The other consequence of self-deception is that individuals high in emophilia dive into relationships without fully thinking them through (another concept we will return to later in the book). Thus, they lack impulse control when pursuing their romantic feelings. Thus, individuals high in emophilia may find flaws in their partners later down the road that they did not anticipate when they first agreed to a serious relationship. They may also find new love interests "perfect" in every way and overlook obvious red flags and flaws. Thus, individuals high in emophilia are blinded to the bad aspects of their partners early on and imagine a much rosier picture of their partner sooner than others, and they are often disappointed by the "reality" of their partner because their "fantasy" partners are so appealing. As a result, relationship dissatisfaction may occur in such situations that often exacerbate their journey toward emotional infidelity.

Jealousy and Emophilia

In his book *The Dangerous Passion*, David Buss (2000) discusses how jealousy is inherently yoked with love. There are some levels of jealousy that are healthy in relationships, and others that are morbid or pathological and are not linked with love. I have found both anecdotally and in my empirical research that those who *intend* to be unfaithful tend to be most jealous of their romantic partners. It is an interesting sort of ironic hypocrisy that those who are consciously aware of their intentions to stray from a relationship tend to *assume* that their partner has similar cognitions or temptations. Specifically, A. J. Figueredo, Sally Olderbak, and I came up with the Intentions Towards Infidelity Scale, or ITIS. The ITIS is a six-item scale that captures conscious intentions to be unfaithful to a romantic partner, active hiding of one's relationship from potentially attractive interlopers, and full intentions to cover-up one's affairs. We found that individuals who strongly endorse this scale are highly suspicious of their romantic partners and what *they* are up to. It is unclear whether it is some form of ironic guilt, the assumption that our partners think like us (i.e., since I'm thinking about infidelity, so must my partner), or it is a centralized strategy to be unfaithful and not suffer any consequences.

However, unlike those with the *intention* to be unfaithful, individuals high in emophilia may never intend to be unfaithful. The Emophilia Scale and the ITIS are typically uncorrelated. Thus, individuals high in emophilia are often blind to their vulnerability to stray and genuinely believe that their relationship will last. Because they are so convinced (each time) that they have met "the one," they do not consider infidelity to be a possibility. However, as the rose tint fades from their glasses and the rush of excitement wears off for highly emophilic individuals, new love interests start to come into focus, and infidelity becomes a high risk.

Nevertheless, individuals high in emophilia do not express higher rates of jealousy themselves. Which perhaps makes sense, they experience love just like everyone else, just faster. Thus, they do not necessarily have a particular concern over sexual or emotional infidelity, and they generally operate under typical auspices of trust. In fact, as I discuss throughout this book, they *prematurely* trust. Individuals high in emophilia are at slightly higher risk of being the victims of infidelity as well, simply because they do not vet their partners and their relationships develop so quickly. Thus, they have higher rates of relationship dissolution and are cheated on more than those low in emophilia.

Monogamish or Cultural Abandonment

I want to present the reader with the following scenario:

> *A husband and wife have been married for 20 years. After having two kids and going through menopause, the wife is struggling with sexual interest. The husband, a very successful businessman, is still quite interested in sexual contact. Because he flies overseas frequently, he very often finds himself tempted to engage in extramarital affairs. Scotland is home to a woman who is interested in sleeping with him with no personal relationship. He decides to take her up on this offer. They have sex a few times a year, but apart from that, he is home with his wife.*

Many people with whom I've discussed this scenario say that what he should do is be faithful to his wife and just deal with the fact that there is little sexual energy in his marriage. I want to be clear that I am not at all arguing for one thing or another. To avoid being unfaithful in monogamous cultures, men and women typically stay and be faithful or leave their partner. Now the issue is, what is the most compassionate thing to do in the above scenario? Being in the relationship and staying faithful is the answer most of us would come up with. But let's assume something is going to happen, one way or the other. Should he abandon his wife and start a new life? Perhaps he could stay single or find someone new? Alternatively, should he engage in this casual arrangement? Marriage counselors may be able to help find ways to better negotiate the situation at hand, but failing that, some argue that the man should be honest and just leave his wife. Others, however, have argued that a silent arrangement is more compassionate. Further, there are cultural norms in some countries that are more permissive of this type of behavior when compared with others. Many of these perceptions also have to do with wealth, gender dynamics, and other cultural variables.

For some, saying you just fell in love with someone new may be more understandable than wanting an affair. Thus, leaving may seem like a reasonable thing to do because love is behind it. Although social perceptions may change, there is a lot of hurt and complexity behind these decisions.

All genders can be lured away from a partner for a variety of reasons. Among those reasons is having a partner who has lost interest in sex. However, there are individual differences here. When someone high in emophilia hits a bump in the road, they are likely to find themselves interested in a new love. In contrast, if this person is the only person with whom you have fallen in love (or perhaps ever will), you are more likely to stay despite sexual dissatisfaction. Thus, not all people stray or leave when relationships get rocky.

I recall one event from my time living in Costa Rica when a group of my friends went out dancing. A woman within the group was quite interested in one of the men who had a girlfriend living in the United States. He was indeed lonely and separated from all the people he knew. When we returned to the apartment complex, she followed him to his room and laid down on his bed, but he resisted her advances. He wound up sleeping on the floor as she fell asleep on the bed. In the morning, she gave up and took a cab back home. He had every opportunity for sex, and no one would have ever known. Nevertheless, he chose to stay faithful. Indeed, some individuals are fiercely faithful to their partners, even in the face of a consequence-free opportunity. Some may even stay faithful when confronted with clear and obvious evidence that it is time to "jump ship." In fact, some may even have a consequence-free exit strategy to a better life and still choose to remain.

As Hunt (1959) discusses, one historical example of incredible fidelity is Elizabetta Gonzaga, the wife of Guidobaldo di Montefeltro (who was Duke of Urbino). Elizabetta was incredibly devout and faithful to an otherwise frail and impotent husband. Making matters worse, Cesare Borgia of Italy had made a descent on the Duke's land, without his defenses fully formed. Borgia, living up to his billing as underhanded, then offered Elizabetta a better life if she left the Duke. She was offered a full Catholic papal annulment of her marriage and the promise of a romantic French husband who would also receive a pension for his husbandly services.

To her amazing credit, Elizabetta refused it all and remained as a fleeing outcast caring for her husband in his poor health. As fate would have it, Pope Borgia died in 1503, his armies were soon after defeated, and the happy couple returned home to a royal welcome. Talk about the tables turning! However, her fidelity and amazing spirit attracted not only the Duke but also the Duke's soldier and (later) Ambassador Baldassare Castiglione, but that is another story.

I would argue that there are three big factors that play into whether someone will stay faithful no matter what: (1) being low in emophilia, (2) having restricted sociosexuality, and (3) being high in conscientiousness. Conscientiousness is a trait that is associated with strong commitments and persistence. Such individuals are likely to see their promises through. Recall that individuals who are low in emophilia and who have a restricted sociosexuality have a very high threshold for developing sexual or romantic feelings for someone else. Thus, they will stay if the relationship is good and will be less interested in an affair with someone else because few people ever pass that threshold of interest for them.

On the other hand, individuals high in emophilia are not only likely to be unfaithful but also do not tolerate infidelity insofar as they are more likely to leave if cheated on. For example, I tested people's reactions to real and hypothetical infidelity. When asked to imagine what they would do if their partner was unfaithful, individuals high in emophilia reported that they would stay and work things out, whereas anxiously attached individuals reported that they would leave. However, in a separate survey, when we asked about actual past behaviors—specifically, participants were asked if a partner had cheated in the past, and if they left because of it—we found that emophilia and anxious attachment reversed their patterns. Individuals high in emophilia were *more* likely to leave the relationship immediately following infidelity, whereas anxiously attached individuals were *least* likely to leave. Thus, although individuals high in emophilia overlook much when it comes to *initiating* a torrid relationship, they let very little slide once the relationship has passed through the initial honeymoon phase. Individuals high in emophilia may initially rally around their partner during hardship, however, over time, they may tire of providing such support when the rush of love wears off.

I have one friend (Paul) from college who dated a woman who had experiences with being abused. He fell in love with her virtually overnight. Initial encounters turned into long phone conversations and mutual pledges of lifelong love. He, at first, was very understanding, respected boundaries, and was patient with her regarding the past trauma. However, over time, she began to lose interest in sex. He stayed incredibly supportive for a period, but he eventually started going on dates with other women. Then those encounters turned into their own long phone conversations and mutual pledges of love as his love interest eventually moved on to different women.

Broken Promises, Not Just Fidelity

There was a recent finding in the psychological literature describing that how much you *promise* a romantic partner is a function of love and commitment. How much you see *them through* and *do* the things you promised is mostly a function of your personality—specifically, how conscientious you are. As aforementioned, conscientiousness predicts sticking to one's commitments. Conscientious people generally do not *over*commit. Instead, they have realistic goals, they are diligent, and stick to the job until it is done. They are generally bound to do their duty, whatever that may be.

Now, it should be noted that emophilia is not correlated with conscientiousness. However, individuals high in emophilia *do*, especially early on in relationships, promise a lot. They offer unconditional and forever love to their new love interest or partner. Now, again, it is important to mention that these promises are not manipulative or intentionally misleading. Indeed, individuals high in emophilia really *believe* it and *want* to deliver such things to their partners. However, immediately finding that forever and unwavering love is often a bit lofty, and the romantic partner of the high emophilia individual is usually met with disappointment.

So, why do individuals high in emophilia do this? Do they not learn from their mistakes? Interestingly, this repeated process goes back to their self-deceptive nature. When they find someone and their emotional side is running at high speed, the promises they sincerely want to give and deliver on for their romantic partner are reinforcing. They feel good. The individual high in emophilia genuinely experiences a rush of positive affect when they make these promises and honestly feel excited about the future with this person. The decision that emophilic individuals engage in to open up and promise the world is a very reinforcing process.

In sum, emophilia is something to consider in predicting and explaining emotional infidelity and infidelity in general. Such individuals may find themselves gravitating toward others, even though their current relationships are working out just fine. Further, if there are relationship troubles, emophilia may accelerate the deterioration by finding someone else. Individuals high in emophilia are self-deceptive. Specifically, they love to make romantic promises that are lofty and unlikely to be kept. Yet, those high in emophilia are sincere in the moment, despite the unrealistic nature of the promises.

5

Selected for Love

Evolutionary and Developmental Explanations for Emophilia

- *Emophilia may be an evolved trait promoting reproductive success through sincere yet short-lived romantic investment*
- *Developmental instability (e.g., mother absence) increases emophilia, likely by pushing individuals toward fast life history strategies*
- *Dopamine hypersensitivity drives the romantic "rush" in emophilia, while serotonin may regulate or dampen it*

At the Society for Personality and Social Psychology meeting in 2009, I chatted with a prominent evolutionary psychologist about my research on emophilia. He was skeptical. He asked a question that I could not immediately answer, which was, "How could something as costly as falling in love over and over again be adaptive?" He posed a good question. According to evolutionary theory on individual differences (Buss, 2009), all heritable personality traits had to have conferred some advantage to our ability to pass on our genes, at least in certain environments. Thus, observable variations must make evolutionary sense depending on one's environment. Consequently, to establish emophilia as a major individual difference, I had to answer this question, and it was not easy at first.

Thinking of a dispositional trait that predicts falling in love repeatedly as "adaptive" does seem absurd at first blush. Love blinds us to alternative (and possibly better) relationships and relationship partners. Further, it creates behavior that is easily classified as irrational and costly, especially in terms of time and money (Aron et al., 1992). Further, love clouds our thinking, leading to a willingness to put another before ourselves and (often) above all others. Thus, love creates an irrational mindset. Yet, across my investigations, many of which I examined in my dissertation (Jones, 2011), I have found Emophilia Scale (EP Scale) scores to be stable and reliable across different time points within the same individuals. Further, the EP Scale shows robust predictions across different cultures and age groups. Therefore, explaining why people may vary on this critical dimension is a theoretical must. This chapter is dedicated to understanding the evolutionary origins of why emophilia may have emerged and what functions it serves in the human condition.

To understand why some may have evolved to fall in love repeatedly, it is necessary to understand how and why people fall in love in the first place. Evolutionary psychologists have argued about love being a human universal, why it may have evolved, and what benefits (and costs) it brings with it. For example, David Buss argues that love is a human universal. In cross-cultural research conducted in 1989, Buss found that people of almost every culture, ethnicity, and country have some experience with the idea of romantic love. Even in cultures of arranged marriage, often individuals either "learn to love" their partner, remarry for love, or learn to live without it.

But why did this concept of "love" emerge in the first place? Some (e.g., Buss, 1988; Frank, 1988) argue that love evolved to solve the adaptive problem of commitment. Buss (2006) notes that if you were with someone for rational reasons, then equally rational reasons would lead you to leave that person. In other words, on a planet of more than 7 billion people, chances are that there is a better match for you in personality, physical appearance, values, and the like when compared to the person with whom you are currently in a relationship. The possibility that a better partner is out there, even if it is just an illusion, may weaken your commitment if not for love. Love is like a drug that diffuses rational thinking and clouds your judgment. It affects your perceptions such that you do not even entertain the possibility of a "better" alternative because you delude yourself into believing you already have the best (Murray et al., 1996). Further, research has shown that individuals who are in love do not even notice attractive potential partners in the environment, even when those potentials express interest. Instead, what we notice is the attractive *rivals* in our environment, ostensibly in the service of guarding our partner against running away with that rival (e.g., Nadler & Dotan, 1992).

This behavior is adaptive because it keeps partners together for longer durations. Thus, it allows them to grow together, raise children, sacrifice for each other, and benefit as a team. Moving aimlessly from one love interest to another may be fun, but it is costly when you are making sacrifices only to move on soon after. Buss (2000) points out that the most important aspect of love and its expression is that it signals long-term intent. Buss further argues that there is a specific circuit in the brain most likely linked with romantic love. Research on the neurobiology of love has confirmed this to be true (Aron et al., 2005). Buss argues that much like love-related behaviors that are more readily observable (e.g., jealousy), the neurological mechanisms linked with love may be triggered in some and never triggered in others.

I would argue that high levels of emophilia occur when that specific circuit is sensitive, triggered often, and triggered with a variety of partners. However, because love is costly, *why* would anyone evolve a sensitive trigger for that sort of thing? I argue that there are reasons that may explain why a hair trigger for love may have been adaptive. One central reason is signaling long-term intent that is (unconsciously) designed to fade.

Fading Intent

As mentioned previously, emophilia is not a manipulative trait. Thus, when individuals signal long-term commitment intent, they are not consciously doing so with the awareness that they will withdraw that commitment later. Instead, they deceive themselves into believing that this relationship (unlike other love interests) will stand the test of time. One of the most effective ways to deceive someone else is to first deceive yourself. Research on self-deception (e.g., von Hippel & Trivers, 2011) has found that there are virtually no cues that someone is deceiving you when they believe the message in the first place—even though that message is false. Self-deception is typically an unconscious process (Paulhus, 1984). By unconscious, I mean that people do not realize what is going on in their heads. For example, individuals high in emophilia would not wake up and think, "How can I get myself to show this person commitment signals without meaning it?" Nor would they think, "How can I increase my evolutionary fitness by finding a guilt-free way of moving between partners and having multiple offspring?" The former may be something that a manipulative person would consider. However, the latter is something most people generally do not consciously consider.

There are several potential reasons why individuals high in emophilia may be self-deceptive when it comes to love. The main reason is that emophilia would help individuals move from partner to partner more effectively with less guilt. Because individuals high in emophilia signal a sincere commitment to a potential partner, it is believable. This sincerity stems from the fact that they have convinced *themselves* they are in love. Thus, all the signals they send, such as *I am in love*, and *I am ready to invest*, are genuine. However, when the initial phase of the relationship is over, individuals high in emophilia often find interest in another partner. This repeated pattern may be evolutionarily advantageous. First, during this time of courtship, a child is likely to be conceived, especially because the two partners believe the relationship will last. Thus, this rapidly developed commitment signals a readiness to invest in the long-term, when in fact individuals high in emophilia are likely to change their minds. Having multiple love interests and genuinely signaling long-term investment to them may be a way to cultivate a hedge-betting strategy in making sure at least one will invest and commit. Further, it may be advantageous in terms of diversifying offspring (i.e., having multiple children with different partners) and parental investment during critical years of development.

Emophilic individuals do not intend to run off with someone else once they fall in love; it just sort of "happens." Evolution turns a blind eye to what is "right," "ethical," or "moral"—it is just about what works. Even if the person left a wake of heartbreak and anger in the aftermath, if it works, people repeat it. By somewhat blinding people to the harm they will cause, the mind may have found a special "trick" that allows people to move from partner to partner without necessarily being callous or manipulative. Further, emophilia also provides individuals with a rationalization for having a child right away. After all, the feeling of love is real, and the idea that this will last forever is real as well. In sum, the experience of genuinely falling in love fast and often may be the unconscious mind's way of getting a partner to invest and stick around (just long enough) when they might not have stuck around otherwise. These events happen because the intentions are genuine—the person *really* is in love. Whether someone is falling in love for the 1st time or the 100th time, the feelings are real, and the person will engage in all the irrational thinking and clouded perceptions of someone in love.

Much like a drug, however, emophilia-driven love has a half-life. When the drug starts to fade, the effects do too. The same is true of love, especially love within an emophilic. Although emophilic individuals rarely fall completely "out of love" or shut the door on an old love interest, the *exclusive* aspects of their love fade. Thus, they begin to open the door to new love interests. In this way, emophilic individuals have more committed relationships, which last shorter than average.

To understand a little more the importance of short- vs. long-term relationships, we must first establish the different adaptive purposes they serve. Overall, people who want to have children do so in long-term relationships. Most often, people will fall in love, raise children together, invest in each other, rely on family and blood relatives, engage in community, avoid risks, and resist alternatives to the relationship. However, there are individuals (who are perfectly healthy) who pursue alternatives to this long-term norm. They seek many sexual partners, move around, and have children with different partners. Such individuals invest less in their children, embrace risky behavior, avoid investment of any kind, and entertain the alternatives at every turn. To understand why emophilia may have evolved, it is critical to understand a little bit about the nuts and bolts of the different strategies humans engage in when having children.

Life History Strategy

In general, the one that bears—at minimum—the most burden for reproducing will always be the choosiest when it comes to casual sex. Among humans, that would be those who get pregnant. Think back to a time when we didn't have courts, houses, addresses, phones, and laws. If, for example, a man and a woman met and decided to have sex, the burden of the child being born is much higher for the woman than for the man. For a man to conceive a child, it only takes the amount of time to have sex, which could be the potential extent of his investment. For a woman, she must carry the developing child inside of her for approximately nine months. Thus, for almost a year, the woman is unable to reproduce again. For the man (depending on his energy), he may conceive another child later that very day. Now, researchers such as Buss and Schmitt (1993) demonstrated that when men plan to *invest* in their offspring (as many men do), then they become equally choosey about with whom they have sex. Note that these findings are consistent with today and across different cultures (e.g., Koohgard et al., 2024). Naturally, modern-day birth control and sterilization techniques have changed the conscious landscape of these behavioral patterns. However, the evolutionary footprint remains.

Research on *life history strategy* began by comparing different species in their approaches to reproduction and parenting (MacArthur & Wilson, 1967). As it turns out, the males and females of all sexually reproducing organisms on our planet can be arranged on a continuum from long term to short term in mating, which corresponds to slow vs. fast development (e.g., Figueredo et al., 2005). On the fast or short-term side of things, you have organisms such as rabbits, snakes, and oysters. Female oysters, for example, expel their eggs into the ocean, and that's all the effort there is when it comes to reproduction. Thus, she is clearly not picky about what male comes along and fertilizes her eggs. Another example of a short-term organism is rabbits. Rabbits are famous for their large litters and rapid reproductive capabilities. Female rabbits have multiple litters of numerous offspring. This high number of offspring is needed because many small rabbits do not reach sexual maturity. In the wild, few bunnies in a large litter will survive. Such animals face high infant mortality. Their environment is unstable, unpredictable, and survival is rare. Another way to put it is, *everything eats rabbit*. Therefore, for a mother rabbit to only have a few bunnies and take extra special care of them would be a bad idea, given that most will not survive. Instead, having as many different bunnies as possible is the optimal strategy. Having many offspring increases the chances that a few survive, go on to have offspring, and continue the genetic cycle. It is also important for baby bunnies to "grow up" fast. Because their lives are short, they must hit puberty and start having their own babies quickly. In other words, they must get hopping (pun intended).

On the other hand of the mating spectrum, there are elephants. A baby elephant dying is a rare occurrence within a herd. Several cases of parental elephants mourning the loss of an offspring for years have been documented. However, unlike rabbits, elephant environments are social, stable, and predictable. Because integrating into a herd of elephants takes social skills and development, having too many calves would not be wise. This is because parental elephants would have to spend time socializing and raising all those calves. The offspring that are not well taken care of generally die out or don't reproduce. Thus, the emphasis is on parental care rather than reproductive output. In line with this long-term mating style, pubertal timing is slowed down for elephants because they are better off "learning the ropes" of their environment and adapting to their climate rather than reproducing too soon.

Humans are more like elephants than bunnies in that they fall on the longer term end of this spectrum. However, people vary on this long-to-short term dimension. Further, this variation correlates with certain traits and individual differences. Thus, long-term individuals are quite attached to parents and partners, delay sex until commitment, have fewer children, invest in those children, and so forth. Now, there are other people who do not attach well to parents or partners, have sex frequently and often, have many children, and/or do not spend that much time raising those children.

Naturally, these statements oversimplify a very complex process. There are individuals who pursue multiple strategies when it comes to relationships (Gangestad & Simpson, 2000), and there are even those who switch strategies. For example, some may have short-term relationships when they are young (e.g., in college) and choose to pursue a long-term strategy after graduation.

Further, cultural norms have a big role to play as well. In the United States, extended family care is not as common as in places such as Mexico or Taiwan. Further, big families are celebrated by the extended family in different cultures, whereas in some places big families are difficult to manage. Moreover, at least within the United States, those with better access to sexual education and birth control typically make more informed decisions when it comes to sex and having children.

Not only do genetics and evolutionary environment matter in shaping life history strategy but developmental environment does as well. For example, Bruce Ellis is a developmental psychologist at the University of Utah who does a lot of work on developmental plasticity and the consequences of instability in a child's developing environment. Ellis has argued that growing up in a father-absent home is a developmental risk factor for children, especially between the ages of birth to six years (see Ellis, 2004). Note that most of these effects are due to the instability that emerges from single-parent homes (Ellis et al., 2021). Ellis and others have consistently found that girls raised in father-absent or tumultuous homes have their first period (menarche) much sooner in life than girls who have a stable and intact family unit. In fact, the presence of stepfathers in the house is often an exacerbating factor for this effect. Now, let me be clear, I believe that when someone who loves nonbiological children and raises them as their own, it is a beautiful thing. However, when stepfathers have antisocial traits, they are an especially huge risk factor for child mistreatment (Hilton et al., 2015). Further, there is instability here that is a problem, and a single parent can make heroic efforts to minimize that impact. However, on average, single-parent households tend to be more unstable than two-parent households.

In the world of emophilia, connections with life history strategy are complicated. Although, in practice, emophilic individuals appear to be pursuing a fast life history strategy, their proximal actions suggest the opposite (i.e., they really do want to commit and make this relationship last). Thus, emophilic individuals may have found an odd middle ground where they stay short enough to diversify but long enough so that they are not here today and gone tomorrow.

Benefits of Offspring Diversification

There are advantages to genetically diversifying one's children in unstable environments. Having children with multiple partners is an evolutionary advantage if you do not know what is coming. To say it differently, it is a form of hedge-betting, and it is a trade-off either way. In stable environments, there are drawbacks to hedge-betting, whereas in unstable environments, there are advantages. Think of it this way: If you *knew* what stocks would go *up* in the next five years, why not invest everything in those and make a ton of money? However, because we *don't* know how companies will perform, we diversify our portfolios, especially when we want to be risk-averse.

I do not mean to trivialize the act of having children. Because we are conscious creatures, we make decisions regarding our behavior that are deliberative. Thus, most of these decisions involve processes such as proximity and emotion in combination with unconscious evolutionary processes. So now, you may be asking the question that I've heard numerous times: "Why didn't we evolve to have as many children as possible?"

As my PhD advisor (Del Paulhus) would always tell me, everything is a trade-off. There are no advantages without disadvantages, and there is no such thing as a free lunch. This has never been more apropos than in the realm of mating. Spending time on children means that you are not spending time finding new partners. Finding new partners means you aren't spending time with children. Having multiple offspring means you are dividing your time among them. Working more means less time with family, more time with family means less time at work, and so on.

Naturally, long- vs. short-term mating is a spectrum, and people vary on that spectrum, even within their lifetimes. The characteristics of potential partners we want will change with age and across individuals. Further, some may recall having different types of relationships in their 20s than in their 40s. People may pursue different mating strategies simultaneously or change strategies as they get older. For example, some individuals choose to have a few short-term relationships or sexual affairs in college but may be happily married now. Others who are happily married now did not have any casual sexual affairs. One type of person is not necessarily more "happily married" than the other. Moreover, some may have children early, even with different partners, but eventually settle down.

Another approach that some engage in is to have a primary partner and have children with that partner but engage in infidelity to have additional offspring. Notably, many societies tend to frown on this type of behavior. It nevertheless has evolutionary advantages, provided the individual gets away without consequences. However, there is still another potential possibility that is a bit of a compromise between the long- and short-term urges: *serial monogamy*. In fact, serial monogamy seems to be of a more common pattern across history and society than traditional monogamy.

Serial monogamy is the idea that a person falls in love, commits, and has a relationship for a while; however, the individual eventually moves on to a new love interest. This move usually occurs after a certain amount of time. For example, there is the colloquial "seven-year itch," which refers to the amount of time in a marriage that passes when people are likely to pursue interests outside the relationship. Often in these relationships, people have children and raise them. But once the children are of a certain age, parenting becomes less critical to development than other factors. As mentioned, Ellis noted that the most critical years of development are birth to six—about seven years. Coincidence? Maybe not. In fact, research seems to support this exact pattern.

Research by Helen Fisher (1989) shows that the most common year to divorce across most societies is year *four*. However, couples who have a biological child together, but still divorce, tend to divorce a few years later. Further, woman-initiated divorce tends to decrease heavily after age 40, whereas roughly the same percentage of men continue to divorce and remarry after 40 as before 40. Thus, reproductive years and differences between men and women seem to play into patterns of serial monogamy. Further, in many ancestral environments where male partners played a critical role in family providing and protection, initiating divorce at an older age could compromise not just the woman's survival but her children's survival as well. Thus, these patterns may have been evolutionarily forged.

Theoretically, it makes a lot of sense that individuals higher in emophilia may end up seeking this compromise between long- and short-term strategies of mating most effectively. Thus, the person falls in love and stays with a partner long enough to raise children through those critical years of development. However, after a while, a new love interest takes hold and the cycle repeats. Although this possibility is still being tested, it is a compelling argument.

The Developmental Environment of the Individual High in Emophilia

I alluded to the fact that the instability of single-parent homes often (but not always) has consequences for the attachment and sociosexuality of children. When the infant (birth–six years) senses instability in their environment, it is an unconscious signal that the world is a risky place, and one better get moving when it comes to development and reproduction. Take for example the average age of sexual initiation. In surveys I conducted in the early 2000s, I found that, even at major state schools, almost half of most college freshmen have never had sex. Note that these are individuals who come from households where there was enough stability to finish high school, earn acceptance to college, and find a way to pay for it. So, the *average age* of first sexual intercourse for that population hovers around 18–19 (obviously some are later in life, and a few are earlier). However, compare that with inner-city youth who struggle with poverty, danger, and hardship. In Baltimore, I was told by several sociologists that the average age for first sexual encounter among children coming from the most impoverished households was around 12–13. A very large difference.

Thus, one's life history strategy gets moved in the "short-term" direction when there is instability in one's environment. That is, the individual gets more unrestricted in their sociosexuality and more insecurely (anxious attachment, avoidant attachment) attached. Recent research examined whether it is specifically father absence or merely a single-parent household that causes these instabilities. In a study of lesbian couples, research shows that there are no developmental consequences for a two-parent household that involves two women (MacCallum & Golombok, 2004). Thus, it is not so much a father but a parent who moves on from an infant that leaves uncertainty in the wake of their disappearance. It is important to note, however, that parents can make heroic efforts to counter this instability, and such amazing parents should be applauded.

But what about mother absence? I decided to test the differential effect of mother vs. father absence and stepmother vs. stepfather presence on my three variables of interest: anxious attachment, sociosexuality, and emophilia. I surveyed well over 600 adults and simply asked them about their environment growing up. The majority of participants indicated that they had grown up with both of their biological parents. However, a small percentage indicated that they had grown up with their biological mother and had a stepfather or stepfathers in the house. As predicted, an even smaller percentage indicated that they had grown up with their biological *father* and had a stepmother or stepmothers in the house. So, what did I find? Well, as predicted, both father absence and stepfather presence predicted insecure attachment (both anxious and avoidant) and predicted a more unrestricted sociosexual orientation. This was true for men and women. OK, fair enough; those findings replicated as predicted. But what about the reverse? Well, as it turns out, *mother* absence and step*mother* presence were the strongest predictors of emophilia. In other words, having a stepmother (or multiple stepmothers) in the house while growing up was the strongest predictor of participants reporting high Emophilia Scale scores. However, given that this is one sample, future research is needed before we can rely on this finding or even know what it means.

Emophilia is a "want" process. Individuals who feel good want to repeat that feeling. Thus, at the conscious level, people feel excitement and seek to repeat what excited them. At the deeper unconscious level, emophilia may have served as a critical niche in the larger picture of evolution. Because we know that falling in love feels good, we seek to repeat it. However, the average person considers what they have and may think better of risking it. It should be noted that this process of anticipating how we will feel down the road is something that people are notoriously bad at doing. Research on "affective forecasting" (e.g., Wilson & Gilbert, 2003) has shown that although we know the gym will make us feel better longer into the day, we discount this by overestimating how good a pizza will taste instead. Further, we underestimate how bad we might feel after the pizza. Much like anything, there are likely individual differences in the ability to affectively forecast one's feelings. Individuals high in emophilia may also overestimate how good a new relationship will feel and underestimate how bad it may feel when that excitement fades.

The Neurobiology of Love

Although it is an oversimplification, there are two major neurotransmitters relevant to romantic relationships. The first is dopamine. Dopamine is a neurotransmitter associated with "feeling good." Whenever you experience pleasure in your life, dopamine plays a role. In fact, my former graduate student, Steven Mueller, always said "That's DOPE! As in, short for *dopamine.*" Dopamine sensitivity is responsible for a wide range of reinforced behaviors. However, it is more complicated than just pleasure. Both an over- or underabundance of dopamine has been implicated in disorders such as Parkinson's and schizophrenia.

Although dopaminergic reinforcement is a major driver behind repetitive approach-based behaviors, such as sexual contact and falling in love, their pathways are distinct (Fisher et al., 2002). Each pathway is a constellation of evolved mechanisms to solve adaptive issues such as choosing appropriate partners (attraction) and initiating sexual contact with a selected partner (sex drive). Despite their distinct neurological and endocrine pathways, both are rewarding to the brain and release dopamine when these drives are satisfied.

Emophilia is associated with behavioral activation in the form of reward focus. High emophilia individuals get a "rush" from meeting new romantic potentials, from falling in love, and from the feeling of a budding relationship. When individuals have a hypersensitivity to dopamine in a certain region of the brain called the "meso-limbic" region ("meso" meaning middle, and "limbic" being part of the emotional system in the brain), they become particularly impulsive and approach rewards more vigorously. This is one of the reasons cocaine is such a risky drug. It saturates the brain with artificial (synthetic) dopamine. Such saturation cannot be matched by any naturally occurring activity. In other words, not even the greatest experiences in the world could generate as much endogenous (or "internal") dopamine as when you flood your brain with the artificial chemical. So, naturally, cocaine highs are a dopaminergic avalanche. However, individuals have reported life-time depression and loss of interest and pleasure after even *just one use* of cocaine. This is because dopamine stretches your scale of how good things feel, and things you *loved* before seem to pale now in comparison.

The second main neurotransmitter involved in romantic relation-ships has to do with emotional stability: *serotonin*. Serotonin may be a little more familiar because this is the neurotransmitter primarily impli-cated in disorders such as depression, anxiety, and obsessive-compulsive disorder (OCD). Drugs, such as Prozac, Zoloft, and Luvox are called selective serotonin reuptake inhibitors (SSRIs) because they block the brain's ability to absorb and disintegrate serotonin, leaving more of it available to your brain. This process then helps treat disorders (such as depression or OCD) that are associated with having too little serotonin in the brain.

At a broad level, serotonin impacts the ability to regulate emotions. So, when someone feels that they are scared or anxious over losing something, it has something to do with serotonin. Right away, the as-tute observer may have made the same connections I have: emophilia is likely associated with hyperactivity in the meso-limbic regions of the brain when it comes to dopamine, and anxious attachment is associated with serotonergic processes. However, this is speculation, and future re-search is badly needed on this topic. Further, emophilia may share an association with conditions such as attention deficit hyperactivity dis-order (ADHD), bipolar disorder, and other types of disorders related to mood or impulsivity. Again, while emophilia is not a pathology and is an independent construct, having hyperactive mood issues or impulsiv-ity problems may exacerbate preexisting tendencies toward emophilia. Again, future research is needed to examine these possibilities.

The Role of Serotonin in Love

Although hypersensitivity to dopaminergic reward drives romantic love and lust, central serotonin can compromise this link (Fisher & Thompson, 2007). As it turns out, the obsessive rumination over a new romantic partner or partners, which would be a frequent occurrence for someone high in emophilia, is attenuated with an overabundance of serotonin. This parallel makes sense given that the region of the brain responsible for repetitive behavior, the anterior cingulate, is activated when viewing erotic films (Karama et al., 2002). Even more striking is that those who have OCD and those who are prone to falling in love have lower levels of serotonin in their blood (Marazziti et al., 1999). Consequently, research has shown that increases in serotonin, such as by taking an SSRI, compromises falling in love. Thus, SSRIs might indeed lower emophilic tendencies—a possibility that should be explored by medical researchers.

Although both sex drive and love drive are fundamental but distinct evolved mechanisms, Fisher and Thomson (2007) argue that the drive for love is more powerful than the drive for sex. For example, a single denied sexual experience seldom produces suicidal ideation and depression, whereas rejected love has had that effect. Further, research has shown that love drives more significant changes in one's priorities, willingness to sacrifice, and daily habits more than sex drive. Thus, Fisher and Thomson (2007) conclude that the craving for emotional union supersedes sexual craving.

Summary

In sum, there are good reasons why we may have evolved differences in our tendencies to fall in love fast, easily, and often. Specifically, individuals with emophilic tendencies likely enjoy dopamine rushes associated with romantic encounters. That rush of excitement may fuel short-term or medium-term relationship pursuits. Because emophilic individuals do genuinely believe they are in love, there is no deception or cues to deception, thus potential partners may feel their sincerity and are more likely to agree to a relationship. However, because emophilia propels individuals toward new love interests, it may encourage a short-term strategy of having children with multiple partners, which confers evolutionary advantages in certain environments.

Although, some of these processes are observable and conscious (e.g., the rush of falling in love), while others are not (e.g., pursuing a short-term strategy that aids with evolutionary fitness). Nevertheless, it is the direct experience of the rush and excitement of love that keeps individuals high in emophilia coming back to restart the process. Further, those high in emophilia may invest more in the children they have (at least for a period of time) more than those who are strictly pursuing a short-term sexual approach to relationships. Further, sex drive and the drive for love are distinct pathways and have separate constellations of neurological, hormonal, motivational, and emotional associations. Nevertheless, because attraction is a key factor in mating, along with sex drive and attachment, there is reason to believe that emophilia evolved as an individual difference trait. However, much of this theorizing is new, and many of these assertions (e.g., dopamine links, life history pursuits) need to be examined more thoroughly in scientific studies.

Finally, emophilia should have a distinct set of neurological patterns and hormonal correlates. Emophilia should be associated with hypersensitivity to dopaminergic reward, especially with respect to the constellation of motivations, hormones, neurochemicals, and emotions associated with love. However, because low levels of serotonin predict impulsivity and down regulate the reward mechanism of dopamine, overabundance of serotonin may mute this dopamine reinforcement. This tamping of dopaminergic reinforcement may be especially pronounced among those taking SSRI medications that produce elevated levels of serotonin in the body.

6

———◦◦◦———

Rose-Colored Glasses and the Emophilic
Frame of Mind

- *Those high in emophilia form intense and idealized perceptions
  of romantic partners quickly*
- *Emophilia is associated with destiny-driven beliefs about love
  and the tendency to overinvest early in romantic relationships,
  the potential for vulnerability to exploitation*
- *Emophilia is associated with hyperbolic statements about love,
  but there is less likelihood of staying when a relationship meets
  challenges*

In the present chapter, we will explore the cognitive processes that are
associated with emophilia. Specifically, we will explore the cognitive
biases and mental associations in which high emophilia individuals engage. The questions we will address include the following: What are the
illusions that they have of love and potential vs. actual partners? Do
they think that relationships are beginning when they are not? How
honest are they with themselves about the likelihood of a relationship
working out?

Positive Illusions

I would argue that love is not logical, even among low emophilia individuals. How we see our romantic partners and potential rivals, and how we view the viability of our relationship all get distorted because of love. This is nothing exclusive to those high in emophilia. What is unique to those individuals high in emophilia, is that this process occurs much faster, and from the start, they generally do not think logically about the people they choose to date. Consequently, emophilia leads to this distorted way of thinking sooner and more frequently.

Back in the 1990s there was a surge of research discussing how positive illusions can be good for romantic relationships (e.g., Murray & Holmes, 1997). This research flew in the face of the zeitgeist of psychology at the time, which focused on cognitive causes of behavior (i.e., Fletcher, 2008). According to this perspective, accurate self- and other perceptions were seen as the gold standard of healthy cognition. Nevertheless, Murray, Holmes, and others demonstrated that having positive illusions about one's relationship partner can be good for the relationship. Further, they found that turning to relationship partners in times of need can be reinforcing, comforting, and healthy. Finally, the presence of these illusions, or "rose-colored glasses," through which one sees one's partner is a strong indicator of romantic love.

So, when do positive illusions become toxic? Lisa Neff and Benjamin Karney (2005) found that although positive global evaluations of one's partner may predict relationship satisfaction, this same principle did not apply to specific details (especially for women). For example, believing that your partner is clean and tidy when they are a slob sets partners up for continual disappointment. However, acknowledging that one's relationship partner is a bit messy, but viewing their "overall value" in a rose-colored way is healthy for the relationship.

What relationship experts in this area of this research never considered was what happens when someone has a hair-trigger tendency to fall in love. Do these same illusions get triggered along with the premature emotional connection? The answer seems to be yes. In a study I conducted on a large internet sample, there was no evidence that individuals high in emophilia were any different from those low in emophilia in their perceptions of how likely their current relationship would work out. The only difference was, those high in emophilia felt these things immediately. When surveyed at the start of a relationship, individuals high in emophilia reported that their partner was 100% honest, ideal, and "different" from all other partners. These same cognitive distortions do emerge when low in emophilia, but later.

I Can't Help Falling in Love with You: Fate or Free Will?

The popular line from the Elvis Presley song about how wise men say only fools rush in seems appropriate when thinking about emophilia. However, empirically speaking, do emophilic individuals believe that they have control over their romantic feelings? Do they believe that it is their "choice" whom they love or is it up to "fate" to decide?

Back in 2011, Del Paulhus and Jasmine Carey published a scale called the Free Will and Determinism scale, or the FAD-Plus, which was published in the *Journal of Personality Assessment*. It broke down into three categories: free will, scientific causation, and fatalistic determinism. Although these aspects are related, they predict unique behaviors when it comes to beliefs about the nature of free will and causes for human behavior. Free will, as the name suggests, tapped individual beliefs in one's own ability to choose their destiny and engage in thoughts and behaviors that are not predetermined. Scientific causation focuses on biological and socialized determinants of human behavior and thought. To elaborate, many psychologists would argue that you are simply a product of your environment, your genes, and the interaction between the two (e.g., Lewin, 1943). For example, the fact that you have opened this book and are reading these lines is just the result of your genes, environment, and upbringing—all of which led you to this point in time. Although these are beliefs that some people have about the nature of humanity and the universe, they are not necessarily *accurate*. The final category, fatalistic determinism, is slightly different from the other two categories. This refers to the belief that an individual has a "fate" or a "destiny" to fulfill.

With respect to emophilia, there is little reason to believe that they will differ in biological explanations for human behavior or thoughts about free will. However, I began to wonder if individuals high in emophilia feel a strong sense of fate or destiny. Often-heard explanations for relationships such as "fate brought us together" or "I just can't help what I am feeling" might point toward a person believing in fate. I conducted a study where I correlated emophilia with the subscales of the FAD-Plus, and emophilia did indeed have a strong and significant correlation with fatalistic determinism.

But what about a sense of control over one's fate? In psychology, there is a construct referred to as "locus of control" that describes whether individuals feel that they have control over their own lives (Rotter, 1966). One can have an *internal* locus of control, or a sense that their life is within their own control and their actions make a difference in how things turn out. One can also have an *external* locus of control. In this case, the individual believes that external forces (e.g., luck, fate, God, the universe, other people, situations, circumstances) determine how things turn out. This research was based on the idea of reward contingency. For example, if I study for a test and score 50%, I may be unhappy. So, I study even harder and still get 50%. If this occurs early and often in life, one might get the impression that no matter what one does, the result will not be affected by efforts expended. Thus, the perception that rewards are random and that efforts may or may not lead to a desired outcome are components of an external locus of control. The result is that the individual eventually develops other explanations (e.g., the professor is inconsistent, the tests are inaccurate, I just can't do this) to address why the grade does not change regardless of studying effort.

However, in 1983, Del Paulhus revised the idea of locus of control to discuss three separate domains where individuals may or may not feel control: internal, interpersonal, and sociopolitical. Internal locus of control taps whether individuals believe that they are capable and able to make changes to their lives, get the outcomes they desire, or that their hard work will pay off. Interpersonal locus of control taps whether individuals believe that they can influence other people, whether they can get people to do what they want or need them to do, and so forth. Finally, the sociopolitical locus of control taps whether people believe that they can "change the world"; change how people are; and/or have an impact on politics, culture, or society.

I decided to test whether emophilia and attachment styles had any relationship to an internal or external locus of control across any of these life domains (self, others, sociopolitical). Interestingly, and contrary to my expectations, emophilia had no significant correlation with overall locus of control or over any of the separate spheres of control. Anxious attachment, on the other hand, had quite a large correlation with an external locus of control. This correlation was especially large when it came to the interpersonal sphere. Thus, it is not the case that emophilic individuals feel that they have no control over their lives, no control over how they influence others, or no control over humanity.

In sum, emophilic individuals believe that they have a fate or that fate has decided where they may go in life. This belief in fate and destiny might suit them well in believing that the universe has brought them to this "special" partner, but that process keeps repeating. However, emophilic individuals are no more or less likely than anyone else to feel that they can control themselves, others, or the world.

I Will Always Be Here for You

We've all said these things like this from time to time. As we discussed in the previous chapters, many cultures are replete with musical lyrics or artistic expressions saying "[I'll be] right here waiting for you," "I will be here for you," and, yes, "I will *always* love you." If one thinks for a moment about the exact nature of these expressions, heartwarming as they may be, they are almost always factually inaccurate.

I will not always be there for my wife. I may *try* to be, I may *want* to be, but if I were, I wouldn't be in my office writing this book right now. Further, I have no idea if my wife and I will always be in love. I would like to think that is the case, but she and I both agree that we take life one day at a time, and whatever comes of it, we enjoy the here and now. However, love is a state, and that state may change for a variety of reasons.

Most of us acknowledge that things happen in romantic relationships that we did not expect. In comparing the cultural scripts surrounding love and the expression of love with the actual, factual *reality* of what we are saying, there are often a lot of empty promises we toss around. In fact, these promises are more than empty, they are *impossible*.

Some of the more common themes include, "I will always be there for you," "I will love you forever," "I will love you no matter what," "Nothing will keep us apart," and "I will always be by your side." Although I realize that these are not literal expressions, I would *hate* if my wife was *always* by my side (for example, it would make my bathroom trips quite awkward). These statements, although figurative, are common in many cultures, and this rhetoric sets up lofty expectations for love and relationships—expectations that are going to disappoint.

To explore the use of these self-deceptive terms, I explored the frequency of use of this type of language with a romantic partner within those high in emophilia. In my survey, I asked participants to indicate how often they used these expressions when in a romantic relationship and specifically noted only to respond with respect to the times when they *really meant it*. In other words, I was not interested in those who might say, "I will love you forever" when they are simply interested in a one-night stand.

Not surprisingly, high emophilia individuals reported a high frequency of expressing these types of sentiments across relationships, and they really did mean it! If one were to look back on this idea, it seems relatively obvious that there are a lot of broken promises coming from individuals high in emophilia. Importantly, neither anxious attachment nor those high in unrestricted sociosexuality expressed the same types of permanent sentiments as often.

Forgiveness

So, what happens when something does go wrong in a relationship? A partner lets you down, spends too much, takes a dumb risk, harms you, harms someone you love, acts thoughtlessly, cheats, behaves in a selfish way, and so on. My friend, Miranda Abild, and I decided to zero in on infidelity. We surveyed individuals on their levels of emophilia, insecure attachment (anxious and avoidant), and sociosexuality and then asked them how likely they would be to forgive a romantic partner if they were unfaithful. Once again, not surprisingly, high emophilia individuals were the only ones to indicate that they would find a way to forgive their partner for the indiscretion. Further, and importantly, anxiously attached individuals indicated a strong intention to leave the relationship if infidelity had ever occurred.

However, none of that matched reality. We conducted a second set of questions asking participants to think back. Have they ever been cheated on? If so, did they forgive the partner and did the relationship continue afterwards? Interestingly, emophilic individuals were not only *unlikely* to have been forgiven, but they were also significantly *more* likely to have moved on from the relationship. Want to know who stayed? Individuals who were high in anxious attachment. Thus, what individuals high in emophilia and anxious attachment do in theory, or think they will do, and what they do in practice is quite the opposite.

Commitment, Premature Investment, and Dissonance

Social exchange theory argues that, in every relationship, there is a natural give-and-take that occurs between two people (e.g., Thibaut & Kelley, 1959). For example, last night, my wife did the dishes because I was just too tired. Tomorrow night, I may do them because she did them previously. When there is an equilibrium, or a natural balance in a relationship, individuals generally report higher levels of satisfaction when compared to times when that balance is off. Naturally, individuals who feel under-benefited in a relationship are unhappy. Whether it stems from monetary exchange in the workforce (e.g., I am doing way more than I get paid for), favors in a friendship (e.g., I *always* give him a ride, he never gives me one), exchanges in a relationship (e.g., I do everything for her!), or students in a class (e.g., she never lets me see her notes, I show her mine all the time), we have a mental "tab" that we use to keep track of others, so we do not get taken advantage of. This may seem perverse, especially in friendships, but it is nevertheless true. A few days ago, I took my friend to lunch, and I paid for us both. Naturally, she did not pull out a notebook and write down that she "owes" me a lunch. But, perhaps, in a few weeks, if we have lunch again, I will let her pay, or we will both pay for our own. If I were to pay over and over, a "balance" may seem off in the friendship.

Interestingly, we also get unhappy in relationships when we are *over-benefiting*. Think of the time that some person was just bending over backwards for you. How did it make you feel, especially if you were not that into the friendship or relationship? I knew a woman while I lived in Vancouver who showered her love interests with gifts and affection early in the relationship. I recall one of these men telling me about it (with me being a neutral party) and saying that he just was not that into her, although he wished he was. Although he did not want to take advantage and tried to slow the process, he said that she insisted on buying him things and taking him places. They eventually parted on amicable terms, but he nevertheless felt guilty and discomfort in that relationship. This was because the balance was off. We have a natural math in our heads that give-and-take is favored over being greedy or taken advantage of. So, very often, people do not want to receive birthday wishes, cards, or presents because they *themselves* do not want to be obligated to remember to do these things.

Emophilic individuals are likely to go overboard early on in a relationship (which was the case for the woman in Vancouver) and wind up under-benefiting. Although, when two individuals high in emophilia meet, it might work out in the early goings. Perhaps you've witnessed partners celebrating seemingly trivial dates (e.g., "This is our three-week anniversary!"). One reasonable explanation for this is that the two are both high in emophilia and have fallen for each other.

Nevertheless, most of us can all relate to a time when we wanted someone's friendship or affection more than they wanted ours. In such cases, we are aware that there is an unequal balance. Similarly, most of us can relate to a time in our lives when someone wanted our friendship or our affection much more than we wanted theirs, and it made us uncomfortable because, again, the balance was off. The only case of which I am aware when someone is at ease with being over-benefited in a relationship is among those high in *narcissism*. In 1999, Campbell demonstrated that narcissistic individuals were mostly concerned with the attractiveness of their partner and how much their partner praised/worshipped them. Affection was not really a critical issue.

However, people may feel better when under-benefited as well. Bill Swann and colleagues found that individuals with low self-esteem in romantic relationships were more likely to report higher levels of commitment when they were not all that valued by their partner. Although it may seem counterintuitive, individuals whose self-beliefs are at odds with their partner's may simply be too uncomfortable. Among those who are under-benefiting in a relationship, those high in anxious attachment are likely to stay.

Based on interdependence theory and social exchange theory, Caryl Rusbult (1980) developed the investment model, which focused on factors predicting relationship commitment. Rusbult argued that commitment was a function of three factors: how satisfied you are in your present relationship, how much you have invested in your relationship, and how many alternatives you think you have outside of your relationship. She defined satisfaction by how much the relationship matched one's expectations and ideals. Investment was defined as any form of input into the relationship, including loss of opportunities or costly investment (e.g., emotions, effort, money, time, etc.). Finally, alternatives were defined as any outside option (even being alone or getting a dog) to the present relationship that might be better. The most common alternative, of course, is other people out there who are seen as possible mates.

From an investment model perspective, there are reasons to assume mixed levels of commitment from individuals high in both anxious attachment and emophilia. However, anxiously attached people are generally more committed than those high in emophilia. For example, with respect to *investment*, we would expect individuals high in emophilia and anxious attachment to invest quite a bit early on in their relationships. This heavy investment should increase their commitment. However, investment is only one of three components. *Satisfaction* is another component. Research has shown that anxiously attached people have their commitment compromised by their lack of trust (Simpson et al., 1990). Consequently, their relationships are typically low in "satisfaction." In contrast, individuals high in emophilia tend to ignore doubts that they probably should not. This immediate trust and certainty results in high levels of initial satisfaction. Finally, there are *alternatives*. Individuals high in anxious attachment cling to partners, which likely mutes their attention to alternatives. However, individuals high in emophilia are the opposite: they see alternatives all around them and may even fall in love with more than one person at once.

Thus, unlike those high in anxious attachment, individuals high in emophilia see alternatives outside of their primary relationship. In many ways, relationship commitment becomes messy in the head of someone high in emophilia: They have invested *a lot* in their primary partner, but they see that there are a lot of great people outside of the relationship, too.

Temptations Online: The Role of Beta Press

Earlier in the book I mentioned the concept "press" (Murray, 1938). Whereas "alpha press" is pressure (e.g., temptation) brought on by real and true pressures from the outside world, "beta press" is the perception of such pressure. If one is a married rock star and has copious offers for affairs, this constitutes alpha press because the pressures and temptations are present and real. However, beta press would be the perception of many possibilities for affairs, such as what can be generated through online dating. Because of online dating forums and platforms, we have made it easier to *express* our emophilic side with less consequence and a lot of opportunity. With apps like Tinder, you need to expend very little energy to find thousands of individuals interested in meeting someone, almost instantaneously. Thus, although the reality of relationships and love hasn't changed, the perception of how many attractive individuals are out there and the ability to gain access to contacting them has.

If You Could Only See How She (or He) Loves Me

One of my favorite songs from the band Tonic makes a similar declaration. I was lucky enough to see this band live when I was an undergraduate student at Stockton University. The lead singer told us (the audience) the story of how this song came to be. He indicated that it stemmed from a disagreement he had with his mother surrounding a woman he loved. He (obviously) declared that her love was much deeper than his mother felt it was, and that it was his duty and honor to pursue an unlikely relationship with her. He laughed as he declared the relationship was over and that his mother was right.

"You just don't know him like I do!" "You don't see how he loves me and all the sweet things he does!" These types of declarations are familiar lines from an adolescent romance script, *especially* when someone is dating a person whom friends or family oppose. Nevertheless, this type of assertion is curious in what it implies. The underlying message is that familiar others, specifically those who are typically quite invested in the happiness of a particular individual, are either unable or unwilling to see the kindness and sincerity of that individual's romantic partner. Although it is entirely conceivable that out of bias or jealousy, family or friends may misjudge an excellent romantic partner to be subpar.

At its most fundamental level, the statement, "You just don't know them like I do!" implies that the person making the declaration is either privy to some knowledge unavailable to the rest of us or is more objective about the available evidence. Although the former is typically true, given that romantic partners have private and public lives, the latter generally is not. Notwithstanding, it is often the case that the person insisting on the sweetness of a partner may have some biases of their own.

Psychological Reactance

Pulling further from a Westernized cultural script, we might say the spark that generally ignites a full declaration that others are simply blind to the sweetness of our current partner, is a statement to the effect of: *"I forbid you to date that person!"*

This statement or statements like it have a toxic effect on the parent-child relationship. Before I define what those are, I first want to say that I am sympathetic to the desire to make such statements. My daughter (still a child as I write this) is my whole world. To imagine her dating in her teen years already makes me quite uncomfortable. What makes me even more uncomfortable is the potential suitors she may come across and their intentions. There may indeed be times in the future when I want to make a declaration that she stops dating that person, "or else." However, these declarations rarely work, and (as I previously mentioned) only work to strain relationships between parent and child. First, it oversteps our culturally defined boundaries of mate choice.

Yes, you should have a say in your child's love life, especially at a young age. Without guidance, children may make poor choices and end up in tough situations. However, heavy-handed declarations may backfire. Both because it puts further enmity between you and your child and because such declarations just made "that young person" a sexy piece of forbidden fruit.

Jack Brehm first conducted his research on "psychological reactance" back in the 1960s (e.g., Brehm, 1966). He discovered that when one of his dogs was hungry, and he fed it, the other dogs immediately wanted to be fed. For those of you who have more than one child, you can relate to this. Something as trivial as a little red ball in the corner may lie untouched for months. One day, Child A wants to play with the ball. Shortly thereafter, Child B insists that they want a turn with the quite often ignored red ball (perhaps this is especially true if the red ball originally belonged to Child B).

Reactance, simply put, is protesting someone's attempt to restrict our options, movements, or choices. One of the classic studies on reactance was conducted in a parking lot (Ruback & Juieng, 1997). Most of us have been there—crowded parking lots (especially during the holidays), endlessly searching for a parking space. *Finally*, someone begins to put their bags in their truck! Terrific! You put your blinker on. How long does it take that person to physically get in their car, turn it on, and vacate the parking spot so you can finally go shopping? Ironically, people who are about to vacate their parking space take significantly *longer* (on average) to leave when someone else is waiting. The explanation is that the person with their blinker on is trying to hurry us, and we will not be bossed around. There are many other examples in modern life from tailgating-inspired slow driving to being told we can't do something and doing it anyway.

In the case of romantic partners, threatening punishment, cost, or imposing some penalty usually only makes people more determined that the partner is valuable. In fact, the more of a cost we pay for a partner (or anyone or anything), the more we value it (or that person)! In the case of emophilia, we find that there is a special vulnerability to forbidden fruit. This attraction stems from the belief that fate draws them to their partners, and their head has little say over what their heart demands.

In summary, individuals who are high in emophilia may seek out information that confirms their view that they are in love. Emophilic individuals may view a budding relationship in overly optimistic and positive ways. They are also more likely to aggressively invest early in a relationship, and this investment may create dissonance with leaving. Thus, individuals high in emophilia may find themselves in situations that are difficult to get out of. Further, they may view new partners in ideal terms, especially early in the relationship. Although, this personal view is unlikely to last as the relationship moves on and other potential partners enter the picture. These partners may create a new positive illusion of a perfect partner, and the reality of an existing partner may fade. Finally, individuals high in emophilia may simply feel that their love was determined by fate, and there is little they can do to change their feelings. In fact, trying to force them out of those feelings may further convince them that their feelings will last.

Rent Money

I was secretly (perhaps not so secretly) a huge fan of the TV show *Judge Judy*. I remember in one episode a woman was suing a former relationship partner for back rent. Judge Judy Shinelan turned to her bailiff in disgust, rhetorically asking, "Burt, how many of these cases do we see in a week?" She was of course referring to the number of women who are forced to take ex-boyfriends to court over lost rent, car payments, loans, you name it. It was clearly frustrating her. Culturally speaking, men are called out more for this type of behavior because of social role expectations (e.g., men are supposed to be the provider). However, parasitic behaviors occur regardless of gender when people exploit others for resources. One article found that exploitative women will engage in what is colloquially referred to as "foodie calls." Simply put, a foodie call is the idea that a woman will use Tinder or a similar dating app and connect with someone, appearing interested. She will allow the guy with whom she has connected to pay for lunch or dinner, have a pleasant time, then block him (Collisson et al., 2020).

Although this behavior is not illegal, it is irksome to those who have been on the wrong side of this equation. However, there are parasitic behaviors in romantic relationships that do cross the line of legality. For example, romance scams have been on the rise since the internet has become more widely available. In such cases, we focus our energy on the offender (and with good reason!), saying, "What kind of person would do this?" Well, much of that was addressed briefly in an earlier chapter on "bad apples." Individuals high in the Dark Triad (Machiavellianism, narcissism, and psychopathy) are quite likely to exploit others for rent, payments, money, and all other kinds of benefits through promises, manipulation, lies, coercion, and even threats. However, among men, there are sometimes other predictors of exploitation beyond personality. For example, insecurity (such as needing to prove something to oneself), low self-esteem, or those who lack a competitive advantage on the dating market may engage in this type of exploitative behavior.

Nevertheless, people will often ask, "What is wrong with the people who put up with that?" As aforementioned, I am not in the business of blaming a victim. However, it does pique a psychologist's curiosity to figure out what draws women to these types of exploitative men (and vice versa) and what leads them to invest so heavily in false promises and take major risks. Further, what leads an individual to double down on an exploitative partner's false promises instead of walking away?

I surveyed over 100 adults about their proclivities toward loaning money to romantic partners. As it turns out, emophilic and anxious attachment are the relationship orientations that push people into this kind of trouble. For example, both emophilic and anxious attachment individuals were equally likely to report that they loaned money to a romantic partner and that money was never paid back. Further, both emophilic and anxiously attached individuals also indicated that they had contributed their own money to help pay down the debt of a romantic partner.

These behaviors seem fair enough. Loving, in fact. If you are going to spend the rest of your life with someone, what difference does it make, right? However, once again, individuals high in emophilia believe that they are going to spend the rest of their life with someone each time they find someone. So, this proposition not only becomes quite expensive for the emophilic individuals who open their wallets for their romantic partners, but it also exposes them to potential exploitation.

Next in our research, we asked, "How *many* romantic partners have you loaned money to?" Indeed, emophilia was the best predictor of this question, and had the highest number.

Summary

Individuals high in emophilia have cognitive biases. They may believe that loaning a romantic partner money will help their relationship and they will see that money back. Similarly, they are more likely to believe that a loved one's concern over a potentially problematic partner is bias on the part of the loved one. Finally, individuals high in emophilia are likely to believe that there are a lot more great matches for them out there than what is realistic. Given these cognitive biases, is it possible that those high in emophilia may actually be drawn to manipulative partners?

7

The Appeal of Bad Partners

- *Emophilia is associated with poor screening of potential partners and inattention to potential relationship red flags*
- *Individuals high in emophilia are vulnerable to manipulation because of their premature investment and emotional decision-making*
- *Emophilia is associated with attraction to individuals with Dark Triad traits, especially those who are high in narcissism, due to their charm and risky lifestyle*

Stephanie was a college friend of mine who always seemed to move headlong from one destructive relationship to the next. She was never interested in just one man at a time either. The men who captured her interest had common personality traits: dominance, recklessness, and egotism. All her romantic partners and romantic interests had at some point conflicted with the law or engaged in activities such as fist fights, binge drinking, and reckless driving.

Her first boyfriend, Andrew, was aggressive and immature, and he pretended to be confident, but it was clear that he was quite insecure deep down. The slightest challenge or disrespect would send Andrew into fighting mode. He frequently engaged in physical confrontations, throwing strange temper fits. The rest of the time, Andrew was charming and fun to be around. He was the lead singer of a rock band and sang in a choir. He was talented at both singing and songwriting and wrote love ballads to show his soft side.

Andrew was Stephanie's first serious boyfriend and her first love. After him, she had a string of boyfriends, all of whom were like him in most respects. Curiously, however, all her relationships ended because she fell in love with someone else, cheating on them, or both.

Perhaps the most obvious example of one of Stephanie's antisocial boyfriends was Peter. Peter was a known thief even in his inner circle, stealing from friends, family, and strangers alike. He had been in and out of juvenile detention centers since he was an adolescent. Despite Peter's casual lies and deceptive nature, his assertiveness and confidence (and his fantastic dancing at nightclubs) swept Stephanie off her feet.

Stephanie woke up one morning to find Peter had left early with no explanation. She also discovered $50 missing from her wallet and her favorite necklace gone. Stephanie called me immediately. She was not worried about the money or necklace but instead over his whereabouts. In fact, she justified Peter's theft by saying he did not have a job and needed the money. She added that he steals from everyone, so she shouldn't take it personally. Peter's robberies did not stop with Stephanie; he soon stole jewelry from a friend of the family and found himself in jail.

Stephanie was heartbroken. Not for the family who lost a family heirloom, or because of the robbery he committed, but because her boyfriend would be locked up indefinitely.

It did not take long for Stephanie to get over her heartbreak. Soon she found a new target to fixate on: Kevin. He was an auto mechanic who graduated high school at age 20. Kevin was recently single, which perked Stephanie's interest, even though his reason for being single would have driven most women away: angry with his girlfriend of three years, Kevin had snuck into her driveway one night and taken a pair of clippers to her brake line. She got into a severe car accident, and he was arrested for attempted manslaughter.

Stephanie saw her opportunity. Bewildered, I questioned her attraction to a clearly antisocial and disturbed individual. Her responses were in his defense, ranging from "she probably deserved it" to "she was really bad to him, and he was just reacting as anyone treated that way would," all the way to "come on, who doesn't notice the puddle of brake fluid under their car? He did it just to scare her and she was an idiot and drama queen for driving."

Stephanie was a talented artist who received a full college scholarship. She smoked pot in high school, but her new circle of friends at college introduced her to new and more dangerous drugs. Stephanie wound up falling in love with a fellow artist in the group who was also a heroin addict.

The last I heard about Stephanie, she had become addicted to heroin and had to leave college for rehabilitation. I have not spoken to her or heard from her since that time. The common theme behind all of Stephanie's relationships was that she fell in love quickly. The good things about these men that emerged in the short-term swept Stephanie off her feet, and she dove into a relationship head first. She did not take the time to screen her partners as many of us do. She ignored red flags that may have given others reason to pause, and each time she felt she had found the one for her. Yet, that cycle repeated over and over. In the end, the force of falling in love with antisocial men had a negative impact on her life and on her relationship with her family.

We should never forget that love is a vulnerable state, and that vulnerability can be used by antisocial individuals for manipulative purposes. When we fall in love, it engages processes of trust, bias, attachment, and irrational thinking. Someone who is aware of these processes may pour on the charm on purpose to engage those processes in others while having a very different agenda.

Failure to Acknowledge Red Flags

Emophilic individuals are likely to let their feelings known early when meeting someone they find attractive. Their efforts to form a relationship with a person upon first meeting leaves them subject to the whims of the individual they are interested in and (perhaps even worse) gives that person power. Similarly, high emophilia individuals do not engage in the typical courtship process that most others experience. Typical courtship involves a level of uncertainty and a screening of romantic partners that takes into consideration red flags and incompatibilities.

For example, if a potential romantic partner hates dogs and you are a dog lover, that might present a problem for a relationship. However, red flags can be even more serious, such as discovering that a potential romantic partner was abusive or unfaithful in previous relationships. For many, such information would be considered, and the relationship would go no further.

However, those high in emophilia are motivated to fall in love. If they feel excitement or chemistry with a particular potential partner, they may rationalize this information. They might question the source of the information. If a previous partner informs them of someone's past infidelity, for instance, they may choose to dismiss that person's information as irrational jealousy or an attempt to sabotage their relationship.

At its most dangerous, individuals high in emophilia are likely to engage in a process called "self-deception." Robert Trivers, a researcher at Rutgers University and an expert in deception and cooperation, first discussed self-deception in humans back in the 1970s. It is a process by which individuals convince themselves of things that are not true (e.g., Trivers, 1971; von Hippel & Trivers, 2011). Self-deception is different from intentional lying because individuals who are intentionally lying understand what they are saying is not true—or that it is an exaggeration. With self-deception, on the other hand, an individual says something untrue but actively believes that it *is* true and convinces themself of the veracity of the information.

Individuals high in emophilia do not usually engage in intentional lying. In fact, they are usually guileless in their approach to others because their transparent emotions lead to brutal honesty. They do, however, tend to engage in self-deception; that is, they convince themselves of things that are not true. Sigmund Freud discussed the idea of "defense mechanisms" as ways of distorting reality to protect the self from information that is hurtful or damaging. Self-deception can also be self-enhancing, but in either case, it is where the individual is motivated to see reality in a way that differs from what objective observation would suggest. I knew a fellow student in college, Josh, who demonstrated these qualities. He once told me that he would be heading to Princeton for graduate school and that his IQ was over 170 (i.e., "off the charts"). When I asked around about Josh, other students corrected me and said that he "applied to Princeton" and just assumed he would get into their program. With respect to his IQ, there was some doubt that the IQ test he took could record a score that high and that (most likely) he was "estimating."

In the case of emophilia, self-deception leads such individuals to believe the lies of a romantic partner because emophilic individuals are psychologically motivated to believe that this person is "the one." This behavior is not entirely uncommon, and early in a relationship, we are all vulnerable to it to some degree. Further, as mentioned, research on romantic couples found that those who idealized their romantic partner (i.e., viewed their partner through rose-colored glasses) had healthier relationships and enjoyed greater relationship longevity (Murray et al., 1996). Thus, to some degree, when in love, many of us make commiserations, exceptions, and excuses for romantic partners. Some of this can be healthy. It is only when individuals distort reality to cover up true problems or red flags that such distortion turns ugly.

In fact, the cycle of violence is perpetuated by beliefs such as "they really love me." A deviant romantic partner has a much better chance of convincing an emophilic partner that a crime he committed was "not his fault" than with any other type of partner. That is because emophilic partners do not acknowledge red flags. In addition, they are self-deceptive in their thought processes. They *convince* themselves that what their partner says is true because they love this person, have invested in this person, and their feelings are so strongly positive toward this person.

High emophilia individuals also tend to fall in love prematurely, and with premature love comes premature trust. Individuals who are overly trusting of a stranger can find themselves in very dangerous situations. Time is required to build trust for a reason. In the process of getting to know someone, we consciously and unconsciously screen individuals: Do they tell other people's secrets? Do they act self-interested at the expense of others? Do they tell stories indicative of malevolence and a lack of remorse? It takes time to truly get the answers to these sorts of questions.

The trouble with emophilia is that individuals make their minds up about a person almost immediately. As a result of this snap judgment, they lack the background knowledge to make appropriate future judgments. Perhaps even more damaging is that even if an emophilic person is exposed to information that indicates that their love interest or partner harbors malevolent dispositions, they may view such information through a rose-colored filter. They will make positive interpretations of, spins on, and explanations for their romantic interest's malevolent behavior.

The Dangers of Early Investment

Early investment is dangerous in other ways as well. In 1957, the social psychologist Leon Festinger described these and other dangers brilliantly with his classic work *A Theory of Cognitive Dissonance*. Festinger and other dissonance researchers demonstrated two very dangerous consequences of premature investment: (a) we are even more invested in things for which we have suffered, and (b) when investments may be lost, individuals often choose to reinvest in bad ideas, rather than abandon them.

It seems counterintuitive that we would come to love more the things we suffer for when compared to the things that come easy. After all, would it not be preferable to find someone who wants to make our lives easy? Or find groups that welcome us with open arms? That does not seem to be the case. A fascinating demonstration of that effect came from a study on initiation into social groups that researchers Aronson and Mills conducted in 1959.

They recruited women for what appeared to be an interesting sexual discussion group. Some of the women had to read highly sexual words aloud in front of an audience before they could join (which was a big deal in the '50s!). Others could simply sign up. The discussion group then turned out to be very boring and technical. The researchers observed who stuck with the group the longest. It turned out that those women who joined the group with no problem dropped out much sooner than the women who were given a harsher initiation process. Indeed, when we invest in something, we tend to stick to it for a longer period.

We also tend to "reinvest" in poor decisions rather than cut our losses and move on with our lives. A real-world example of such reinvestment comes from observing members of a religious cult. In 1954, a group of researchers, led by Festinger, infiltrated a dooms-day cult. The cult claimed that the world would end on December 21, 1954. The authors were anxious to see how the group would respond when the world did not end on that day. Would the in-dividuals feel foolish? Go back to their families? Admit they were wrong? No. In fact, the researchers were stunned to discover that their faith and commitment to the group *increased* because of the prophecy not coming true. The group, which had never engaged in proselytizing or missionary work before the failed prophecy, began to invest significant time and energy into community outreach ini-tiatives (such as distributing fliers and taking out newspaper ads) after the prophecy failed. In other words, they reinvested in a cult that was already proven to be definitively wrong (Festinger et al., 1956).

Against the backdrop of these findings, it becomes clear that people high in emophilia can find themselves in very compromising situations. Given their propensity to dive into relationships and commitments, they may find themselves defending bad choices in which they have heavily invested and often with little forethought. Then, like most of us engaged in such high investments, they waste time and energy in attempts to maintain dead-end relationships with less-than-optimal partners.

These two processes (loving what we suffer for and reinvestment in bad decisions) play themselves out in interesting ways for emophilic individuals. For example, they are likely to decide early that they are in love and make compromises to court a particular romantic partner. Consequently, when abusive or antisocial behavior begins to surface, they tend to stay longer to justify the effort, excitement, and energy they have already put into their new partner. This justification may, in turn, lead to future investments rather than a withdrawal. Even from a practical perspective, moving out or ending a relationship is always tricky, especially when there are children involved. In fact, research sug-gests that emophilia predicts having children with more partners, thus it is entirely possible that emophilic individuals are more likely to have children earlier in a relationship, and such breakups may more often involve children.

High emophilia individuals will already have committed more, sooner, to a new partner. Because of this commitment, reinvestment and future commitment is likely to ensue rather than a re-evaluation of the situation or a breakup. Consequently, highly emophilic individuals may find themselves *more* committed to less-than-optimal partners than others would be within a certain time period. In sum, doubts about a partner or a discovery that a romantic partner might be antisocial will leave the emophilic individual in a position that motivates them to justify an exorbitant commitment. Such justification would not exist among individuals who took their time to make decisions or commitments, evaluated partners, and acknowledged red flags. Ziva Kunda, of Princeton University, put it best: "People are more likely to arrive at those conclusions that they want to arrive at." Kunda was a pioneer in research and theory demonstrating that motivation is a major factor in information acquisition and distortion (Kunda, 1990, p. 495). When outcomes and accuracy are important, individuals do engage in cognitive mechanisms and actions aimed at objective reality. However, when individuals are psychologically motivated to arrive at a particular conclusion (e.g., they do not want to look bad), they will often only pay attention to information that leads them to that conclusion.

Based on what we know about the doomsday study and others like it, the more we invest in a particular outcome, the harder and harder it becomes to step back and acknowledge wasted time, energy, and effort. For example, not only are we motivated to stay with a course of action when we feel we have invested so much and there is no going back, but we also avoid and ignore information that would make us change our minds. Dieter Frey (1986) and others have published numerous papers showing that individuals "selectively expose" themselves to information based on whether that information would support the decisions that those individuals already made. Individuals in romantic relationships may avoid finding out where their partner was on Thursday night or argue with individuals that present information suggestive of relationship problems.

When investments come quickly and prematurely, individuals may convince themselves of things that aren't true about their new partner. They may argue that their partner is not "really like that" or "didn't mean it that way." In addition, such individuals may feel trapped or invested to a point where they do not want to "throw away" the relationship. Finally, such individuals may overlook or ignore negative signs that the relationship is taking a turn for the worse or their partner is not good for them. Instead, emophilic individuals may actively engage in ways that enable or even help their antisocial partner because of their already perceived investment.

Going back to the opening example of Stephanie, she committed to her partners early and doubled down on her efforts when things looked shaky. Stephanie did have several non-antisocial boyfriends while I knew her, but she quickly discarded these men. They were good guys, and as a result, Stephanie's premature commitment had no negative consequences. Because they did not warrant a reinvestment or justification, she moved on quickly to the next partner.

The Manipulative Wedge

Eddie slammed the door to his bedroom. His best friend, Tina, stood in the hallway trying to explain that she was only trying to protect him. I met Eddie when I lived in Baltimore, Maryland. Tina was a mutual friend of mine and Eddie's. Eddie had been dating Colin for several months, and in that time, Tina (and I) had grown increasingly concerned. Colin had earned a reputation within his circle of friends as an exaggerator, if not a full-blown liar. Colin dismissed these criticisms, claiming we were merely jealous. He was a decent amateur guitar player and technology expert. I met him several times through friends (being an amateur guitar player myself, we had a bit to talk about). Colin used musical terms I was unfamiliar with. At first, I was impressed with him; however, over time it became apparent that he had very cursory knowledge of the topics he discussed. Colin also claimed to have other remarkable talents such as having "perfect pitch" (i.e., he tuned his guitar precisely without a tuner), which clearly was not the case.

Colin was convinced he would make it big with one of his bands, which according to him, his skill would have to carry. When Eddie and Colin went on their first date, Colin played a remake of the song "Earth Angel" that he had made for Eddie. He told Eddie that he was the first thing he thought of when he woke up in the morning and the last thing he thought about when he went to bed at night. Eddie thought he had found the man of his dreams.

The trouble with Colin was that he did not spend much time on things other than video games. This left him perpetually short on cash. Many of our friends would complain that they had to pay for him when he participated in group activities. Colin was full of promises about when he would repay people for everything from Chinese food to rent. He would occasionally work a job for a few weeks at a local grocery store or McDonald's, but he would insist that such jobs got in the way of his future.

Colin moved in with Eddie two weeks after they met because he was being evicted from his current apartment. Eddie was happy to have him, and they agreed that as soon as he was back on his feet, they would split the rent. Colin would always add that once he made it big, he would buy Eddie two houses (one up north for the summer and one down south for the winter).

For the third straight month, Colin failed to help at all with the rent. Eddie had noticed that he did, however, purchase a new amplifier for his guitar. When Eddie approached the subject, Colin would get angry, insisting that he just needed to give him more time. Eddie was a social worker who dealt with underprivileged preteens and adolescents. The demands of his work required him to be absent from the house at odd times, often working back-to-back shifts. Often, Eddie would come home to the smell of cannabis with Colin passed out on the couch.

Eddie's friends grew increasingly concerned. Eddie was very conscientious with his bills and always paid the rent on time. However, between paying for food, beer, and "miscellaneous" expenses for Colin (along with the occasional party he would throw), Eddie had fallen behind twice in the electricity, once in rent, and his car was overdue for several critical maintenance issues.

Tina had come over while Colin was at band rehearsal to plead with Eddie to kick Colin out. Tina barely saw her friend anymore, and when she did, Eddie would cry, complain, or get drunk. Tina likened Colin to a parasite who was sucking the life out of Eddie. Eddie protested, insisting that Tina "did not understand" Colin. Eddie always went on to say that Colin was a loving man, and money doesn't matter when you love someone. Eddie would also point out that Colin's musical career was important and that it was only a matter of time before he made it big and paid Eddie back with interest. Although I fell out of touch with this group, I do not think things ended well for Eddie.

Why the Truth Just Does Not Work

We worry when we see friends moving in with someone a week after meeting them or preparing to commit to people they barely know. When our friends tell us that they have found "the one" or are falling in love quickly when they don't know a person that well, we fear that our friend will get hurt, or worse, used, abused, taken advantage of, or stuck in a horrible situation. We feel helpless and compelled to do something to slow the process down and get our friend to take a moment and *at least* think things through.

Many of us may feel the temptation to warn or dissuade friends to slow down when they are falling for someone who is not much more than a stranger or someone who is already raising red flags. Tempting as it may be, getting a friend to cool off for a moment is tricky. Although well intentioned, warning or dissuading can backfire. People do not like being told what to do, especially when they are in a state of high positive arousal. This state can blind people to potential catastrophes. High levels of positive arousal can also turn to rage easily when someone tries to "interrupt" or "interfere" with that happiness. Think about the last time you were elated about something, and someone interrupted you. Frustrating, right? Well, the individual high in emophilia you are trying to warn is in a state of bliss and often will not be able to understand why you do not want to just "see them happy." They may even accuse you of being jealous, misunderstanding, or being overprotective (particularly when it is parents trying to warn their children).

As discussed in the previous chapter, we do not like our options to be limited. My high school physics teacher was a kind woman named Marylou Ciavera. She would always enthusiastically say that, in physics, forces are like shoes—they come in pairs! In psychology, just as in physics, forces come in pairs. If you push on a wall, there is resistance. Humans are the same way. Thus, the same is true of human attraction and desires. "I forbid you to date that person!" is like a magical spell that makes that person the sexiest human on the planet. (More on this later).

I should say at the outset that the best solution for concern over someone's mental health, interpersonal relationships, or future is a professional therapist. Therapy is not only for the mentally ill but also for people who find themselves at an impasse in life. One would not think twice about taking one's child to a doctor if that child was having an allergic reaction to a type of food, so why would we hesitate to take someone to a therapist about life problems? First and foremost, I recommend offering to go with someone to see a counselor or trained therapist when concerns of this type (or any type) arise. My advice below is based on theory and research, yes, but nothing can replace professional guidance and training for handling these situations.

Therapy notwithstanding, there are two ways around reactance, and they require time and cooperation on the part of the individual falling in love. The first is to play the "if you were me" game. By getting the individual to step outside of the situation and see the risks about to be taken, the individual may think twice. This strategy operates under the principle of perspective-taking. Perspective-taking is a powerful tool derived from research in social psychology that engages the empathy centers of the brain and gets individuals to step outside of self-centered thinking. One might say, "OK, imagine I am with a guy who is just not good for me, but I am telling you all the things you are telling me. What would you say to me to protect me?" By engaging these perspective-taking mechanisms, the individual might begin to realize the concern that you are feeling, and that these concerns are not "jealousy," "overparenting" or somehow an attempt to sabotage the individual's happiness. This strategy opens the door to demotivating the distorted mind (as discussed earlier) because the individual is engaging in a hypothetical scenario and is playing the role of the "concerned." The individual then begins to explain, without the irrational defense mechanisms, why this type of behavior might be counterproductive. However, the individual may still cling to the idea that their situation is entirely different for a series of reasons. Thus, it should be noted that rarely will a one-time talk lead to a knee-dropping confession of "you were right!" People have far too much pride for such displays. However, such an exercise may get the individual thinking.

The second strategy is to ask the person to play devil's advocate for a moment. Cognitive dissonance literature has found that asking people, even as just a favor, to write, advocate, or list ideas in a manner counter to their existing attitudes can create attitude change (e.g., Harmon-Jones & Mills, 1999). Thus, you might ask your son, daughter, or best friend to sit down and list all the things that could go wrong with their premature relationship or all the problems ("small" as they may be) with the partner that they know so little about. However, for this task to work, individuals must do it of their own free will.

Emotional Intensity Among Emophilic Individuals

Emophilia is a trait that allows early emotional connections to be either misinterpreted as love or amplified with such intensity that feelings of love are evoked. Research on relationships has shown that danger, fear, excitement, or even exercise can amplify the signal of interpersonal attraction for most people. In a classic study, researchers Donald Dutton and Arthur Aron put these assumptions to the test. Instead of the laboratory, these researchers took their study to a tourist attraction in Vancouver, Canada known as the Capilano Suspension Bridge. At the time, it was a rickety old bridge that seemed highly unstable. It served as an attraction for thrill-seekers across the globe. Dutton and Aron (1974) asked a series of female research assistants to approach men crossing the bridge with a few questions. They did so either at a safer, sturdier, northern bridge or while the men were standing on the swaying and unstable Capilano bridge. At the end of the study, the women tore off a small portion of paper and gave the man her phone number.

Among the men approached on the stable bridge, only a handful (about 12%) called the researcher later. However, among the men approached on the seemingly dangerous bridge, half called the female assistant! The phenomenon is referred to as "trauma bonding." The authors even demonstrated this effect in the lab, finding that people are significantly more attracted to another person when about to experience painful shocks. Follow-up research has found that anything that elevates your heart rate (from excitement, to fear, to shock, to exercise), even if it is *unrelated* to a person, can create a bond with someone.

When the arousal is unrelated to a person, but the excitement is associated with a person anyway, this process is called "misattribution of arousal." Such misattribution gets focused on a person instead of its actual origins.

So, what happens when someone is exposed to an exciting, dangerous, shocking, or arousing situation *and* has a predisposition for misinterpreting such emotions and feeling them more strongly than others? The allure of charming and egotistical partners for emophilic people can partly be explained through this process. Men and women who are more likely to engage in overconfident, risky, dangerous, or even illegal activities are likely to romantically arouse someone high in emophilia more than they would the average person. Antisocial personalities have predispositions toward leadership, authority, and risk-taking. These attractive and exciting traits are especially likely to arouse excitement in others who have a predisposition to misattribute arousal for love.

I once observed two male teenagers as they were cliff-jumping into pools of water near Tucson, Arizona. In particular, they decided it would be a good idea to do back flips into a four-foot x four-foot x four-foot pool of water from at least 15 feet up. With little room for error and high risk of serious injury, most of us would consider this behavior a dumb risk. However, this type of behavior does have the effect of raising the heart rate of observers, either out of fear or excitement. Often, young men will engage in such behaviors for the benefit of a young female observer. Indeed, in the case of the two teenage cliff-jumpers, there was an attractive young woman watching with an adoring gaze as they behaved in what (at least to us) appeared to be needlessly risky actions.

This behavior is referred to in the evolutionary psychology literature as "mate display." Such displays may lead the young woman to feel either fear (because of the risk of his injury), excitement (over the thrill of his extreme actions), or both. Regardless of the source of arousal, the young woman with these feelings or sensations might unconsciously interpret them as attraction. Individuals who are high in emophilia may be especially vulnerable to such feelings and feel them so strongly that they end up with a strong romantic attraction to the person at risk.

Excitement, however, is only one piece of the puzzle. Individuals high in emophilia often wear their hearts on their sleeves. Because they fall in love quickly, easily, and often, they are prime targets for manipulation and abuse. They also feel romantic connections more intensely, making it harder for them to hide the emotions they feel. As a result, individuals who are predisposed to selfishness, egotism, and deception may seize these signals and decide how best to "use" the high emophilia person to their own advantage.

The Dark Triad of Personality

Individuals who engage in short-term charm, deception, and "anything it takes" strategies to find sexual partners may find success with emophilic individuals or others who are drawn to short-term encounters. Because emophilic people fall in love fast and easily, they are often drawn to such individuals. Research on attraction to "bad apples" has an empirical foundation. I have found that emophilic individuals find themselves drawn to individuals high in traits known as the "Dark Triad" of personality. Del Paulhus, my PhD advisor at the University of British Columbia, is an expert on destructive personalities. In 2002, Paulhus and his graduate student Kevin Williams began research on the three most researched destructive personalities and how they differ from one another. This cluster of dark personalities came to be known as the "Dark Triad" of personality: psychopathy, Machiavellianism, and narcissism. These three traits are particularly informative when examining those who might be predisposed to using others for selfish gain. Psychopathy and narcissism are both considered clinical syndromes as well as subclinical personality traits, which means that the individual functions in society. All three of these traits can be assessed using questionnaires. People with them share a common theme: they all strive for selfish success, and none of them care about whom they hurt in the process.

Psychopathy. Psychopathy has several definitions and conceptualizations. Most, if not all, derive in some form from the work of Hervey Cleckley and his groundbreaking 1941 book, *The Mask of Sanity*. Cleckley was a pioneer in psychopathy research. Cleckley recognized that most of his patients were perfectly in control of reality and their decisions. However, they lacked fundamental aspects of compassion such as empathy and guilt, which led them to behave in erratic, violent, callous, and destructive ways.

Robert Hare, an expert on psychopathy, indicated in his book *Without Conscience* that psychopaths never accept the blame for their misdeeds. In fact, many of them do not believe that they did anything wrong and that they are being unfairly punished or singled out for behaviors in which everyone engages. When they are caught and punished, psychopathic individuals will blame everyone else for their lot (parents, family, friends, victims, society) but never themselves. Psychopathic individuals are quick to explain away their antisocial behavior with excuses and rationalizations aimed at mitigating their culpability or punishment. In the psychopath's mind, it is often another person's fault, and *they* were a victim of the situation. Psychopaths go so far as to blame the victim(s) of their crimes. One individual who was highly psychopathic and engaged in a hit-and-run driving incident explained that he was really the victim. He bemoaned how unfair it was that the man he hit would probably get all kinds of insurance money, while he was going to rot in prison for six months.

The first, and perhaps most recognized, empirical definition of psychopathy is one that Robert Hare and colleagues put out in 1980. Hare created a checklist of 30 or so features that describe a prototypical psychopath, which came to be known as the Psychopathy Checklist (later revised as the Psychopathy Checklist-Revised, or PCL-R; Hare, 2003). Hare's argument was that it was insufficient to simply "ask" individuals who are suspected of being pathological liars whether they have a psychological condition that might be harmful to others. It was more accurate to engage in a semi-structured interview with these individuals and have trained coders extract scores for themselves. Hare's overall model has been refined through the years, starting with two factors (personality and behavior), to three (personality, affect, and behavior), to its current state, which assesses four, interrelated factors: interpersonal manipulation, callous affect, erratic lifestyle, and antisocial behavior.

Psychopathic individuals live fast, die young, and manipulate others for short-term immediate gratification—or just for the fun of it. They are constant liars, and (according to Hare) often lie after a contradiction and keep talking as though it all makes sense! They are reckless and engage in antisocial behavior freely with no concern about the consequences. Psychopathic individuals are callous to others' pain and emotions. Many have compared them to being "color-blind" when it comes to emotions; they can fake emotional expressions, but they do not really "get it" at a deep level. The callousness that results is akin to a neurological impairment where they simply cannot resonate with the suffering of others or take their perspective on things.

Narcissism. The second trait in the Dark Triad is narcissism, which is much more common than psychopathy. Narcissism was a trait first recognized by Sigmund Freud in the early 1900s. Narcissism was named after the mythological Greek character "Narcissus" who fell in love with his own reflection and died staring at it. Narcissism was originally conceptualized as a disorder that was associated with a fragile sense of self and insecure ego (Freud, 1914). Researchers have found that this definition is only half true. Some types of narcissism are indeed associated with low self-esteem, fragility, and vulnerability (Pincus et al., 2009). Other types, however, are rooted in overconfidence, egotism, and approach-oriented self-aggrandizement (Krizan & Herlache, 2018).

To orient the reader, I will point out an infamous case of narcissistic behavior, which comes from a criminal case against a famous actress and singer. After she walked into a jewelry store and took a necklace, she claimed in her defense that people gave her free things all the time. This type of entitlement is commonly seen among individuals high in narcissism. Note that I have never met this singer, nor do I have the qualifications to diagnose her. Thus, I have no idea whether she has behaved in other ways that fit the description of a narcissist, but that type of entitled behavior is indicative of elevated levels of narcissism. Young and Pinsky (2006) conducted research suggesting that celebrities are higher in narcissism than the public. Because correlations do not imply causation, it is unclear why this link exists. For example, fame could make someone more narcissistic, narcissistic people may be more likely to seek fame, or there may be some additional variable (privilege) causing both.

Narcissism differs from psychopathy in three ways. First, narcissistic deception is based on self-deception (Paulhus & Williams, 2002). As discussed earlier, self-deception means that individuals truly believe (or convince themselves) positive things about themselves that aren't true. Interestingly, although individuals high in emophilia engage in self-deception to enhance their relationship, narcissistic individuals engage in self-deception to enhance others' perceptions of them. Although these processes are similar, it is the emphasis on repeated romance vs. self-enhancement that distinguishes emophilic individuals from narcissistic individuals in their behaviors. For example, narcissistic self-deception that results in self-enhancement involves thoughts or statements such as the following: "I'm the smartest person in the room," "I am the most attractive person in this bar," "It was not my fault," or "I never get the respect I deserve." This type of self-deception leads individuals to be overconfident, cocksure, and extremely assertive.

A second key characteristic of narcissism is that the callousness associated with the trait is derived from grandiosity and entitlement, not a deficit as with psychopathy. In fact, research has found that narcissistic individuals can indeed show empathy if they are led to take another person's perspective for a moment (Hepper et al., 2014). By abandoning their self-centered and egotistical perspective on the world, they can resonate with other people's feelings.

A third key characteristic of narcissism is that such individuals are not antisocial under normal circumstances but engage in such behaviors when they feel that something is owed to them, they have been insulted, or their ego has somehow been undermined. Research and theory have suggested that narcissistic individuals become very angry and aggressive when insulted (Kjærvik & Bushman, 2021). Perhaps even more disturbing is that they are likely to engage in sexual coaxing or physical aggression when denied a sexual experience (Bushman et al., 2003).

Machiavellianism. The third trait of the Dark Triad is Machiavellianism. Machiavellianism was partially based on the original writings of Niccolò Machiavelli, the fifteenth-century Italian philosopher (Machiavelli, 1513/1998). Machiavelli's philosophy was one of pragmatic advice to leaders and rulers. This advice included the use of ruthless and unethical force when necessary (but only when necessary) to maintain power and control. Many have summarized Machiavelli's philosophy with the phrase "the ends justify the means."

In the late 1960s, a researcher by the name of Richard Christie began to realize that agreement or disagreement with Machiavelli's ideas was associated with other stable individual differences. For example, individuals who agreed with Machiavelli tended to engage in less ethical behavior in the service of bottom-line goals and had a cynical view of humanity. With the help of his collaborator Florence Geis, they began research on defining and examining the construct of Machiavellianism. They found that Machiavellianism consisted of manipulative tactics, amoral thinking, and a cynical worldview. They conducted a series of experiments showing that Machiavellian individuals looked people in the eye when they lied and were able to manipulate people into taking more money from others. In sum, they found that Machiavellian individuals were dishonest with and callous toward others and seemed to have a knack for homing in on accomplishing their goals, using any means necessary (Christie & Geis, 1970).

Machiavellianism was based partially on political philosophy (i.e., Machiavelli) and partially on militaristic philosophy from East Asia. Indeed, manipulative tactics have a lot in common with militaristic deception. Machiavellianism is defined by three key components: amorality, manipulation, and cynical worldview. Recent theory and research have argued that some necessary (but previously unidentified) characteristics of the trait include morally flexible and expedient thinking, situational sensitivity, and strategic planning (Jones & Mueller, 2022).

Although Machiavellian individuals (like psychopathic individuals) have no empathy and are comfortable lying to others, Machiavellianism differs from the other two Dark Triad traits in at least two ways. First, individuals high in Machiavellianism differ from those who are high in psychopathy because they engage in manipulation and lying in the service of long-term tangible goals (such as money or power) rather than immediate gratification (psychopathy) or egoistical praise (narcissism). Similarly, individuals high in Machiavellianism are cautious in their misbehavior, and they will not engage in a behavior that gains in the short term but is risky in the long run.

Although both psychopathy and Machiavellianism are linked with manipulation and direct deception (not self-deception), the manipulation style is different. Whereas psychopathy is linked with quick scams and short-term lies (e.g., "You won a free trip to Hawaii!"), Machiavellianism is linked with long-term careful lies involving rapport building. It is not that either has moral qualms about manipulation, they just differ in their approach to it.

Dark Triad and Relationships

In 2009, Peter Jonason and colleagues conducted a study to examine the sexual history and relationship styles of people who vary on these three traits. He found that all three personality traits were positively related to one-night stands, and all three reported having had more sexual partners throughout their lifetime when compared to individuals low in any of these traits. This was especially true for men. They concluded that the Dark Triad traits may have evolved to help men get more short-term sexual partners.

As it turns out, this finding is an oversimplistic representation of the Dark Triad. There are several ways that the Dark Triad traits differ in their approach to relationships. For example, individuals high in psychopathy are usually after anything that they desire in the moment. Food, sex, money, power, whatever they crave, they seek it instantly. Thus, they are driven by immediate gratification and are not deterred by fear, punishment, or consequences. Further, such individuals will use reckless tactics (lies, coercion, even assault) to get what they want (Camilleri & Quinsey, 2009).

Narcissistic individuals are a little different in that they seek anything that reinforces their ego. If having a successful long-term relationship garners praise, that's what they will seek. If a one-night stand with a particular person is ego reinforcing, that's what the person will seek.

Machiavellian individuals are slightly different. They have instrumental goals. Although Machiavellian individuals will manipulate and lie, they do not do so at their own peril. In fact, such individuals are quite cautious and reserved in their misbehavior when there is the chance for punishment or harm to themselves. A Machiavellian may have the goal of many sex partners or a successful long-term relationship, it just depends. Nevertheless, individuals high in any of these three traits are likely to use manipulation to get a partner to do whatever it is they want them to do.

As it turns out, emophilia is the best predictor of attraction to Dark Triad individuals. Although, it should be noted that insecure attachment and unrestricted sociosexuality may also lead to a vulnerability to Dark Triad traits as well.

An honor student of mine, Jacqueline Lechuga, and I decided to test who was most likely to have romantic interest in individuals who are high in the Dark Triad (Lechuga & Jones, 2021). To do this, we conducted two studies. The first one was relatively simple. We had people fill out assessments of sociosexuality, emophilia, and insecure (i.e., anxious & avoidant) attachment (along with a few other measures) to learn more about their dispositional traits. Next, participants filled out a measure called the "Short Dark Triad," or SD3 (Jones & Paulhus, 2014). The SD3 is a scale that Del Paulhus and I developed to briefly (but accurately) assess the Dark Triad traits. However, there was a twist. Instead of filling out the SD3 for themselves, they filled it out as they would want an *ideal romantic partner* to fill them out. We found that, overall, individuals high in emophilia reported higher scores for their ideal romantic partner on all three Dark Triad traits. In addition, we found that anxious attachment and sociosexuality were also correlated (although the correlations were weaker) with wanting partners higher in the Dark Triad. Indeed, each of the three relationship styles (emophilia, sociosexuality, and anxious attachment) predicted a desire for elevated scores on the Dark Triad. Sociosexuality, for example, makes sense given that that the reckless, short-term, and impulsive nature of psychopathic individuals means that they will be willing to engage in "no strings attached" sexual behavior that is here today and gone tomorrow. The findings pertaining to anxiously attached individuals also make sense, given that individuals high in anxious attachment are seeking someone to latch onto who would never leave them. Such insecurity and sense of need make them an easy target for someone who is seeking to manipulate. Machiavellian individuals, for example, are likely to sense the needs of the anxiously attached and convince them of lies. This assertion stems from the fact that Machiavellian individuals generally do a good job of detecting others who are in distress (although they do not feel bad for them). Further, it is critical to note that because Machiavellian individuals are effective long-term liars, they are likely to be believable in what they tell others. Individuals high in emophilia and anxious attachment may be especially eager to believe the lies if the circumstances are right.

In this way, the disposition of individuals high in emophilia to dive into a relationship, and the correlated tendency for them to be anxiously attached and cling to partners, may leave them vulnerable to being accessories to crime. Given their premature trust and early emotional bonds, emophilic individuals may "vouch" for antisocial individuals. This process may occur because manipulative individuals sense an opportunity for exoneration through false alibi, and emophilic individuals are blinded by their passion and premature trust.

I became curious about how far these findings extended. So, we conducted a second study. This time, we surveyed hundreds of individuals and asked them for their scores on the SD3, along with some other basic demographics. For simplicity, we focused this time on Dark Triad men. Although, it should be pointed out, we expected these findings would generalize equally across men and women.

After filling out the SD3 and basic demographics, we simply asked participants to tell us about themselves in a "dating profile" type format. Specifically, we asked them to tell us "About you," "Your hobbies," and "Your ideal date." We told them to answer these questions as they would a serious dating website. From there, we isolated the top-scoring men on each of the Dark Triad traits. Thus, we came up with three Machiavellian targets, three narcissistic targets, and three psychopathic targets. Finally, we also isolated the bottom scorers on all three Dark Triad traits, so we had three non-Dark Triad targets.

Machiavellian Targets:
1. **Interests:** Fun, good-looking, physically fit, charming, caring, and passionate.
   About You: I am a fun-loving person that has a sense of humor but understands responsibility. I am an easygoing man who likes to play sports, weight lift, and dance.
   Ideal Date: Going dancing after having dinner.

2. **Interests:** Smart, funny, intelligent, fun, sociable, well mannered, and outgoing.

   About You: Smart, funny, outgoing, fun, well mannered, respectful, organized, responsible, and loyal.

   Ideal Date: I think an ideal first date would be going to a romantic dinner and going to the movies or go walk at the park after.

3. **Interests:** Video games, hiking, camping, shooting range, cookouts, family gatherings, and children.

   About You: I am the type of person that generally listens to what you have to say rather than be the one talking. I am very cool tempered and will be slightly bothered by certain pet peeves. I enjoy going out with friends to different places, as I do not enjoy having a routine. I am quiet when around a large group of strangers, but when it comes to people I am already acquainted with, I am very chatty.

   Ideal Date: The ideal first date would be with someone whom you have a lot of similar interests with. The reason for that would be not having silence during the first date since it is when you are seeing if you would like to continue further. A simple dinner and a movie is usually ideal since it gives you a little sense of what the other person is like.

Narcissistic Targets:

1. **Interests:** Any kind of sports, video games, outdoors activities, working out, and relaxing with friends or family.

   About You: I am a fairly quiet person, but I can be very funny and social once I am comfortable around you. I am very family oriented and love spending time with my family. I like being active as well as just taking time to sit back, relax, and enjoy what is going on around me.

   Ideal Date: An ideal first date would be going to a rodeo where I would be comfortable and things are not going to distract me from my date, but at the same time there are things going on. At the end of the event there is a live band that we could dance to and have a good time. After all we could go to a nice quiet restaurant to eat.

2. **Interests:** I like the outdoors, cycling, MMA, hotrods, tattoos, swimming, music shows, and roller derby. Pretty much anything fun.

   About You: I have traveled quite a bit. I lived in Austin, Texas, for the majority of my adult life. I like to cycle, and I have worked for roller derbies as a referee. I am fun and outgoing, but I do not mind just hanging out and watching TV. Music is a big passion of mine and I enjoy seeing it live.

   Ideal Date: Going to see a music act that is interesting to both of us.

3. **Interests:** Someone fun, has an open mind to life, is positive, caring, and loving.

   About You: Fun to be around, I try my best to be a gentleman, I am positive, and I have a good sense of humor.

   Ideal Date: Going dancing, showing confidence, but also taking the time to get to know one another.

Psychopathic Targets:

1. **Interests:** Physical activities, art, family, and social events.

   About You: I'm a good guy that is easy to get along with. I love soccer. I started playing since I was three and started officiating at thirteen. I like to meet new people. I put others before myself. I enjoy making other people happy. I am a great listener and I give some good feedback. If you have any problems, anything you want to discuss, or even just someone to listen to you, I'm always available.

   Ideal Date: I would take my date on a small city tour of the town that finished at a small hole in the wall restaurant, followed by a visit to a local performance.

2. **Interests:** Smart, funny, good personality, and healthy.

   About You: I am generally a shy and quiet person, but I do open up rather easily. I enjoy conversations that are stimulating in an intellectual manner, and I enjoy spending time outdoors. I can be funny and I enjoy a wide variety of activities, from video games to exercising.

Ideal Date: Getting to know each other in a quiet and comfortable restaurant, without the need of anything drastic.

3. **Interests:** School, education, hiking, jogging, and reading.

   About You: I really enjoy doing outdoor activities such as hiking, jogging, and biking. I am reliable, when I say I'll do something, I'll do it. I am always willing to hang out, and I am open to a lot of activities and ideas.

   Ideal Date: An ideal first date would take place at a park (no one else there) having a picnic. Just talking and having fun all day.

Low Dark Triad Targets:

1. **Interests:** Someone that takes a relationship seriously and is not afraid to fall in love.

   About You: Self-motivated individual who has a positive attitude most of the time. Very friendly and kind.

   Ideal Date: If possible, on the rooftop of a building as the sun sets on the horizon.

2. **Interests:** Playing guitar, writing music, singing, old school arcade games, relaxing, spending time with friends, watching old movies, eating, drawing, and creating.

   About You: I'm a really simple kind of guy. I enjoy doing things that don't involve a lot of hyperactivity, but rather, prefer writing music while noodling on my guitar. Maybe singing a few lines to pull a song together. I spend many nights before bed out on the roof of my house with my headphones on listening to music and watching the stars shine above me. I spend a lot of time with my friends and family. I think it's important to have those kind of close relationships with people because that way there's always someone to talk to, or laugh with, or just to keep company. I'm always ready to make plans or head out and try something new.

   Ideal Date: First dates usually say too much or too little about a person. My ideal first date would be with a girl who doesn't really care what we do as long as we get to talk to each other. Maybe a semi-fancy dinner or a walk in the park would give us enough time to realize that maybe we'd want to see each other again. As long as we get to talk and have some fun, I'm sure any place is good enough for a first date.

3. **Interests:** Music, photography, hiking, cycling, traveling, history, movies, learning, reading, computers, and gadgets.

    About You: I am a nice person. I'm a laid back guy. I'm a pretty calm and caring individual. I am confident and funny. I have a strong belief in having close and affectionate relationships within my family.

    Ideal Date: A trip to a zoo where we can have plenty of time to talk to each other and interact. Followed by lunch at a small quiet restaurant.

A cursory glance over these profiles indicates that nothing is terribly out of the ordinary for any of them. However, it is the subtle cues that one must look for, with respect to the Dark Triad personalities that will stick out. Notice the Machiavellian target #3, and his interest in "family gatherings" and "children." Although it is entirely possible that this individual really does enjoy family gatherings and being around children, it is also highly likely (given his score on Machiavellianism) that these "interests" are listed to evoke a certain sense of trustworthiness and mate quality in the mind of the reader. Similarly, notice the narcissistic targets focus an awful lot on their accomplishments, how much they have traveled, and their abilities. Again, I realize that these are very subtle cues, but they are nevertheless small telltale hints of what is to come.

So, the larger question, now, is who is attracted to whom? We gave these 12 profiles to a brand-new sample of women and asked how attractive each man was on a scale of 1 (not attractive to me) to 10 (extremely attractive to me). What we found was quite fascinating. First, emophilic individuals had the highest levels of attraction across all the targets in total. In other words, emophilic individuals were more likely to see more of the targets attractive when compared to anyone else. However, there was a noticeable and significant bump when it came to the first nine profiles—those of the Dark Triad individuals. Women high in emophilia were particularly drawn to these men, indicating high levels of attraction. The same was not true for any of the other variables we studied, with one exception: avoidantly attached individuals were drawn to the Machiavellian profiles.

Loving the Egotistical

Narcissistic entitlement can reach extreme levels, such as leading individuals to feel entitled to kill. One example of a convicted killer who has expressed this type of narcissistic entitlement was Larry Dasilva. Dasilva was convicted of first-degree murder and executed using the electric chair. Although it will never be known if Dasilva was a psychopath, narcissist, or Machiavellian, he was certainly callous and entitled. When asked if he felt any remorse for a particular victim, he responded with, "All I wanted was her goddamn wallet; the bitch had to give me a hard time."

Individuals high in emophilia are particularly likely to buy into explanations, rationalizations, excuses, and victim blaming that some narcissistic individuals will provide. Such faith in the narcissist comes from the gut-level attraction emophilic individuals may feel toward their new love interest. Indeed, narcissistic individuals are extremely charming upon first encounter. In 2010, Mitja Back and colleagues conducted a study on narcissism with people who knew nothing about each other before meeting. They found that narcissistic individuals won the day with their immediate charm. My friend Kate Rogers and her coauthors in 2018 demonstrated similar findings with narcissistic individuals being seen as most likeable and sadistic individuals being least likable. In both studies, individuals high in narcissism walked away from the group interaction as the most liked and most attractive. Research has also found that narcissistic individuals do extremely well on first dates (Jauk et al., 2016), job interviews (Paulhus et al., 2013), and other encounters that involve first-time, short-term meetings (Rogers et al., 2018).

Perhaps the best example of this charm comes from research by Dark Triad expert Del Paulhus. Paulhus (1998) had participants rate each other, once per week, on likability over a series of months. Paulhus made a startling discovery about narcissistic charm. He found that individuals who recorded high scores on narcissism were significantly *more* liked during the first few weeks of interaction. They were rated as the most exciting, engaging, and charming of the group. They often spoke up, sought leadership roles, and took charge of group discussions. However, over time, not only did narcissistic individuals drop in their attractiveness, but they also wound up the most disliked of the group by the time the study was done! There is an Italian expression my grandfather taught me (although I had to find a translator because I do not remember the original Italian), which was approximately, "*Quando la neve si scioglie, la merda è ancora lì,*" which roughly translates in English to "when the snow melts, the crap is still there." Perhaps the Italians were thinking of narcissistic entitlement when they coined this phrase. At best, Paulhus (1998) argues that narcissism is a "mixed blessing." Although they do well in early encounters, they wear on people after a while and end up disliked in the long run.

Recall that high emophilia individuals feel comfortable falling in love with others immediately. Such premature love also leads to early commitment and diving head first into relationships. Consequently, individuals high in emophilia may find themselves "stuck" with a narcissistic partner. Perhaps even more problematic is that emophilic individuals are self-deceptive, so narcissistic individuals are likely to be able to convince emophilic individuals of their entitlement and authority. Such self-deception among individuals high in emophilia may lead them to *want* to believe the narcissistic grandiosity and overconfidence rather than question it. From the example at the beginning of the chapter with my friend Stephanie, it seems clear that individuals high in emophilia are vulnerable to believing in the excuses and the deservingness of a narcissistic lover.

Individuals high in any Dark Triad or Dark Tetrad trait are often difficult to leave. There is little evidence that their reluctance to let partners leave has to do with love or affection, however. Instead, they see partners as *property* and will resort to a myriad of toxic tactics to reclaim such perceived property. Some of these strategies appear desperate, such as love bombing a partner.

"Love bombing" is a term that has been circulated in the media to describe excessive behaviors, expressions, and assertions of love that are designed to overwhelm and flatter a target. Love bombing often emerges among those high in narcissism when they fear losing something that is "theirs" such as a romantic partner. Although these assertions are flattering and appear unwavering, they are a form of abuse, coercive control, and manipulation. Although a common tactic for those who perceive they are about to lose their partner, among abusive or toxic partners, love bombing often fits into a cycle of idealization followed be devaluation or abuse. The love bombing emerges to maintain the relationship, sometimes referred to as a "honeymoon" period of charm, gift giving, tenderness, and apology.

To be clear, there are many reasons why someone becomes abusive in a romantic relationship, the Dark Triad and Dark Tetrad are just a few traits that can lead to abuse. However, anxiously attached individuals also can become abusive out of desperation and fear of loss. Although they do not see their partner as a "possession" necessarily, instead, they see them as a life raft in a huge ocean. They feel that if they lose their partner, they lose all that is good in their life and may "pull out all the stops," including love bombing and abuse, to keep that partner. Research has also demonstrated that men who feel insecure, low-quality, have anger issues, or control issues all may become abusive as well. Although many of these reasons focus on men, it is also worth noting that people of all genders can engage in abusive behavior toward partners.

In sum, the difference between someone high in the Dark Triad/Tetrad who abuses, and someone who abuses for a reason that does not involve being dispositionally callous and manipulative, has to do with genuine loss and remorse. Whereas someone high in anxious attachment (for example) will genuinely feel bad about being abusive, someone high in narcissism (for example) probably will not. Further, someone high in narcissism also would not fear the loss of intimacy or security as much as anger over losing someone they see as a possession.

From the Subclinical to the Criminal Attraction

My graduate student, Sampada Karandikar, and I decided to investigate who among us may feel attraction toward convicted murderers, such as serial killers. We investigated relationship variables such as attachment styles, sociosexuality, and emophilia. Then we examined personality variables such as the Dark Tetrad, which is the three Dark Triad traits plus subclinical or everyday sadism (Paulhus, 2014). In brief, sadism is like psychopathy, but sadism predicts a desire to harm. This desire can be so strong that they are willing to pay a price to engage in harming others (Buckels et al., 2013) and find themselves spending exorbitant amounts of time trolling others online just to agitate people (Buckels et al., 2014).

We then correlated these traits to attraction to serial killers, fascination with serial killers, and actual attempts to reach out to or contact serial killers. Although we found that emophilia did indeed correlate with attraction to serial killers, the three strongest traits that predicted attraction were sadism, psychopathy, and avoidant attachment. Although all three are equally strong predictors of attraction, sadism is not only correlated with attraction but fascination as well. Thus, I suspect when emophilia and sadism mix (although they are mostly unrelated) serial killer "groupies" emerge.

Take for example the famous case of Sondra London. London was taken in so thoroughly by many of the narcissistic serial killers she met when she visited prisons that she wrote and published their stories, confessions, childhoods, life traumas, and even their ideologies. London tried to help several serial killers (such as Gerard Schaefer and Keith Jesperson) tell their stories through fiction and nonfiction writing. Dubbed the "queen of serial killer groupies," London seemed a slave to her emotions. She moved from killer to killer and developed rapid attachments to men who had committed horrible crimes. For example, London and "Gainesville Ripper" Danny Rolling professed their love for each other and announced plans to be married less than six months after London met Rolling in prison. In general, London moved on quickly to a new love interest (often a serial killer) when the old relationship was made impossible either through government restriction or execution.

In fact, many serial killers and violent offenders in prison end up with love letters and love interests that develop after they are incarcerated. This "serial killer groupie" mentality is one of the strangest phenomena among romance and love. London embodies many of the behaviors of a person who is high in emophilia. First, London has many relationships that are short in duration and develop rapidly. Second, London seems differentially attracted to excitement and attention. Third, London appears to commit herself to impossible relationships and does so in a rapid time frame. Finally, when the relationship became impossible (not just inconvenient), London swiftly moved on to another love interest.

It is important to note that men will often fall in love with women killers as well, and London is by no means the only "groupie" of serial killers to fit this pattern. There are other women who tend to move from killer to killer in a rapid and torrid fashion, too. Take for example the case of Veronica Compton. Veronica attempted to incriminate herself in order to cast aspersions upon the guilt of her then love interest Ken Bianchi. When things took a turn for the ugly with Compton and Bianchi, Compton moved on to a new love interest: serial killer Douglas Clark.

It should be noted that the emophilic trait of these women was only part of the story. The men they were interested in were not at a loss for female interest, especially once convicted. The excitement that surrounds these men, for many women, is a romantic adventure. They are obviously master manipulators as well, effective at concealing their true intentions or convincing others of their innocence. Take for example the girlfriend (at the time of his murders) of serial killer Ken Bianchi; she claimed to have been taken completely by surprise with respect to Ken's crimes, describing him as a "gentle" man.

It should also be noted that not all serial killer groupies fit a high emophilia pattern perfectly. Take for example the case of Doreen Lioy, who fell in love with the notorious "night stalker" killer, Richard Ramirez. Although she wrote 75 letters to Ramirez professing her love (before ever meeting him), there were other aspects of her behavior that did not fit typical emophilic behavior. The unusual aspect of Doreen was her unwavering fidelity to Ramirez, especially despite his meeting and engaging with many women once incarcerated. Many accounts report that Ramirez had "lines" of women waiting to meet him. Reports were released that at least one woman requested Ramirez get her pregnant. Despite her situation, Lioy would rail against the "unfair bias" in the media against Ramirez. In the end, Lioy's efforts to stand by Ramirez "paid off" when they ultimately became husband and wife on October 3, 1996.

Recently, the notorious convicted murderer Charles Manson heard wedding bells. The late Charles Manson, when he was 79 years old, was married to a 25-year-old fan by the name of Afton (Star) Burton. Although Star was not allowed a life with her husband nor more than a hug when she visited, she swore fierce loyalty to Manson. She argued that Manson was innocent and planned to stand by him, filing papers and pleas on his behalf. Star believed that marrying Manson was her life's purpose. Star claimed that Manson, often considered a master of mind control, was not at all a manipulative person. Star argued instead that Manson was an environmental advocate and never manipulated anyone.

Individuals high in emophilia are vulnerable to antisocial partners, especially those high in narcissism. Narcissistic individuals, those who are entitled, grandiose, authoritative, overconfident, and egotistical are superficially charming in the short term. They are especially appealing to those who feel romantic connections immediately and intensely, such as individuals high in emophilia. This vulnerability toward entitled and grandiose individuals is especially pronounced among those who feel romantic attraction toward people who have committed crimes. Although individuals of all genders may fit this pattern, we have mostly studied the topic of women who are attracted to men. Women end up vulnerable to such men, being convinced that they are innocent, do not deserve their punishment, or are "deep down" good guys. Individuals high in emophilia may go as far as covering for or helping these men because of their premature investment in a relationship. Further, when falling in love, emophilic individuals may fail to screen partners for potential issues that may emerge later in the relationship. In the end, emophilic individuals are vulnerable because they are looking for their "princess" or "knight in shining armor." Narcissistic or manipulative individuals may seize upon this fantasy by playing the part for a while, only to eventually turn the fairy tale into a nightmare.

8

Till Death Do We Part
The Dangers of Emophilia

- *Because love reduces the perceived need for protection, those high in emophilia have more unprotected sexual partners because they fall in love quickly and repeatedly*
- *Emophilia is associated with being initiated into drug use by romantic partners and are at greater risk of being abused*
- *Even early in a relationship, those high in emophilia will lie or commit perjury to protect an antisocial partner from harm or punishment*

In this chapter, I will discuss some of the very real dangers to which emophilic individuals often expose themselves. For example, sexually transmitted infections (STIs), unwanted pregnancy, domestic abuse, drug initiation, and psychological trauma. Individuals high in emophilia experience rapid feelings of love for someone they just met. With love comes premature trust, which, as it turns out, can produce risks to one's mental or physical well-being. For example, if sexually active, individuals high in emophilia tend to dispense with sexual protection such as condoms, dental dams, and other safe-sex tools when they feel that they can trust their partner and are in love. After all, we only protect ourselves from diseases from strangers, right?

Love Is Not the Same as Protection

I often point out to my students that no reasonably cautious individual would go out and have unprotected sex with six to eight strangers over the course of a week. However, most college students in the United States, *on average*, finish their college experience with about that many sexual partners. Note that this is an average range that varies by college, individual differences, and region. We, as a society, focus a lot of attention on risks and dangers of casual sex such as one-night stands and short-term affairs. For example, for many, we emphasize the need to use a condom when having sex with a stranger because "you don't know" what their history is and that you are sharing yourself not just with that person but all the people that person had sex with. These educational efforts seem reasonable. When I have surveyed students in the past, most indicate that for a casual affair, condoms are simply nonnegotiable, which is a good thing. However, when I ask about being in love, and about the necessity and desire to use protection, things change. People generally report less desire to use any form of physical protection (e.g., condoms, dental dams) when in love with someone *and* report that they feel less of a need for them. Thus, the real trick does not seem to be convincing people of the need to use protection when the primary motive behind a relationship is sex. Instead, it seems that the real challenge is getting people to realize that love, in and of itself, does not remove any of the risks. Those individuals who report having had sex within the confines of a committed relationship are the ones most often to report that they had neglected to use protection at least once or had done away with protection altogether.

There are at least four ways that this logic is flawed. First, you do not know your partner is being faithful. Most people do not believe infidelity will happen to them, but around 3% of married people report having been unfaithful to their spouse *within the past year* (Buss, 2000), and those numbers go even higher (15%–20%) if we ask about during the life of their relationship (Jones & Weiser, 2014). Those numbers continue to rise if we ask non-married couples, especially couples in college (Buss, 2000). Second, you do not know that your partner has been fully forthcoming about their sexual past. It may be that they have "softened" the blow about their history because they may fear that the "true number" of past partners, or past *unprotected* partners, may cause concern. Third, you do not know that your partner *can* fully be honest about their sexual past because they may not know the sexual past of all *their* partners. Fourth, even if you are certain that your partner is being honest, and you are certain your partner is being faithful, and your partner can articulate the exact past and nature of sexual relationships of all their previous sexual partners, you do not know if someone was a latent carrier of an STI and that no one knew. Admittedly, the safest way to have unprotected sexual contact is to go without sex for three to four months, have a full battery of STI tests, and be faithful.

Naturally, everything is a risk. Going out of my house to the office today presented dozens of risks to my health and mortality. However, as any good health psychologist will tell you, some risks are more reasonable to take than others. Going back to the issue of unprotected sexual contact, if people are more likely to have unprotected sex in the confines of serious, committed romantic relationships, then the next logical question is, how many of these relationships does someone have?

If the average college student has several committed relationships that include unprotected sexual activity, then that alone is a risk factor. Now, introduce emophilia into the equation. If someone is comfortable having sex soon within a relationship, *and* someone falls in love fast and easily, then they will be in committed relationships more often and faster than others. That coupled with comfort having sex sooner means that protection is less likely to be used in more situations. The logic stems from the fact that individuals feel protected within the confines of a committed and serious relationship. They trust their partners more and they want to be closer with their partners, so it seems logical that protective barriers may not be necessary and, in fact, may just be perceived as a barrier to intimacy.

As it turns out, this logic can lead to high-risk behaviors. In a study we published in 2012 in the journal *Psychology & Health*, Del Paulhus and I found that individuals who were high in both sociosexuality and emophilia were at the highest risk for accumulating many unprotected sexual partners in a year or even over the course of their life. Individuals who feel that they are "safe" with their partner because of their strong emotional connection, but also have sex sooner in a relationship, move from partner to partner in an unprotected fashion.

Making matters worse, individuals high in emophilia were more likely than others to be attracted to drug-using partners. In fact, in a survey I conducted, I found that individuals (especially women) high in emophilia were most likely to try drugs for the first time with a romantic interest. These findings together paint a picture of the dangers that emerge from premature love. Thus, emophilia can present very real, physical risks to one's health.

However, is it that individuals high in emophilia do not ask their partner about their sexual histories? Or is it that they are unaware that their partner may have an STI? There may have been some truth to that, so I tested those assumptions directly. I surveyed over 100 adults and asked them a simple hypothetical scenario: *Imagine you had met someone, and this person was perfect in every way as a romantic partner. After the first week of dating (prior to having sex), the person tells you that she or he has herpes. How likely would you be to have a relationship (both physical and emotional) with this person?*

I found that individuals high in emophilia were more likely than anyone else to indicate a willingness to go ahead and have a physical and emotional relationship with that person. Now, please understand that I am not criticizing those who have a relationship with partners who have herpes or any other STI. It makes sense that if you love someone, most infections are treatable or manageable. However, it is a critical decision one is making. Importantly in my research discussed above, the prompt says, "After the first week of dating . . ." Individuals high in emophilia have already made up their minds that this person is the "future." Those lower in emophilia seem to report that they would take a little more time before deciding to have a physical relationship with this person. Again, I want to emphasize that there is nothing wrong among those who have partners with an STI. However, because a sexual relationship risks exposure to an STI in the above scenario, it might be judicious to simply wait to make sure the relationship is indeed turning into something special.

However, most risks are not something that emophilic individuals weigh carefully when they are in the early stages of a relationship. In Chapter 6, we established the trouble of premature commitment, especially with partners who are antisocial in nature. However, even non-antisocial partners may not know that they are carrying an STI.

First Time Drug Use

I have a friend and colleague, Jennifer Eno Louden, who has spent a lot of her career working with offenders with mental health issues. In particular, she and James Wood (professor emeritus and friend at the University of Texas at El Paso) have spent much time working with juvenile offenders. I was chatting with Jennifer one day over lunch about the chapter in this book on the relationship between emophilia and the law. The concerns about adolescents with respect to their romantic partners seemed to resonate with her. She noted that teenage girls—in particular—tended to get sucked into the criminal justice system because of their early onset relationships with antisocial boys. So, when teenagers fall in love fast and easily, they are at greater risk for tolerating bad behavior from a romantic partner. Specifically, it seems like a common story among adjudicated youth that these teenagers find a partner early (which is likely facilitated by high scores in emophilia), then they find out their partner may use or deal drugs. If they stay in their relationship, they may end up eventually lying to the police, "covering" for them, and even helping them with their operation. Perhaps after more time, if they are dating a drug-dealing partner for example, they may begin cutting drugs, bagging them, or even making deliveries on a partner's behalf. Making matters worse, these partners are often significantly older or even adults, leading the teen to become reluctant to come forward.

Although anyone of any gender and sexual orientation may fall victim to this scenario, I have found in my research that women high in emophilia seem especially at risk for drug initiation at the hands of a romantic partner. Research on addiction has shown that addiction often begins with social influence. For example, Katherine Urberg (1992) found that adolescents were most likely to smoke if their best friend (or the person they *wanted* as their best friend) smoked. For those high in emophilia, drug influence initiated by a romantic partner is likely to occur for a myriad of reasons. First, my research indicates that the emophilic individual falls in love with drug-using partners more readily. Also recall from the previous chapter that emophilic individuals (women in particular) are disproportionately attracted to those high in any of the Dark Triad traits, thus, they seek "bad apples." Second, emophilic individuals do not take the time to screen romantic partners, the way someone lower in emophilia might. As a result, they find out after making significant commitments (e.g., after they have cancelled a lease and moved in) that their partner is into drugs or other dangerous activities. Third, even if emophilic individuals do know about the drug addiction, they are less likely to address the situation if they think they have found their soulmate.

Domestic Abuse and Partner Mistreatment

From the start, it should be directly noted that by talking about emophilia and abuse, I am in *no way* blaming the victim here. Abuse is a disgusting act, and 100% of the culpability lies with the perpetrator and the perpetrator alone. That said, there are characteristics abusers seek, such as rapid attachment and commitment, that place those high in emophilia at disproportionate risk of abusiveness. These risks, such as emophilia, are not "weaknesses" or "pathologies" or anything that should cause someone to blame the victim. But there is a significant association between being high in emophilia and being the victim of abuse. So, just like people with lighter skin are at higher risk for skin cancer, or people with high blood pressure are more likely to have heart attacks, people high in emophilia are at an increased risk of finding themselves with an abusive partner.

Beth the Brave

In my final year at the University of Arizona in my master's program, I taught a personality class in the final summer to make some extra money. It was there I met Beth. Beth was a very talented artist. She also happened to be ridiculously smart (one of my top students). A few weeks into our summer session, I gave a lecture on relationships and harmful personalities. Once the class ended, she asked if she could talk to me. When the classroom emptied, she was clearly doing her best not to cry as she began to speak. She told me that recently her boyfriend had gone from verbal and emotional abuse to physical abuse. She was particularly concerned because he had beaten her so badly that the police had to get involved.

I advised Beth to seek professional help right away, both because this was both urgent and beyond the scope of my skills. Like many abuse victims, this was no easy task because her abuser was a skilled manipulator. Her boyfriend's gaze was enough to send shivers down her spine, so the mere thought of his temper was scary stuff. The boyfriend would use threats to scare her out of pressing charges. He eventually realized the threats would get him into more trouble, so he poured on the charm. He began writing her poetry and persisted in making amorous advances toward her. He promised her anything in the world, just to be together once again. Finally, when neither of those strategies seemed to work, he guilted her by saying this type of incident would get him thrown off campus permanently, placing responsibility on her for "ruining his life," "destroying his future," and "shredding his reputation"; what he did not do was take responsibility for his behavior or make authentic attempts to change.

In fact, the abuser had already been seeing a few other women during this period. He had one steady and one semi-steady woman on the side, but he insisted that he loved Beth the most and would die if she did not come back to him. Beth would occasionally keep me posted after class about the progress with the charges. She had moments of doubt when she felt what he was saying was all true and she was indeed "ruining his life." I did my best just to be a mentor and listen and remind her that his actions and his actions *alone* were responsible for his outcome, not hers. Further, as a Dark Triad researcher, I did what I could to teach her that these patterns of behavior are both pervasive and typical of manipulation. What she described to me were behaviors that were prototypical of a person high in narcissism. Although, I was careful not to diagnose the abuser, I am not a clinician, nor did I meet him. I also avoided using any labels (although she voluntarily did so). What I did was describe the traits and behaviors that were prototypical and likely to be forthcoming. I did my best to inform her of how these patterns ultimately play out. In sum, what I did was point out that these types of claims and attempts to escape punishment are typical parts of manipulative behavior.

Beth also missed her ex. She felt incredibly guilty for what she did, and she hated herself for mourning the loss of her relationship. Again, while I am not a therapist, I did offer my opinion that when a relationship ends, even a bad one, sometimes there will be periods of missing a partner, the relationship, and whatever good times there were. I still hold to that; it is natural to miss someone, even someone toxic, when a relationship ends.

Beth proved to be tough. Her resolve was that other women may suffer the way she did if he was not punished. She held on to the hope that, at the very least, it may deter him from harming other women, even if just one. Although we don't keep in touch any longer, I am still very proud of her. Overcoming the charm of a narcissist is akin to breaking a spell one has cast over you. Individuals high in a Dark Triad trait are familiar with all forms of manipulation in the service of twisting the truth. So, when reality has been so completely twisted before your very eyes, it can seem like you are the truly "evil" one. This is not an easy mindset to break free from. In our conversations, Beth revealed that she had many relationships, and she fell hard each time. She told me she meets someone and then cannot get them out of her head. Shortly after ending things with her ex, Beth told me that she did jump into another relationship, which is consistent with someone high in emophilia. However, Beth is likely more aware than she was before, and I am hopeful that she will not find herself with an abuser again. For many, what Beth went through could have lasted much longer with additional negative outcomes. Beth was self-aware enough and strong enough to take a stand. Unfortunately, there are others who suffer much more.

Risk of Abuse

After reflecting on all this, the first question I asked was, What is the relationship between emophilia and partner mistreatment? As it turns out, emophilia is one predictor of being in an abusive relationship, alongside low self-esteem and other psychological variables.

When combined with a lack of appropriate screening and premature commitment, risks increase.

There are several reasons why emophilic individuals may find themselves in abusive relationships. The first is that emophilic individuals are drawn to antisocial romantic partners. Further, they may ignore the early "red flags" like temper and aggression. It is important to note that emophilic individuals are not masochistic. They don't select these partners because they want to be harmed, abused, or punished. Further, they are not low in self-esteem, so it is not the case that they think that they "deserve" the punishment or stay because they think that they cannot do any better.

No abusive partner walks around with a sign that indicates such. Further, abusive individuals will *not* advertise their malevolent streak when you first meet them. In fact, those (like someone high in one of the Dark Triad traits) will do their best to pour on the charm and seem like a "dream come true" upon first impressions. They will come across as sweet and charming, and hide their temper, callousness, or manipulative tendencies. Now, as we know, these things cannot be hidden forever, so they will eventually emerge. However, if emophilic individuals do not spend the time necessary to screen and date and court in a way that allows those red flags to emerge and be acted upon, it may be the case that the emophilic individual has already moved in with, committed to, or somehow found themselves in a difficult spot early on because of their premature trust in an unstable partner. Finally, emophilic individuals are willing to trade-off romance for safety by getting involved sooner with those who may pose health risks, such as an STI. Thus, they are willing to risk exposure for a relationship that has yet to develop.

Selective Attention to Red Flags

Further, because romantic bonds form quickly among those high in emophilia, they are likely to dismiss or ignore red flags. In the face of a manipulative, abusive partner with ready-made excuses, the red flags that emerge are deemed "coincidences" that are "not at all typical" of them. The manipulative individual will try to convince the new partner that this type of thing has never happened before and will not happen again. They are adept at blaming their victim and often have a history of doing this to others. Thus, a motivated mind may be more receptive to such lies.

Summary

There are real physical dangers that can emerge from emophilia. These dangers are mediated by the premature connections, love, and bonds emophilic individuals may feel with someone they just met. The natural consequence of these, sexually speaking, is early abandonment of protection, such as condoms. Further, there are many partners that are likely to fit this pattern throughout the life of someone high in emophilia.

Adding to the physical risks, emophilic people are more likely to be with someone who is involved with drugs and do not screen for that behavior. Instead, emophilic individuals may find themselves drawn into the life of a drug-using individual. Individuals high in emophilia may also rush into relationships with someone who is a reason for concerns about physical abuse. Thus, potentially abusive partners do not seem to raise the appropriate warning signs in the mind of someone high in emophilia. This lack of screening does not mean they deserve abuse, nor does it mean that they are at fault. However, it is an addressable concern that may be surmountable.

9

Emophilia as a Risk Factor for Harming Others

- *Emophilia may lead to inappropriate romantic behavior that causes discomfort, harassment, or perceived stalking*
- *Emophilic individuals are more likely to commit unethical acts (e.g., false alibis) to protect romantic partners—even in early relationships*
- *Love-driven actions can be harmful if they are not reciprocated or violate social and legal boundaries*

A friend of mine, who was named Katie, worked at a large university in the Southwest United States. She was from out of state, meaning she paid out-of-state tuition, so she could not afford a parking space on campus. Thus, she would park off campus on the street and walk to her classes. Apparently, a lot of students at this university did this. Consequently, she had plenty of company walking to and from campus, occasionally chatting with fellow students.

A few weeks after her first day, there was a note on her car. Immediately, she panicked, thinking that she had received a parking ticket. No, no ticket—it was notebook paper. Inside was a love letter stating, "Ever since I've seen your beautiful face, I've been thinking about you." Upon reading it, she felt a wave of discomfort wash over her. She whipped her head around. No one was there. She darted into her car and took off. One week later, she saw another note on her car's windshield, only this time it was a folded piece of sketching paper. Unbelievably, it was a sketched picture of her home state and written inside was an arrow saying, "I want to see your beautiful hometown and your beautiful face in it."

"Oh my God!" she thought. "How does this person know my home state? Have they been stalking me? Do they have other information on me?" She went to her friend, who told her to go to the police right away. At this point, four to five notes had accumulated, and she turned them all over to the local authorities. She was, from that point forward, instructed to walk to and from her car *only* with a friend or law enforcement officer. This was tricky because she worked late into the night on occasion. Thus, there were a couple of times when she would walk, tense and ready, on her way to her car by herself. It was getting to the point that she did not feel safe on campus or at home and was considering leaving school because she was in danger.

Weeks passed with no notes. She was hoping maybe ignoring them would eventually make these notes go away. One day, she decided to leave school early to prepare for her boyfriend's birthday celebration. As she approached her car, there was a young man standing in the vicinity. She recognized his face as one of the nice students she chatted with in her early days of going to class. Not at all putting the situation together, she asked, "Can I help you?" The young man answered, "OH, hi! Did you get the letters I wrote for you?" She was stunned for a moment and thought, "Notes? What? . . . Wait! *YOU*?!?" She stood with an incredulous look on her face, not believing that this guy would be so brazen to approach her! She responded, "They are with the police." The young man looked at her broken hearted and muttered, "Oh, I guess you took them the wrong way. I just liked you." He took off shortly thereafter, and she never heard from him again.

In this story, the young man clearly believed that there was a romantic connection with my friend when they first talked. When this sense of immediate connection repeatedly occurs, it is an indication that someone is high in emophilia. Although it is unclear if this man repeated this behavior, he clearly got ahead of himself (and my friend) with respect to the level of connection he thought he had vs. the one he *actually* had. People who do this sort of thing are likely to think that they are being romantic or sweet by leaving anonymous notes or letters. If the level of mutual connection was deep, it is possible that leaving love notes would be seen as romantic. However, if both parties are not feeling the same strength of connection, it can result in discomfort for the other party. Interestingly, although stories like this remain common, people's attempts to be romantic can be misinterpreted as awkward or even creepy.

Although men have typically played the role of "pursuer" in our society, it is not just men that engage in these types of behaviors. Women, too, can pursue a romantic connection in a way that can be perceived as awkward or overly aggressive. Many years ago, my friend Matt was taking several courses at a local state college. He met a woman in one of his classes who seemed friendly, and the two went for coffee a few times and even lunch once or twice. In recalling the story, he told me that he did not think much of it until one evening when he came home to his apartment to find 15 hang-ups on his answering machine (this was the year 2000). "Odd," he thought to himself, "it may have been an emergency." However, after mulling it over, that seemed unlikely because there probably would have been a message left. "Wow, or someone really wanted to talk to me," he concluded. Regardless, without caller ID on landlines back then, it remained a mystery. Not too long thereafter, the phone rang, and it was this nice young woman with whom he had coffee and lunch. He greeted her and asked how she was. He was just about to tell her how weird it was that he received all these hang-ups on his phone when she got very nervous and said she had to go. She later admitted that all the calls to his answering machine were from her. She said that she "just wanted to hear his voice" and kept calling to listen to the answering machine. He told me that he really felt uncomfortable and did not know what to say.

Shortly thereafter, they met for coffee one last time. According to his recollection, he tried to politely turn her down, indicating that he would be moving soon to pursue a degree in another city *far* away from there. Apparently, she looked at him and asked, excitedly, "Oh, what school?" Now, at the time, he had not officially decided on a school or even a region of the world, but he responded quickly with "Stanford," which was the graduate program he was considering that was farthest away from them. She looked at him with utmost sincerity, touched his hand, and said, "If you wanted, I would sell my house and move with you; all you need to do is say the word." He told me that he felt fear followed by a little bit of guilt. He couldn't imagine what this woman must have been feeling to think that some student she met over coffee a few times was the answer to all she was looking for. Further, he searched his memory for something he may have done to make her believe that they were on the same page. To the best of my knowledge, they did not speak after that day, but my friend tells me he still wonders if she wound up being OK. He assures me that he does not think she was a bad person or that she meant to scare him (although she did). However, given her vulnerability, he hopes she will end up with someone with a good heart. He believes she truly thought she was being romantic and was demonstrating her commitment to having a relationship with him. When her behavior is taken in the context of sincerity and with the understanding that she was trying to be romantic, these actions were meant to flatter. However, human radar in such situations often tells us to keep our distance because this magnitude of desire is not typical after only meeting someone a few times over coffee.

It should be stated that if both parties *did* feel a strong romantic connection, such as what would be likely if both were high in emophilia, then these romantic advances may be quite welcome and strike the right tone. Although it may seem bold to go out on a limb and take a chance, it carries with it a high probability of creating discomfort and fear. Such was the case with both Katie and Matt. Like Katie was with the windshield notes, Matt was uncomfortable with the aggressive advances of the woman from his class. I am certain she meant her advances to be endearing and romantic. After all, what a romantic notion it is to give up everything you know and take a chance on a romantic connection faraway? It is clear she felt a much deeper and serious connection quickly with Matt, but Matt was not on the same page, which created discomfort. One contributing factor that encourages these types of romantic advances comes from film and other forms of media. They work out in Hollywood, but much of the time, in real life, it creates an awkward dynamic. Although there are many examples of this type of aggressive romantic behavior being modeled in popular media, I will highlight just a few. For example, as mentioned in Chapter 3, the protagonist in the movie *Bed of Roses* sends a woman he hardly knows a dozen roses every hour, on the hour. While his intentions are revealed as romantic, and it works out in the end, his behavior in the real world would most likely scare someone rather than facilitate a romantic connection.

Making matters worse, if someone gets it in their head that this person could be the "one" or that "fate" brought them together, then the person may see it as their duty to be "persistent" or "hang in there" because "love will always prevail." This type of persistence often borders (and sometimes crosses) the boundaries of legality. In legal and social psychology, we refer to one product of this type of persistence as the "rape myth": the idea that (typically a woman) will say, "No, no, no, no . . . OK, I give in!" if one just persists long enough. This is a terribly damaging misnomer in our culture, especially in our media (Kahlor & Morrison, 2007). "NO" is just that. It doesn't mean "convince me," "maybe," "we'll see," "depends," or "keep trying," and it certainly doesn't mean "yes."

However, one can find this type of myth even in comedies, such as the movie *Super Troopers*. One of the main characters expresses his crush on a female officer in the same precinct (which, that's right, demonstrates poor judgment). However, after getting "shot down" time after time, she tires of rejecting him and gives in. Now, don't get me wrong, *Super Troopers* is a great movie, and it makes me laugh just like everyone else, but modeling this type of behavior only leads to trouble in the real world. Of course, there are people who play hard to get, and they do it intentionally. I am not saying that engaging in this dance is necessarily wrong, just risky. Typically, I would advise folks that it is OK to miss out on a phone number here and there from someone playing "hard to get"—far better than the alternatives of frightening someone or legal issues.

From the perspective of the workplace, I became curious about the effect that emophilia might have on proclivities toward sexual harassment in the workplace. If sexual desire, desire for power, and physical attraction could lead to unwanted advances in the workplace, why couldn't love? We found convincing evidence, across several different conditions, that individuals high in emophilia scored high on a sexual harassment proclivity scale. To be sure, these dynamics are probably not identical to those who are driven by sexual desire, power, or coercion.

People who think they are in love are not typically trying to make a power play or intimidate another co-worker but are genuinely interested in a person with whom they work. Nevertheless, just because it is love doesn't mean it cannot be inappropriate, be perceived as uncomfortable, or be illegal. In fact, starting any relationship at work, especially one with a power discrepancy, presents a myriad of legal and ethical problems for the parties involved and the organization.

Nevertheless, unlike power and sexual interest, in the situation where an emophilic person commits sexual harassment, it is likely that they thought a special connection was being formed, or that because a relationship is starting, it would be OK to pursue. Moreover, an individual high in emophilia may know that the consequences may be dire but may still feel that their love is not able to be controlled (or is not worth controlling) in the end. In our survey, we found that individuals high in emophilia were more likely to lose a job over amorous advances, even when controlling for other risk factors. I would like to reiterate that this dynamic is not the same stereotypical case of brazen sexual harassment that sticks out in our minds. As mentioned, emophilic individuals are likely pursuing a genuine sense of connection. Nevertheless, if the advances are unwanted, then they are sexual harassment. Further, even if they are mutual, it may still involve bad judgment and lead to unfavorable outcomes.

Aside from money affairs, however, there are other serious legal concerns that arise with emophilia. Given that emophilic individuals, as well as anxiously attached individuals, do *not* want to see their relationships end, find themselves in bad relationships with suboptimal partners, and are usually led astray by their romantic choices, it may not be a surprise to suspect that they are at the highest risk for *lying* and other antisocial behaviors in order to protect their romantic partner.

Emophilia and the Risk of False Alibi Testimony

In the legal system, we often do not trust husbands or wives to give accurate testimony pertaining to their romantic partner. For the question, "Where were you last night?," the response of "home with my wife" may carry similar weight in the eyes of a juror as the response, "I was home alone." Most people are motivated to sacrifice for their partner. In fact, that is a component of love and commitment, right? In good times and bad? For richer or poorer? Further, some individuals may be motivated through self-interest. Such self-interest may take the form of partner needs (e.g., "Who will take care of me if she goes to jail?"), a desire to cover-up collusion (e.g., what if the person was an accomplice previously?), financial or emotional needs provided by the partner, or even a need for a sense of stability. However, another key reason may be because the person falls in love too quickly and feels that it is the right thing to do.

Across two studies, my first graduate student, Adon Neria, and my friend and collaborator Harmon Hosch conducted two studies to test which relationship-relevant individual differences might put people at a high risk for "covering" for a romantic partner. We sampled over 500 adults on an internet website and asked them simple questions, such as, "Have you ever lied for your romantic partner?" "Have you ever told someone your partner was with you, when they were not?" All the way up to, "Have you ever lied to the police to protect your romantic partner?" The findings across both studies were very clear that emophilia was a strong predictor of this type of behavior. However, what made emophilic individuals most unique was they were willing to do this for a romantic partner much sooner in their relationship.

Now, it is important to note that anxious attachment was also a strong and consistent predictor as well. We decided to test these ideas a bit more directly in the lab. We hired a talented actor, Roger Estrada, to work with us as our confederate (meaning someone who pretends to be just another participant but is doing what we instruct them to do). I also put my best research assistants, Ruth Massey and Theresa Benavidez, on the study as well. The study design was a "bonding task." We invited women into the lab to bond with Roger, who they thought was just another student participating for course credit. Ruth and Theresa would randomly assign the two to engage in a bonding task or a nonbonding task. Two things are important here. First, neither Ruth nor Theresa *knew* which condition they just assigned. They simply handed a packet with instructions to Roger. In this way, we kept them from knowing what to expect and possibly contaminating our results! Second, this process was random. So, we shuffled the packets. Some of these packets had bonding instructions in them, and some of them had the nonbonding instructions in them.

The bonding task was modeled after Arthur Aron and colleagues' "getting to know you" task (e.g., Aron et al., 1995). This task involves answering a series of increasingly intimate questions. They start small (e.g., "What is your major?" "What do you like about our school?") and end up being quite deep and probing (e.g., "What are three things we have in common?" "What is a secret you have never told anyone?"). In the other condition, which was of equal length, we had participants take turns reading Shakespeare's *A Winter's Tale*. This way, they did not exchange any information but spent an equal amount of time with each other.

Regardless of the task they were assigned to, the two were alone in the room for 15 minutes. Roger, however, had a cell phone that had a timer on it. A silent alarm went off in his pocket at 12 minutes. At that point, he was instructed to "notice" a flash drive located in the USB hub attached to an adjacent computer. His instructions were to reach over, remove the drive, look it over, and then hold it up in front of the participant's face and say, "Oooo! Don't tell anyone!," making sure participants noticed the device in his hand. He proceeded to put the device in his pocket, and they finished the activity.

The two were quickly separated when the 15 minutes were up. Roger disappeared into my office, and the other participant sat and answered a few filler questionnaires. Ruth or Theresa (depending on who was on duty) would then go into the lab. Her instructions were to tap her pockets, search some shelves, search around the computer, turn and say to herself, "*Shit!*" and then ask the participant, "Did you see a flash drive around here?" If the participant indicated "no," she was instructed to ask one more time, "Are you sure?"

Our dependent variable was who would give Roger up? As it turned out, more than half of the women in the control (i.e., nonbonding) condition indicated that Roger took the flash drive. In the bonding condition, only 22% named Roger. However, the data get more interesting when we examine personality. Anxious attachment interacted with condition, such that women high in anxious attachment who bonded with Roger did not give him up at all!

Now, there are two major drawbacks to this study. The first was that we did not have enough people (40 participants in total). This was because our actor, Roger, had to move to another state, and my two research assistants moved on to graduate school. Nevertheless, it is an indication that, even within the confines of a laboratory bonding task, these traits may put people at risk for engaging in false alibi behaviors.

In sum, emophilia and anxious attachment can put people at risk of being perpetrators of harm and often find themselves in legal trouble. Because individuals high in emophilia are willing to take these risks much sooner in a relationship, they may feel that breaking the law or amorous pursuits are needed. Individuals high in emophilia may also think their romantic advances are the shining beginning of a happy relationship when, in fact, they may end up making another person extremely uncomfortable. Similarly, early investment and other risk factors of premature commitment may lead an individual to pair-bond with someone who is criminally involved and may end up involved themselves. In the end, these tendencies can lead to very real and permanent legal consequences.

10

The Future of Emophilia Research

- *Emophilia has a profound influence on behaviors beyond relationships, including parenting, trust, and family dynamics*
- *Although emophilia may increase the risk of impulsive romantic decisions, premature commitment, and emotional manipulation, there are strategies that people can use to manage these tendencies*
- *Those who have emophilia-related struggles should consider therapy, journaling, using relationship calendars, and advice from trusted loved ones to navigate the risks associated with emophilia*

This book only scratches the surface of emophilia research. There are many implications, studies, and discoveries yet to be made. Here, I discuss what I think are going to be some more interesting and important directions going forward. Some of these directions include the impact on family and how to deal with someone (especially a friend, child, or significant other) who has especially high or low levels of emophilia.

High School Romance, Is It Really Love?

Many individuals look at high school romance and say something to the effect of, "They don't know what love is yet." In many cases this is true, but in some cases it is not. Indeed, people often revise their perceptions of love later in life (e.g., Kephart, 1967). There are studies that find high school sweethearts are psychologically vulnerable, and those experiences can often predict future patterns of attachment and relationship functioning. A serious bond at a young age can predict anxiety and depression down the road (e.g., Monroe et al., 1999).

In fact, an emeritus professor named David Lester at my alma mater—Stockton University—once told us that he worked with a suicide hotline. Workers at the hotline found that they had to separate those who took adult calls from those that took calls from teens. Why? Adults would often call in with issues such as, "I lost my job, my house was foreclosed, my wife left me, took the kids, and now I'll be on the street next week." In especially painful times like that, people often fail to see a way forward and contemplate suicide because it seems like a way to stop the suffering. Conversely, a teen may then call after and say, "I'm thinking of killing myself, my boyfriend just left me for my best friend." It happened all too often that the operator did not take the call seriously enough, assuming the teenager would eventually "get over it" or "snap out of it"—and should call back when she has "real problems." However, as is often the case, perceptions are strong. To that teen, their world *is* crashing down. Such teens cannot see beyond the moment that they are suffering through, and suicide may unfortunately be seen as a way out, just as with adult callers.

Thus, it is important to realize that love at the teen stage may be very serious. Further, high levels of emophilia may exacerbate the complexities of teenage dating. Life experience, maturity, and forethought often have not set in yet, but the emotions are still very real. Thus, these struggles may be a particularly difficult and confusing time for a teen to negotiate, especially with high levels of emophilia. This difficulty and confusion may also be true for teens that are especially low in emophilia. They may feel like the "odd one out" when their friends are pairing up and going to dances or parties with partners when they always go alone. Pressure may eventually get to that individual as well.

The Impact of Emophilia on Family

Emophilia in a parent can also have dire consequences for the family dynamic. I provide the case of Helen and David: Helen and David fell in love almost overnight. David was a little nervous to be moving in with a woman that had two daughters and a son (14, 12, and 8, respectively) but was so excited to be with Helen. This was especially true since things were not going so well in his own life. David worked for a telecommunications company but was only hired for contract work. Because David did not plan his budget well, he was destitute during off-periods. David found himself on the doorstep of homelessness when he and Helen first struck up a conversation in a Subway restaurant. After two dates, Helen decided that she loved David so much that he should move in with her and her three children. Helen was so incredibly happy at first. David even started cooking for all of them. By the time she got home from work, there was a fresh meal on the table. It was like a dream come true!

On the flip side, her children were less than excited. David was around *all* the time. According to the 12-year-old, he was bossy and acted like he owned the place. Further, he was a bit of a slob, so his clothes and personal belongings were strewn across the house. Her children complained that they couldn't bring friends over because of how messy the house was. Over time, David grew increasingly mean toward Helen's children. The eldest, the 14-year-old, spoke up and finally told her mother that the three of them were just not comfortable with David being there anymore. Helen couldn't understand. David made her so happy, so why could her children not see this? Didn't they want their mother to be happy? Helen pressed back and insisted that David was staying. Her oldest daughter soon found ways to rebel. She stayed out late, smoked pot, and ended up running with a bit of a dangerous crowd. When Helen came down hard on her eldest one night because she was out late and Helen smelled alcohol on her breath, her daughter violently screamed, "Screw you, you never gave a shit about us anyway!" Helen was beside herself. She had let David (who now spent most of the week playing video games in the den) ruin her relationship with her children. David soon left Helen for a waitress at IHOP on the other side of town.

Keep in mind that emophilic individuals, such as Helen, do not mean to be self-centered. In fact, to my knowledge, Helen is quite regretful of how she prioritized David over her children. However, as we discussed before, emophilic individuals have a difficult time calibrating what they find rewarding. They often get "tunnel vision" when it comes to the harm or risk that they are putting themselves in or exposing others to when they fall in love so quickly.

Sometimes, these stories turn out even more tragic. Statistics suggest that stepfathers are sometimes a big danger to young children when it comes to physical and sexual safety (e.g., Buss, 2012). Now, a quick note about stepdads that I mentioned before. Those men who love a nonbiological child as their own, treat the child with love and respect, and put their heart into helping to raise that child are commendable. I believe that it can be classified as "true love" when someone loves a nonbiological child as their own. Indeed, there are many cases when people get into relationships where their new partners already have a child. Although they may enter the relationship with the purest intentions, things can often go wrong. For example, they may find that the child is a handful, their new partner spends all their time with the child, or the tension in wanting to help parent but not knowing the appropriate boundaries all wear on them over time. Further tensions may arise in the relationship, perhaps even ending it, leading to the question of, "What now? What role do I play in this child's life?"

Perhaps further complicating the issue is if the stepparent and the partner have a biological child together. Very often, parents will "favor" their biological child over their adopted child or stepchild, and that, too, can create tension in the family dynamic (De Leeuw et al., 2022). So, those high in emophilia may be self-deceptive regarding how much they love a new partner with a child and how much they think they can make the dynamic work; they may find themselves in over their heads. Perhaps even more likely with the individual high in emophilia is that they may find that when the going gets tough, they want to get going (on to another relationship that is). Finally, individuals high in emophilia may be self-deceptive in how easy or pleasant the arrangement will be. A person's priority is usually (and should be) her child, so playing second fiddle to a demanding nine-year-old may not be something a love-struck partner is ready to deal with.

I decided to test this idea empirically. I asked participants a simple question: *Imagine you met someone and the two of you seem like you were meant for each other and had perfect chemistry. However, this person has a child from a previous relationship. How likely are you to get into a relationship with this person?* Participants indicated a 1 (*not at all*) to 7 (*extremely likely*) response. None of the typical relationship variables (avoidant attachment, anxious attachment, emophilia, or unrestricted sociosexuality) had a correlation with this variable. They were all relatively neutral. However, I also looked at an interaction between sociosexuality and emophilia. A perfect crossover interaction emerged. Individuals high in emophilia but *low* in unrestricted sociosexuality were likely to indicate an eagerness to be with a person who already has a child. Similarly, individuals who were high in unrestricted sociosexuality but *low* in emophilia were also likely to report an eagerness to be with a person who already has a child.

The likely reason here is that two different relationships are being considered. Individuals high in emophilia may be thinking about a serious relationship, while those high in unrestricted sociosexuality may be thinking about a short-term affair. Future research is needed to disentangle these associations. Nevertheless, there seems to be a case where these two variables, under certain circumstances, may be drawn to partners with children.

However, we have not yet discussed dark personality suitors, or those who are callous, indifferent, or even *predatory*. Sometimes, a person (often men, but not always) may enter a relationship with someone who has a young child and has very evil intentions. Cassie was one of these young children.

I met Cassie in college in my sophomore year. She had never had a boyfriend before college. Although there was nothing terribly unusual about that, her reason for not having a boyfriend was. She would get close to someone, maybe even share a kiss goodnight after a date, and then have a breakdown. These breakdowns were angry spells of vicious spite aimed at the man she just dated. Perhaps spurred by a lack of calling, an unclear arrangement (maybe he was dating her and others), or a sense of rejection, she would fall into a fit of rage and call the man she went out with, cursing him. Naturally, this behavior was unusual, and few endured the punishment to ask her for a second date. Needless to say, it was clear that something was seriously wrong.

Eventually, I learned Cassie's tragic story. Cassie had three stepfathers growing up. Her mother would fall in love with someone and prioritize him over her children (similar to Helen in the story above). However, stepfather #2 had a dark agenda. As it turns out, although Cassie's mother was desperately in love with Cassie's stepdad, Cassie's stepdad had an eye for Cassie. At 13, Cassie was both physically and sexually abused. To this day, I do not know what happened to stepdad #2. I do know that Cassie was strong and found herself a therapist to try and work out some of these issues. However, it is clear to me that this man was a predator and likely played along in the relationship with the mother to get access to Cassie. Similar to Helen, the mother just thought the children were rebelling and simply acting out. Only until much later did she realize how much damage her ex had done.

As mentioned, emophilia can blind us to reality at times. Although often unintentional, emophilia blinds us to clear and present dangers to ourselves or even to our children. Again, I am not blaming the victims here. Both Cassie's mother and Cassie were victims of a predator. Further, the damage done was due to him and him alone. However, I bring this story up as an example of how individuals high in emophilia may be unknowingly exposing themselves and those around them to danger.

I understand that one may be very psychologically motivated to find a romantic partner and that the quest may be exponentially complicated when a child from a previous relationship is involved. For most people, at any level of emophilia, hearing "I will love you and your child" is a seductive line. However, although it may be true, it may indeed be just "a line." Because of their optimism, self-deception, and premature trust, individuals high in emophilia may be at a disproportionately high likelihood for exposing their children to new parental figures. Sadly, and unfortunately, if one rushes in too quickly and a partner is not properly vetted, there is an increased risk for that person to be a predatory (or at the very least, disappointing) stepparent figure.

Low Emophilia and the Struggle to Find a Partner

I first met Katie when I was 25. She was a great soccer player and overall talented athlete. She was a decent student and had a rewarding life and network of friends around her. On occasion, Katie and I would hang out and play video games together. She was a lot of fun and was always a great friend to me. However, at 27, Katie was still a virgin, both emotionally and physically. She had never fallen in love or been physically intimate with anyone.

Many in our friend group would offer to set Katie up on dates, but she was exceedingly picky. She just "didn't feel it" when it came to most guys. It came to the point where one of my friends asked her out directly one day because he thought Katie was great (as we all did) and really wanted to get to know her in that way. Katie immediately felt uncomfortable and awkward. She did not know how to tell him that she simply was not interested. It created a rift in our group because Katie did not feel comfortable coming to a gathering if he was going to be there.

Katie eventually did find someone on whom she developed a crush: Steve. Steve was an aspiring actor at the university nearby. Katie would send me excited texts that she was going to meet Steve that night for coffee and a movie. She would even get giddy—was this *finally* the guy? She told me that for the first time in her life, she felt like she found someone she could be emotionally intimate with, have intercourse with, and build a relationship with. However, Steve turned out to be, well, a bit of a "flake." He would ditch Katie to hang out with his friends or abandon plans with her on short notice. Sometimes, he would just not show up to a date and provide no explanation. Katie immediately crawled back into her shell and refused to come out.

There was one other guy, much later, who I recall Katie potentially liking, but she quickly lost interest. This guy was "smooth," and when I met him, I immediately knew why he liked Katie—she was a challenge. Katie was still a virgin, never had a boyfriend, and in my eyes, he wanted to demonstrate his prowess for charm and saw Katie as a conquest. Katie was (and still is) perceptive and ended it quickly. Katie and I still message from time to time and every now and again. She rarely tries to "get out there" but, to my knowledge, still has never had a boyfriend.

Katie is not pathological. She doesn't have family or parental issues. She is not "cold" or unemotional. Quite the contrary, I have found her to be a very warm and loving friend from day one. But she is just not free with romantic emotions and does not dive in easily. In fact, she is very reserved, very picky, and quite focused on practical or day-to-day matters. She is not one who would let her life's dreams, goals, and aspirations get interrupted by a romance that could never be or that would be improbable. In fact, she is very practical, and that has interfered with her ever taking too much of a risk on someone. She does lament from time to time about how she really wishes she could find someone with whom to settle down. Further, Katie is also extremely realistic, to a fault. She knows what is going to make her happy and what is not. She knows what she wants, it is just that what she wants is quite specific, rigid, and (I suppose) rare in the general population.

Katie is an example of someone who is extremely low in emophilia. It isn't the case that she *doesn't* want a relationship, she doesn't want love, or does not want romance or to be romanced. As I mentioned, she is not avoidant or somehow cold to others. However, the alternative of being alone or simply just having a lot of friends always appealed to her more than making a wrong decision with the wrong guy. However, as conventional wisdom tells us, if you are never willing to be vulnerable or look past a few things, you are likely to end up alone quite often. This is not to be confused with asexuality, which has to do with a lack of other-targeted sexual arousal (e.g., Bogaert, 2004). Theoretically, one can be low or high in emophilia and low or high in asexuality. Thus, someone can be asexual and fall in love, or someone can be extremely low in emophilia and have a great interest in sex. However, the processes are likely similar to each other: extremely low emophilia would have to do with disinterest in romance, not necessarily sex. One potential outcome of extremely low emophilia might be aromanticism. Aromanticism may indeed be a romantic parallel to asexuality and possibly worth exploring in future research.

As I stated at the beginning of this book, I do not consider emophilia a pathology. That goes for both high and low individuals on the emophilia spectrum. Someone who takes a long time to fall in love or only falls in love once (or never) is rare, but so is someone who falls in love over and over. As I have emphasized, most people fall somewhere in the middle. We may have more than one love in our life, but it takes some time to develop, and we are usually moderately picky about who we trust, commit to, make ourselves vulnerable to, and love.

Counter to that point, there *are* pathological causes for behaviors that *look* similar to emophilia. For example, if someone had avoidant attachment, family issues, abuse, schizotypal or schizoid personality characteristics, then these individuals might feel uncomfortable being intimate with others. Further, such individuals may be awkward in human interactions and may not feel the need to be close with others, unlike those high in extraversion or high in agreeableness. They have trouble forming real connections with others. However, these are identified issues that are unrelated to emophilia. To be sure, someone can be high or low in emophilia and have these issues or not. The same is true of those high in emophilia. Yes, family issues such as repeated attachment figures, abuse, borderline personality, and other types of developmental abnormalities or pathologies may account for behaviors that are identical to those caused by high emophilia. However, they are not the same thing.

One key takeaway from this book is that emophilia is much like extraversion or neuroticism. There are outcomes and consequences associated with the trait whether high or low. However, much like introverted individuals, or those who are highly neurotic, can live very happy, fulfilling, and meaningful lives. It is important to keep in mind that love is an *intense* motivational force. It commands a tremendous amount of attentional direction and focus. Further, it distorts thinking and leads to extraordinary drives.

One topic that is particularly tragic is the potential for depression and even suicidal thoughts that can sometimes accompany romantic dissolution, rejection, or separation. There are species across the planet that are so fiercely monogamous that when the partner dies, the other goes into mourning. In fact, in the baya weaver bird, when one partner dies, the other shortly follows. Likewise, there are some humans who take the loss of a partner much harder than others.

In addition to sleepless nights, fluctuations in appetite, obsessive attention demands, and constant thinking and worrying about one's partner, love can take a toll on our mood as well. This toll may be especially pronounced when things are not going well. Falling in love fast and often may put people at situational risk for affective roller coasters. Falling in love quickly may, in some cases, create a risk of self-harm.

Leaving Someone and Why

It has become relatively accepted in the modern era to divorce someone when we do not feel the same way about them anymore. In fact, there are even terms such as the "starter marriage," which assumes that marriage is a process that will repeat itself. Relationships are a lot of work, and they take a lot of patience, time, and dedication. It is a nonjudgmental observation of mine that, many times, individuals assume that a new relationship will take care of the issues of old. However, much of the time, these new relationships turn out to be the same situation but on a different day. It reminds me of people who look at their phone when they are already engaged in a face-to-face conversation. Texting, IMing, or emailing may be a "quick fix" for social contact and attention, but often a true conversation takes some energy and effort. Naturally, this is a controversial point. There are texts that can be quite fulfilling; I am focusing on those that are quick fixes for attention.

The same is true of relationships. Most people will tell you that it cannot be fun all the time. Nevertheless, we search for greener pastures elsewhere even though we may have already found what we were looking for—we just did not work for it. These patterns may be especially pronounced among individuals high in emophilia. They are addicted to the rush of love, so their attention is drawn to the greener pasture quite quickly. However, they may find that they are simply plowing the same turf over and over, just with different people.

Can You Complete Me?

Emophilia may alter an individual's perceptions of the self. People who feel that their partner completes them may feel fragmented as they move in and out of relationships. It is critical to note that these individuals may also withdraw from social relationships, friendships, and even family as their love interests become their all-consuming focus. I would recommend to anyone with a friend that is particularly high in emophilia to be patient with that person. Understand that the individual does not mean to behave selfishly. Perhaps more important, it may be critical to be there for the person if the relationship goes south.

I think it is equally critical to be respectful of individuals who are particularly low in emophilia as well. Many of us expect our friends, children, whoever, to "settle down" with the right person. We want that person to find "the one" and live happily ever after. However, pushing someone to get involved may lead to discomfort, poor choices, and assumed fits that are suboptimal. Thus, they may end up with "the one for right now," but not with someone that will last.

I think the best course of action is to understand that many of us have different drives, wants, and needs in our lives. Some individuals may be exceedingly choosey about who they settle down with, and, in some cases, it may happen once or even never. One can live a very fulfilling life without romance. As great as love is, forcing it may be equally horrible.

Yet, individuals may find themselves being pushed, "set up" on dates, and otherwise scorned for not having a partner, family, and so on. It is important that we accept people for what they want and who they are in their orientations toward relationships—both sexual and emotional.

How Do I Know If Someone Will Stick Around?

In the evolutionary psychology literature, there is a thing called "costly signaling" (McAndrew, 2002; Zahavi, 1975). The idea of costly signaling comes down to the idea that talk is cheap, and actions speak louder than words. When someone invests heavily in another person with finite and precious resources (time, money, energy), we can be relatively sure that this person is serious. This concept is one of the reasons why "sorry, I was busy" irritates us so much when we do not get a return phone call or even a text. It takes only a moment to reply to someone, and not returning communication implies, "I had better things to do."

In a lot of cultures around the world, expensive jewelry is a sign of affection. In the United States, we generally spend "three months' salary" on an engagement ring to show true commitment and sacrifice. Although I've heard complaints about this, we get off easy in our culture. In some historical cultures, around the world, things get rougher. There are several tribes that believe pearly white teeth are unattractive to a new partner. Thus, when a young man falls in love, he takes a rock or hard object and whacks out his front teeth to show affection and willingness to marry (e.g., Pietrusewsky & Douglas, 1993).

Although costly signals can still be faked, they are tougher to fake overall. Individuals high in emophilia are likely to both misrepresent and misinterpret signals. As mentioned, individuals high in emophilia are likely to self-deceive. Thus, there is no trace of insincerity in their promises. Further, they may spend most of their time ruminating and investing in a newly found love partner at first, giving the appearance of costly signaling early on. The same is true on the receiving side. One high in emophilia may see the tiniest gesture as a sign of affection and see minor investments through rose-colored glasses.

Remember, intentions to commit, even sincere intent, are not the same as commitment. Potential partners who have been in love many times before may require extra caution. Further, individuals high in emophilia may not fully shut the door to ex-partners, which should be a telltale sign that someone you are meeting, dating, or broke up with may be high in emophilia. Finally, caution over having children is critical. Feelings are not the same as facts. Individuals high in emophilia sincerely want to commit, but there are reasons outlined throughout this book that describe why those promises often do not pan out. Thus, if a committed partner in parenting is what you seek, then patience may be of utmost importance.

In general, a good way to determine whether someone is sincere is through costly signaling (perhaps, we can forgo the tooth removal). Nevertheless, a reasonable guide for sincerity has to do with asking yourself these three questions: "Does the person claim commitment?" "Does the person show costly investment in their commitment?" And "Do the two line up?"

Another clue as to whether a person is "long-term" relationship material is to assess the longest term relationship they ever had. Humans are creatures of habit; moving from partner to partner and never having spent much time in a serious committed relationship may be an indicator of how challenging it may be for that person to settle down.

This indicator may be relevant for two reasons: motivation and ability. On the motivational end, someone who has never spent much time in a committed romantic relationship may be high in some dispositions (e.g., sociosexuality, avoidant attachment, emophilia) that drive them away from commitment after a short period of time. Second, the individual, even if fully motivated to engage in a committed romantic relationship, may lack some of the communication and relational skills required. Relationships do take work, and often that work requires practice to get good at it. While everyone must start somewhere, it may require additional patience and risk to engage in a relationship with someone for whom it is uncharted territory.

Life Stages and the Power of the Situation

As mentioned earlier in the book, Kurt Lewin noted almost 100 years ago that all behavior is the function of the person, the environment, and the interaction between the two. There are times in our lives when we may be susceptible to love, intimacy, and passion than we are at other times. I recall one conversation I had in Tucson with a woman who was happily married for 13 years. She glowed most of the time about her husband and how kind and gentle he was. By all accounts, she had a great relationship. However, one night out among co-workers, she told me and some other trusted friends that he was not, however, the best *lover* she ever had. She spoke with deep conflict as she explained that he is the man for her, but about five years before she met him, she dated a man who was just incredible in bed. She felt guilty even saying it and wished it were not so.

Although I was a novice in relationship research at the time, as a young social psychologist, I explained the power of the situation. I told her that the sexual passion she felt for her former lover may indeed simply be the product of that time, that place, and that age. People crave sexual contact more at different stages than they do others and even crave different types of partners at different life stages. As we have discussed in this book, fear, anxiety, life changes all make someone more (or less) attracted to someone in each slice of our life. This is not even to mention endocrine system changes (i.e., hormonal surges). Thus, given that her former lover was exciting and met her in a time in her life where fun was her focus, it may have had more to do with the circumstances than the person. In fact, had she the chance to have sex with him again, it would likely not spark the same passion as before. After explaining this, she was almost drawn to tears of joy and told me that she felt a weight lifted off her chest.

Future Applications of Emophilia Research

Given that I have transitions to a management department at the University of Nevada at Reno, I have had to search for ways to make my research more applied, as well as trying to make it appealing to those in organizational settings. One way that I have done this is to examine a construct I call "premature trust." Premature trust utilizes the same principles of emophilia but applies them to the sensation of trust rather than romantic connection. We have met with some early success in validating this psychological construct. We have found that individuals high in premature trust feel closer to someone after a bonding activity and are more likely to declare the person trustworthy for a variety of tasks sooner.

Another potential application has to do with investment in an organization and the speed at which someone identifies with their new company. Research has shown that people express different attachment styles toward leaders at work (Harms, 2011), so the same may be true of the speed of their identification with an organization and the organizational citizenship behaviors in which they are willing to engage.

In fact, I have been asked if emophilia could apply to nonromantic relationships, such as the speed with which someone makes friends or engages in trust. The research seems to be clear that anything for which there is an emotional threshold, that threshold can be assessed. Although the Emophilia Scale (see Chapter 2) and the assessments and research discussed in this book are associated primarily with romantic connections, the EP Scale can likely be reworked or reworded to assess these other forms of emotional connection just as easily.

Joys, Warnings, and Risks

As alluded to throughout the book, there are upsides and downsides to being high in emophilia, much like every trait. They are likely to experience the rush of love more often, which is a great feeling. Further, those high in emophilia are likely to be more resilient in some contexts, such as getting over breakups faster. Finally, they are more likely to enjoy more intimate encounters and people throughout their lives. However, there are potentially negative consequences that follow those high in emophilia. For example, romance schemes continue to plague modern society. Recently, "wrong number" scams are on the rise. Someone will text with an order for wine, gold, or valuables, attempting to confirm an order. This text often comes out of the blue, and the recipient had placed no such order. However, given this "funny coincidence" the texter will play nice and ask about the person whom they texted. They will apologize profusely and after engaging in enough rapport building, will try to strike up a relationship with the recipient, given how "sweet they are."

From there, a happy coincidence gets manipulated into a predatory scam. The individual continues to build their relationship with their wrong number partner; the scammer typically has many others at various stages building. Requests for money to meet, stories of financial hardship, sick family members, and the like ensue. The person will spend money to try and help their downtrodden love interest, but that money is never to be seen again. Although I have not studied if emophilia places individuals at higher susceptibility for these scams, and there could be other factors such as loneliness or idealistic thinking that also contribute, emophilia seems like a logical risk factor.

Emophilia also presents relationship trade-offs from within. Those high in emophilia will dive into their relationships and will even lie to protect their partners from very early on in the relationship. Such individuals also view their partners idealistically much sooner in a relationship. Finally, they are willing to sacrifice for a romantic partner much sooner, even without a history of trust or commitment from that partner. They are also more likely to do away with protection in a relationship, putting them at a much higher risk for unwanted pregnancy, STIs, and other related consequences.

However, despite these passionate pushes for a partner, we have found in a recent dataset that those high in emophilia are likely to be chronically unfaithful. Further, not only are those high in emophilia an infidelity risk, they are also often unfaithful despite typical levels of relationship satisfaction, commitment, and investment. They simply find someone attractive and feel a connection with that person. Thus, someone high in emophilia may be unfaithful despite their earnest and sincere pledges of love and fidelity. This may lead to self-inflicted damage to one's relationship as well as the risk of harming a loved other.

Because those high in emophilia follow their emotions and fall strongly and quickly for partners, they are likely to fall for the most charming among us: those high in narcissism. Further, because they act readily on these romantic feelings, they invest right away and fail to screen or attend to potential warning signs that a partner may be problematic in the future.

Given These Risks, What Do We Do?

For those who struggle at all with emophilia, whether it be high or low, I always recommend seeing the right therapist. Finding the right therapist for you will take time and research. I recommend seeing several before settling on someone to commit to for the long term. It is not only the therapeutic approach but also the alliance and chemistry that make it successful. I still see a therapist and have seen a therapist since I was 14. There is no shame in it. There are so many benefits to seeing someone with whom you connect and who has the right skills and approach for you.

For those high in emophilia, who fear these consequences, I also have several recommendations for managing the risks and issues that may follow. First, I am a big advocate of diaries. Put down on paper all the pros and the cons that a person or a relationship presents. This may best be done with a therapist or a close friend. Force yourself to write down all the risk factors, negatives, and things that could go wrong. No one can tell you that you are at risk; most people need to see it for themselves to give such risk factors the weight they deserve. Keeping a journal or a diary of your emotions places them somewhere, and it gives you an opportunity to think about them and manage them using your head, not just your heart.

I also advocate that people keep a calendar of emotions. Meeting someone and ruminating about them overnight may drive you to want to tell them all about those feelings the very next time you meet. Perhaps, some may be better suited to have a paper calendar on the wall. Take three to four weeks before expressing these feelings. It may be helpful to use the calendar in conjunction with a journal. Write down what you are feeling daily, note when the three to four week mark is up (or whatever time frame you calmly and cognitively designate as appropriate), and then start expressing your feelings.

I also recommend listening to your trusted loved ones. Parents, siblings, children, friends, and anyone who has your best interest in mind. These people may caution you about the dangers of the paths you are going down. They may challenge your choice of partners and worry about the speed, frequency, or risks involved in romantic relationships. Rather than shut them out, do your best to sit down with them and listen. Involve them in the journal process and even involve them in therapy sessions. You will find that they see things you do not, and that can be incredibly helpful.

Further, if you have someone in your life who is high in emophilia and has made dubious choices in the past or is currently involved in such situations, it is important to support your loved one as well. Get them to a therapist. The best way to do so is to offer to help them find one and attend sessions with them if need be. I have had several friends throughout my life who have lost everyone and everything because they chased their emotional connections, and some of those emotional connections were with undeserving people who took advantage. Many of us are tempted to walk away in disgust and shrug with a statement such as—"It's their life, whatever." While it *is* their life, and we cannot live it for them, leaving a door open for someone who may really need support is an act of true love. I have had friends come back into my life because no one else would listen. I always try to get them to a therapist and provide support, even if they are at high risk for future mistakes like the one that they are recovering from.

Among those high in emophilia who are at risk of infidelity, there are also certain strategies that one can use to avoid repeating the infidelity process. First, when you meet someone who is attractive and is making a connection with you, draw a line. Because suppressing a thought will backfire (as the famous study shows, try not thinking of a white bear, and that's all that pops into your mind), we need to acknowledge the attraction. If you acknowledge that yet do not pursue it by refusing to cross a certain line, you stand a chance of staying faithful and avoiding what could be heartbreaking consequences. There are times when a new partner may be a better choice or a new love may lead to greater happiness—that is up to the person. However, if the infidelity risk is going to be a repeat and lead to nothing positive, many would advocate avoiding it.

When I teach business ethics to my students, I often share several strategies for maintaining an ethical culture. The first thing I tell them is to follow your thoughts through to their long-term consequences. Sure, we could take this money from account A and move it to account B to hide our losses, but what if the root problem is not fixed? What if we are found out? What if this leads to further borrowing? In the end, a one-time indiscretion could cost not only bigger losses but also reputational damage, and even the company going under.

I say the same is true of meeting someone. Regardless of the situation, what is the endgame here? If it is just to have a conversation or chat, then it does not need to go further. If you exchange numbers, why? Where will this end up? Often, a one-time great conversation can and should stay just that—one time. Another procedure I often tell my students is to ask, "Would I say this out loud if the media were sitting right here?" Trade secrets aside, if the answer is no, then *why* not? What am I saying that I would not want others to hear? That is a red flag for an ethical violation. In relationships, would you leave your unlocked phone with your partner for three days while you were out of town. If not, *why* not? That is often a sign that we are going down the wrong path.

Finally, because individuals high in narcissism and other Dark Triad/Tetrad traits are ruthless, they are likely to manipulate and lie to get what they want. They also treat partners as property and will often become aggressive if you try to leave. This is when family support, therapy support, or proper involvement with law enforcement is necessary. Be safe but get away. As sad as it is, moving (even temporarily) is a great way to stay safe and get the person out of your system.

Individuals high in narcissism are especially toxic in this regard because they are so charming in first encounters. I liken the interaction with a narcissistic charmer to taking social cocaine. Because cocaine fakes dopamine, and floods your brain with it, no genuine experience (e.g., cookies, sex, success) will generate the same amount of dopamine. The trouble is, it sets up unrealistic expectations of what feeling good really means. The same is true of the narcissistic charmer. They come off so confident, so experienced, and so high potential, that most honest people will pale in comparison. However, much like cocaine in the brain, it is all artificial and does not reflect any substance. Unfortunately, after dating a few people high in narcissism may mean that a genuinely sincere person may come across as "boring" or "uninteresting" because you are used to the social cocaine of those high in narcissism.

Consequently, after a first date, we often have to decide whom to give a second one to. My personal recommendation on "giving someone a second chance" boils down to this: What were the downsides? If his abusive behavior toward the server was an issue or arrogance and interpersonal style was off-putting, then stay away. Those things are unlikely to improve with time and are most likely to get worse. However, if the person was boring, shy, or not very talkative, that is who may deserve a second chance. Often introverts may struggle with nerves or discomfort on a first date, but once they become familiar, they warm up and may end up being some of the most interesting and funny people you'll ever know!

General Conclusion

Research on emophilia is a new line of investigation that promises to bring new insights into the individual differences in speed and frequency of falling in love. For those who enjoyed this book, there are additional resources and reading that can be found on my website: www.darktriad.co.

Emophilia is an individual difference much like general personality, self-esteem, or sociosexuality. It predicts a variety of important outcomes related to relationships, workplace behaviors, legal behaviors, health behaviors, and life outcomes. Emophilia may predict real physical risks, and emophilic individuals tend to dive into romantic situations. At times, these quick decisions may be dangerous and at other times innocuous. Nevertheless, knowing that these tendencies exist empower us to inform, educate, and understand what is going on when a friend says, "I think I've found the one!"—except, we have heard that before . . .

REFERENCES

Aron, A., Aron, E. N., & Smollan, D. (1992). Inclusion of other in the self scale and the structure of interpersonal closeness. *Journal of Personality and Social Psychology, 63*(4), 596.

Aron, A., Aron, E. N., Tudor, M., & Nelson, G. (1991). Close relationships as including other in the self. *Journal of Personality and Social Psychology, 60*(2), 241.

Aron, A., Fisher, H., Mashek, D. J., Strong, G., Li, H., & Brown, L. L. (2005). Reward, motivation, and emotion systems associated with early-stage intense romantic love. *Journal of Neurophysiology, 94*(1), 327–337.

Aron, A., Paris, M., & Aron, E. N. (1995). Falling in love: Prospective studies of self-concept change. *Journal of Personality and Social Psychology, 69,* 1102–1112.

Aronson, E., & Mills, J. (1959). The effect of severity of initiation on liking for a group. *The Journal of Abnormal and Social Psychology, 59*(2), 177.

Back, M. D., Schmukle, S. C., & Egloff, B. (2010). Why are narcissists so charming at first sight? Decoding the narcissism–popularity link at zero acquaintance. *Journal of Personality and Social Psychology, 98*(1), 132.

Barta, W. D., & Kiene, S. M. (2005). Motivations for infidelity in heterosexual dating couples: The roles of gender, personality differences, and sociosexual orientation. *Journal of Social and Personal Relationships, 22*(3), 339–360.

Baumeister, R. F., & Vohs, K. D. (2004). Sexual economics: Sex as female resource for social exchange in heterosexual interactions. *Personality and Social Psychology Review, 8*(4), 339–363.

Berridge, K. C., Robinson, T. E., & Aldridge, J. W. (2009). Dissecting components of reward: "Liking," "wanting," and learning. *Current Opinion in Pharmacology, 9*(1), 65–73.

Bleske-Rechek, A. L., & Buss, D. M. (2001). Opposite-sex friendship: Sex differences and similarities in initiation, selection, and dissolution. *Personality and Social Psychology Bulletin, 27*(10), 1310–1323.

Bogaert, A. F. (2004). Asexuality: Prevalence and associated factors in a national probability sample. *Journal of Sex Research, 41*(3), 279–287.

Bowlby, J. (1982). *Attachment and loss:* Vol. 1. *Attachment.* Basic Books. (Original work published 1969)

Brehm, J. W. (1966). *A theory of psychological reactance.* Academic Press.

Brennan, K. A., Clark, C. L., & Shaver, P. R. (1998). Self-report measurement of adult attachment: An integrative overview. In J. A. Simpson & W. S. Rholes (Eds.), *Attachment theory and close relationships* (pp. 46–76). The Guilford Press.

Buckels, E. E., Jones, D. N., & Paulhus, D. L. (2013). Behavioral confirmation of everyday sadism. *Psychological science, 24*(11), 2201–2209.

Buckels, E. E., Trapnell, P. D., & Paulhus, D. L. (2014). Trolls just want to have fun. *Personality and individual Differences, 67*, 97–102.

Bushman, B. J., Bonacci, A. M., Van Dijk, M., & Baumeister, R. F. (2003). Narcissism, sexual refusal, and aggression: Testing a narcissistic reactance model of sexual coercion. *Journal of Personality and Social Psychology, 84*(5), 1027.

Buss, D. M. (1988). Love acts: The evolutionary biology of love. In R. Sternberg & M. Barnes (Eds.), *The psychology of love.* Yale University Press.

Buss, D. M. (1989). Sex differences in human mate preferences: Evolutionary hypotheses tested in 37 cultures. *Behavioral and Brain Sciences, 12*(1), 1–14.

Buss, D. M. (2006). The evolution of love. In R. J. Sternberg & K. Weis (Eds.), *The new psychology of love* (pp. 65–86). Yale University Press.

Buss, D. M. (2000). *The dangerous passion: Why jealousy is as necessary as love and sex.* Simon and Schuster.

Buss, D. M. (2009). How can evolutionary psychology successfully explain personality and individual differences? *Perspectives on Psychological Science, 4*(4), 359–366.

Buss, D. M. (2012). The evolutionary psychology of crime. *Journal of Theoretical and Philosophical Criminology, 1*, 90–98.

Buss, D. M., & Schmitt, D. P. (1993). Sexual strategies theory: An evolutionary perspective on human mating. *Psychological Review, 100*, 204–232.

Buss, D. M., & Shackelford, T. K. (1997). Susceptibility to infidelity in the first year of marriage. *Journal of Research in Personality, 31*(2), 193–221.

Camilleri, J. A., & Quinsey, V. L. (2009). Individual differences in the propensity for partner sexual coercion. *Sexual Abuse: A Journal of Research and Treatment, 21*, 111–129.

Campbell, L., Simpson, J. A., Kashy, D. A., & Fletcher, G. J. (2001). Ideal standards, the self, and flexibility of ideals in close relationships. *Personality and Social Psychology Bulletin, 27*(4), 447–462.

Campbell, W. K. (1999). Narcissism and romantic attraction. *Journal of Personality and Social Psychology, 77*(6), 1254.

Christie, R., & Geis, F. (1970). *Studies in Machiavellianism.* Academic Press.

Cleckley, H. (1941/1976). *The mask of sanity* (5th ed.). Mosby.

Cohen, J., Cohen, P., West, S. G., & Aiken, L. S. (2013). *Applied multiple regression/correlation analysis for the behavioral sciences.* Routledge.

Collins, T. J., & Gillath, O. (2012). Attachment, breakup strategies, and associated outcomes: The effects of security enhancement on the selection of breakup strategies. *Journal of Research in Personality, 46*(2), 210–222.

Collisson, B., Howell, J. L., & Harig, T. (2020). Foodie calls: When women date men for a free meal (rather than a relationship). *Social Psychological and Personality Science, 11*(3), 425–432.

De Leeuw, S. G., Kalmijn, M., & Van Gaalen, R. (2022). The dilution of parents' nonmaterial resources in stepfamilies: The role of complex sibling configurations in parental involvement. *Social Forces, 100*(4), 1671–1695.

Diamond, L. M. (2004). Emerging perspectives on distinctions between romantic love and sexual desire. *Current Directions in Psychological Science, 13*(3), 116–119.

Dickman, S. J. (1990). Functional and dysfunctional impulsivity: Personality and cognitive correlates. *Journal of Personality and Social Psychology, 58*(1), 95.

Drigotas, S. M., Safstrom, C. A., & Gentilia, T. (1999). An investment model prediction of dating infidelity. *Journal of Personality and Social Psychology, 77*(3), 509.

Dutton, D. G., & Aron, A. P. (1974). Some evidence for heightened sexual attraction under conditions of high anxiety. *Journal of Personality and Social Psychology, 30*(4), 510.

Edlund, J. E., & Sagarin, B. J. (2017). Sex differences in jealousy: A 25-year retrospective. In J. M. Olson (Ed.), *Advances in experimental social psychology* (Vol. 55, pp. 259–302). Academic Press.

Ellis, B. J. (2004). Timing of pubertal maturation in girls: An integrated life history approach. *Psychological Bulletin, 130*(6), 920.

Ellis, B. J., Shakiba, N., Adkins, D. E., & Lester, B. M. (2021). Early external-environmental and internal-health predictors of risky sexual and aggressive behavior in adolescence: An integrative approach. *Developmental Psychobiology, 63*(3), 556–571.

Eysenck H. J. (1976). *Sex and personality.* Open Books.

Festinger, L. (1957). *A theory of cognitive dissonance.* Stanford University Press.

Festinger, L., Riecken, H. W., & Schachter, S. (1956). *When prophecy fails.* University of Minnesota Press.

Figueredo, A. J., Vásquez, G., Brumbach, B. H., Sefcek, J. A., Kirsner, B. R., & Jacobs, W. J. (2005). The K-factor: Individual differences in life history strategy. *Personality and Individual Differences, 39*(8), 1349–1360.

Fincham, F. D., & May, R. W. (2017). Infidelity in romantic relationships. *Current Opinion in Psychology, 13,* 70–74.

Fisher, H. E. (1989). Evolution of human serial pairbonding. *American Journal of Physical Anthropology, 78*(3), 331–354.

Fisher, H. E. (1998). Lust, attraction, and attachment in mammalian reproduction. *Human Nature, 9,* 23–52.

Fisher, H. E., Aron, A., Mashek, D., Li, H., & Brown, L. L. (2002). Defining the brain systems of lust, romantic attraction, and attachment. *Archives of Sexual Behavior, 31,* 413–419.

Fisher, H. E., & Thomson, J. A. (2007) Lust, attraction, attachment: Do the side effects of serotonin-enhancing antidepressants jeopardize romantic love, marriage and fertility? In S. Platek, J. P. Keenan, & T. K. Shackelford (Eds.), *Evolutionary cognitive neuroscience* (pp. 245–283). MIT Press.

Fletcher, G. J. (2008). *The new science of intimate relationships.* John Wiley & Sons.

Fraley, R. C., Waller, N. G., & Brennan, K. A. (2000). An item response theory analysis of self-report measures of adult attachment. *Journal of Personality and Social Psychology, 78*(2), 350.

Frank, R. H. (1988). *Passions within reason: The strategic role of the emotions.* W. W. Norton.

Freud, S. (1914). *On narcissism: An introduction.* Hogarth Press.

Frey, D. (1986). Recent research on selective exposure to information. In. L. Berkowitz (Ed.), *Advances in experimental social psychology* (Vol. 19, pp. 41–80). Academic Press.

Gangestad, S. W., & Simpson, J. A. (2000). The evolution of human mating: Trade-offs and strategic pluralism. *Behavioral and brain sciences, 23*(4), 573–587.

Guitar, A. E., Geher, G., Kruger, D. J., Garcia, J. R., Fisher, M. L., & Fitzgerald, C. J. (2017). Defining and distinguishing sexual and emotionalsz w'1w infidelity. *Current Psychology, 36*(3), 434–446.

Hare, R. D. (1996). Psychopathy: A clinical construct whose time has come. *Criminal Justice and Behavior, 23*(1), 25–54.

Hare, R. D. (1999). *Without conscience: The disturbing world of psychopaths among us.* Guilford Press.

Hare, R. D. (2003). *The Hare psychopathy checklist* (2nd ed.). Multi-Health Systems.

Harmon-Jones, E., & Mills, J. (1999). *Cognitive dissonance: Progress on a pivotal theory in social psychology.* American Psychological Association.

Harms, P. D. (2011). Adult attachment styles in the workplace. *Human Resource Management Review, 21*(4), 285–296.

Harris, C. R. (2003). A review of sex differences in sexual jealousy, including self-report data, psychophysiological responses, interpersonal violence, and morbid jealousy. Personality and Social Psychology Review, 7(2), 102–128.

Hatfield, E., & Sprecher, S. (1986). Measuring passionate love in intimate relationships. *Journal of Adolescence, 9*(4), 383–410.

Hazan, C., & Shaver, P. (1987). Romantic love conceptualized as an attachment process. *Journal of Personality and Social Psychology, 52*, 511–524.

Hendrick, C., & Hendrick, S. (1986). A theory and method of love. *Journal of Personality and Social Psychology, 50*(2), 392.

Hendrick, C., Hendrick, S. S., & Dicke, A. (1998). The love attitudes scale: Short form. *Journal of Social and Personal Relationships, 15*(2), 147–159.

Hendrick, S., & Hendrick, C. (1987). Multidimensionality of sexual attitudes. *Journal of Sex Research, 23*(4), 502–526.

Henrich, J., Heine, S. J., & Norenzayan, A. (2010). The weirdest people in the world? *Behavioral and Brain Sciences, 33*(2–3), 61–83.

Hepper, E. G., Hart, C. M., & Sedikides, C. (2014). Moving Narcissus: Can narcissists be empathic? *Personality and Social Psychology Bulletin, 40*(9), 1079–1091.

Hilton, N. Z., Harris, G. T., & Rice, M. E. (2015). The step-father effect in child abuse: Comparing discriminative parental solicitude and antisociality. *Psychology of Violence, 5*(1), 8.

Horney, K. (1945). *Our inner conflicts.* W. W. Norton.

Hunt, M. M. (1959). *The natural history of love.* Knopf.

Jackson, J. J., & Kirkpatrick, L. A. (2007). The structure and measurement of human mating strategies: Toward a multidimensional model of sociosexuality. *Evolution and Human Behavior, 28*(6), 382–391.

Jauk, E., Neubauer, A. C., Mairunteregger, T., Pemp, S., Sieber, K. P., & Rauthmann, J. F. (2016). How alluring are dark personalities? The Dark Triad and attractiveness in speed dating. *European Journal of Personality, 30*(2), 125–138.

Jonason, P. K., Li, N. P., Webster, G. D., & Schmitt, D. P. (2009). The Dark Triad: Facilitating a short-term mating strategy in men. *European Journal of Personality, 23*(1), 5–18.

Jones, D. N. (2011). The emotional promiscuity scale. In T. D. Fisher, C. M. Davis, W. L. Yarber, & S. L. Davis (Eds.) *Handbook of Sexuality-Related Measures* (3rd ed., pp. 226–227). Routledge.

Jones, D. N. (2015). Life outcomes and relationship dispositions: The unique role of emophilia. *Personality and Individual Differences, 82*, 153–157.

Jones, D. N. (2016). The *Chasing Amy* bias in past sexual experiences: Men can change, women cannot. *Sexuality & Culture, 20*(1), 24–37.

Jones, D. N. (2017). Establishing the distinctiveness of relationship variables using the Big Five and self-esteem. *Personality and Individual Differences, 104*, 393–396.

Jones, D. N. (2019). Defining emophilia through the Emotional Promiscuity Scale. In R. Milhausen, J. Sakaluk, C.M. Davis, W.L. Yarber, T.D. Fisher (Eds.), *Handbook of Sexuality-Related Measures* (p. 436). Routledge.

Jones, D. N. & Curtis, S. R. (2017). Emophilia, sociosexuality, and anxious attachment: Approach and inhibition differences. *Personality and Individual Differences, 106*, 325–328.

Jones, D. N., & Mueller, S. M. (2022). Is Machiavellianism dead or dormant? The perils of researching a secretive construct. *Journal of Business Ethics, 176*(3), 535–549.

Jones, D. N., Olderbak, S. G., & Figueredo, A. J. (2011). The intentions towards infidelity scale. In T. D. Fisher, C. M. Davis, W. L. Yarber, & S. L. Davis (Eds.), *Handbook of Sexuality-Related Measures* (3rd ed., pp. 251–253). Routledge.

Jones, D. N., & Paulhus, D. L. (2012). The role of emotional promiscuity in unprotected sex. *Psychology & health, 27*(9), 1021–1035.

Jones, D. N., & Paulhus, D. L. (2014). Introducing the short Dark Triad (SD3) a brief measure of dark personality traits. *Assessment, 21*(1), 28–41.

Jones, D. N., & Weiser, D. A. (2014). Differential infidelity patterns among the Dark Triad. *Personality and Individual Differences, 57*, 20–24.

Kahlor, L., & Morrison, D. (2007). Television viewing and rape myth acceptance among college women. *Sex Roles, 56*(11), 729–739.

Kanazawa, S., & Still, M. C. (2000). Teaching may be hazardous to your marriage. *Evolution and Human Behavior, 21*(3), 185–190.

Karama, S., Lecours, A. R., Leroux, J. M., Bourgouin, P., Beaudoin, G., Joubert, S., & Beauregard, M. (2002). Areas of brain activation in males and females during viewing of erotic film excerpts. *Human Brain Mapping, 16*(1), 1–13.

Kelley, J. (1978). Sexual permissiveness: Evidence for a theory. *Journal of Marriage and the Family, 40*(3), 455–470.

Kenrick, D. T., Neuberg, S. L., Zierk, K. L., & Krones, J. M. (1994). Evolution and social cognition: Contrast effects as a function of sex, dominance, and physical attractiveness. *Personality and Social Psychology Bulletin, 20*(2), 210–217.

Kephart, W. M. (1967). Some correlates of romantic love. *Journal of Marriage and the Family, 29*, 470–479.

Kinsey, A. C., Pomeroy, W. P., & Martin, C. E. (1953). *Sexual behavior in the human male.* Saunders.

Kjærvik, S. L., & Bushman, B. J. (2021). The link between narcissism and aggression: A meta-analytic review. *Psychological Bulletin, 147*(5), 477–503.

Koohgard, S., Tan, L., Li, N. P., & Hashemi, M. (2024). The impact of modernization on mating strategies in Iran: A comparison across cities versus small towns. *Personality and Individual Differences, 221*, 112546.

Krizan, Z., & Herlache, A. D. (2018). The narcissism spectrum model: A synthetic view of narcissistic personality. *Personality and Social Psychology Review, 22*(1), 3–31.

Kunda, Z. (1990). The case for motivated reasoning. *Psychological Bulletin, 108*, 480–498.

Lechuga, J., & Jones, D. N. (2021). Emophilia and other predictors of attraction to individuals with Dark Triad traits. *Personality and Individual Differences*, *168*, 110318.

Lewin, K. (1943). Defining the 'field at a given time. *Psychological review*, *50*(3), 292–310.

Li, N. P., Bailey, J. M., Kenrick, D. T., & Linsenmeier, J. A. (2002). The necessities and luxuries of mate preferences: Testing the tradeoffs. *Journal of Personality and Social Psychology*, *82*(6), 947.

Lieb, K., Zanarini, M. C., Schmahl, C., Linehan, M. M., & Bohus, M. (2004). Borderline personality disorder. *The Lancet*, *364*(9432), 453–461.

Lombard, M. and Jones, M. (2015). Defining presence. In M. Lombard, F. Biocca, J. Freeman, & R. J. Schaevitz (Eds.), *Immersed in media: Telepresence theory, measurement & technology* (pp. 13–34). Springer International Publishing Switzerland.

MacArthur, R. H., & Wilson, E. O. (1967). *The theory of island biogeography*. Princeton University Press.

MacCallum, F., & Golombok, S. (2004). Children raised in fatherless families from infancy: A follow-up of children of lesbian and single heterosexual mothers at early adolescence. *Journal of Child Psychology and Psychiatry*, *45*(8), 1407–1419.

Machiavelli, N. (1513/1998). *The Prince*. University of Chicago Press.

Madsen, S. D., & Collins, W. A. (2011). The salience of adolescent romantic experiences for romantic relationship qualities in young adulthood. *Journal of Research on Adolescence*, *21*(4), 789–801.

Marazziti, D., Akiskal, H. S., Rossi, A., & Cassano, G. B. (1999). Alteration of the platelet serotonin transporter in romantic love. *Psychological Medicine*, *29*(3), 741–745.

McAndrew, F.T. (2002). New evolutionary perspectives on altruism: Multilevel selection and costly signaling theories. *Current Directions in Psychological Science*, *11*, 79–82.

McCrae, R. R., & Costa, P. T., Jr. (1999). A five-factor theory of personality. In L. Pervin & O. John (Eds.), *Handbook of personality: Theory and research* (pp. 139–153). Guilford Press.

Messick, S. (1995). Standards of validity and the validity of standards in performance asessment. *Educational Measurement: Issues and Practice*, *14*(4), 5–8.

Meston, C. M., Heiman, J. R., Trapnell, P. D., & Paulhus, D. L. (1998). Socially desirable responding and sexuality self-reports. *Journal of Sex Research*, *35*, 148–157.

Milhausen, R. R., & Herold, E. S. (1999). Does the sexual double standard still exist? Perceptions of university women. *Journal of Sex Research*, *36*(4), 361–368.

Miller, D. T., & Ross, M. (1975). Self-serving biases in the attribution of causality: Fact or fiction? *Psychological Bulletin*, *82*, 213–225.

Monroe, S. M., Rohde, P., Seeley, J. R., & Lewinsohn, P. M. (1999). Life events and depression in adolescence: Relationship loss as a prospective risk factor for first onset of major depressive disorder. *Journal of Abnormal Psychology, 108*(4), 606.

Murray, H. A. (1938). *Explorations in personality.* Oxford University Press.

Murray, S. L., & Holmes, J. G. (1997). A leap of faith? Positive illusions in romantic relationships. *Personality and Social Psychology Bulletin, 23*(6), 586–604.

Murray, S. L., Holmes, J. G., & Griffin, D. W. (1996). The self-fulfilling nature of positive illusions in romantic relationships: Love is not blind, but prescient. *Journal of Personality and Social Psychology, 71*(6), 1155.

Nadler, A., & Dotan, I. (1992). Commitment and rival attractiveness: Their effects on male and female reactions to jealousy-arousing situations. *Sex Roles, 26*, 293–310.

Neff, L. A., & Karney, B. R. (2005). To know you is to love you: The implications of global adoration and specific accuracy for marital relationships. *Journal of Personality and Social Psychology, 88*(3), 480.

Patton, J. H., Stanford, M. S., & Barratt, E. S. (1995). Factor structure of the Barratt Impulsiveness Scale. *Journal of Clinical Psychology, 51*(6), 768–774.

Paulhus, D. (1983). Sphere-specific measures of perceived control. *Journal of Personality and Social Psychology, 44*(6), 1253-1265.

Paulhus, D. L. (1984). Two-component models of socially desirable responding. *Journal of Personality and Social Psychology, 46*(3), 598.

Paulhus, D. L. (1998). Interpersonal and intrapsychic adaptiveness of trait self-enhancement: A mixed blessing?. *Journal of personality and social psychology, 74*(5), 1197–1208.

Paulhus, D. L. (2014). Toward a taxonomy of dark personalities. *Current Directions in Psychological Science, 23*(6), 421–426.

Paulhus, D. L., & Carey, J. M. (2011). The FAD–Plus: Measuring lay beliefs regarding free will and related constructs. *Journal of Personality Assessment, 93*(1), 96–104.

Paulhus, D. L., Westlake, B. G., Calvez, S. S., & Harms, P. D. (2013). Self-presentation style in job interviews: The role of personality and culture. *Journal of Applied Social Psychology, 43*(10), 2042–2059.

Paulhus, D. L., & Williams, K. M. (2002). The Dark Triad of personality: Narcissism, Machiavellianism, and psychopathy. *Journal of Research in Personality, 36*(6), 556–563.

Penke, L., & Asendorpf, J. B. (2008). Beyond global sociosexual orientations: A more differentiated look at sociosexuality and its effects on courtship and romantic relationships. *Journal of Personality and Social Psychology, 95*(5), 1113.

Pietrusewsky, M., & Douglas, M. T. (1993). Tooth ablation in old Hawai'i. *The Journal of the Polynesian Society, 102*(3), 255–272.

Pincus, A. L., Ansell, E. B., Pimentel, C. A., Cain, N. M., Wright, A. G., & Levy, K. N. (2009). Initial construction and validation of the Pathological Narcissism Inventory. *Psychological Assessment, 21*(3), 365.

Rogers, K. H., Le, M. T., Buckels, E. E., Kim, M., & Biesanz, J. C. (2018). Dispositional malevolence and impression formation: Dark Tetrad associations with accuracy and positivity in first impressions. *Journal of Personality, 86*(6), 1050–1064.

Rotter, J. B. (1966). Generalized expectancies for internal versus external control of reinforcement. *Psychological Monographs, 80* (Whole No. 609), 1–28.

Ruback, R. B., & Juieng, D. (1997). Territorial defense in parking lots: Retaliation against waiting drivers. *Journal of Applied Social Psychology, 27*(9), 821–834.

Rusbult, C. E. (1980). Commitment and satisfaction in romantic associations: A test of the investment model. *Journal of Experimental Social Psychology, 16*(2), 172–186.

Sabini, J., & Green, M. C. (2004). Emotional responses to sexual and emotional infidelity: Constants and differences across genders, samples, and methods. *Personality and Social Psychology Bulletin, 30*(11), 1375–1388.

Schmitt, D. P. (2005). Is short-term mating the maladaptive result of insecure attachment? A test of competing evolutionary perspectives. *Personality and Social Psychology Bulletin, 31*(6), 747–768.

Selterman, D., Joel, S., & Dale, V. (2023). No remorse: Sexual infidelity is not clearly linked with relationship satisfaction or well-being in Ashley Madison users. *Archives of Sexual Behavior, 52*(6), 2561–2573.

Shackelford, T. K., LeBlanc, G. J., & Drass, E. (2000). Emotional reactions to infidelity. *Cognition & Emotion, 14*(5), 643–659.

Simpson, J. A. (1990). Influence of attachment styles on romantic relationships. *Journal of Personality and Social Psychology, 59*(5), 971.

Simpson, J. A., & Gangestad, S. W. (1991). Individual differences in sociosexuality: Evidence for convergent and discriminant validity. *Journal of Personality and Social Psychology, 60*(6), 870.

Spielmann, S. S., MacDonald, G., Maxwell, J. A., Joel, S., Peragine, D., Muise, A., & Impett, E. A. (2013). Settling for less out of fear of being single. *Journal of Personality and Social Psychology, 105*(6), 1049.

Spinella, M. (2007). Normative data and a short form of the Barratt Impulsiveness Scale. *International Journal of Neuroscience, 117*(3), 359–368.

Sprecher, S., & Metts, S. (1989). Development of the Romantic Beliefs Scale and examination of the effects of gender and gender-role orientation. *Journal of Social and Personal Relationships, 6*(4), 387–411.

Sprecher, S., & Metts, S. (1999). Romantic beliefs: Their influence on relationships and patterns of change over time. *Journal of Social and Personal Relationships, 16*(6), 834–851.

Sprecher, S., Regan, P. C., McKinney, K., Maxwell, K., & Wazienski, R. (1997). Preferred level of sexual experience in a date or mate: The merger of two methodologies. *Journal of Sex Research, 34*(4), 327–337.

Sternberg, R. J. (1986). A triangular theory of love. *Psychological review, 93*(2), 119.

Swann Jr, W. B., Hixon, J. G., & De La Ronde, C. (1992). Embracing the bitter "truth": Negative self-concepts and marital commitment. *Psychological Science, 3*(2), 118–121.

Tennov, D. (1979). *Love and limerence: The experience of being in love.* Stein & Day.

Thibaut, J. W., & Kelley, H. H. (1959). *The social psychology of groups.* Wiley.

Tracy, J. L., Shaver, P. R., Albino, A. W., & Cooper, M. L. (2003). Attachment styles and adolescent sexuality. In P. Florsheim (Ed.), *Adolescent romantic relations and sexual behavior: Theory, research, and practical implications* (pp. 17–159). Lawrence Erlbaum.

Trivers, R. L. (1971). The evolution of reciprocal altruism. *The Quarterly Review of Biology, 46*(1), 35–57.

Urberg, K. A. (1992). Locus of peer influence: Social crowd and best friend. *Journal of Youth and Adolescence, 21*(4), 439–450.

Von Hippel, W., & Trivers, R. (2011). The evolution and psychology of self-deception. *Behavioral and Brain Sciences, 34*(1), 1.

Webster, G. D., & Bryan, A. (2007). Sociosexual attitudes and behaviors: Why two factors are better than one. *Journal of Research in Personality, 41*(4), 917–922.

Weeks, G. R., Gambescia, N., & Jenkins, R. E. (2003). *Treating infidelity: Therapeutic dilemmas and effective strategies.* W. W. Norton.

Wei, M., Russell, D. W., Mallinckrodt, B., & Vogel, D. L. (2007). The Experiences in Close Relationship Scale (ECR)-short form: Reliability, validity, and factor structure. *Journal of Personality Assessment, 88*(2), 187–204.

Wilson, T. D., & Gilbert, D. T. (2003). Affective forecasting. In M. P. Zanna (Ed.), *Advances in experimental social psychology* (Vol. 35, pp. 345–411). Academic Press.

Young, S. M., & Pinsky, D. (2006). Narcissism and celebrity. *Journal of Research in Personality, 40*(5), 463–471.

Zahavi, A. (1975). Mate selection: A selection for a handicap. *Journal of Theoretical Biology, 53*, 205–214.

Zuckerman, M. (1971). Dimensions of sensation seeking. *Journal of Consulting and Clinical Psychology, 36*(1), 45.

INDEX

For the benefit of digital users, indexed terms that span two pages (e.g., 52–53) may, on occasion, appear on only one of those pages.

Tables and figures are indicated by an italic *t* and *f* following the paragraph number.

abandonment
  cultural, 103–106
  fear of, 48–49
Abild, Miranda, 129–130
abuse, 8, 145, 167, 180
  domestic, 171–172, 176–180
  of drugs, 40–41
  narcissism and, 177–178
  risk of, 178–180
adam4adam, 78
addiction
  drug, 6–7, 40–41, 112
  nicotine, 100
  romantic relapse and, 100
  social influence and, 175–176
ADHD. *See* attention deficit
    hyperactivity disorder
adolescence, 13
affair partners, 86
affairs, 86
affection, 69, 131
affective forecasting, 119–120
Agape, 35–36
aggression, narcissism and, 156

agreeableness, 49–50, 101, 198
alpha press, 78–81, 133
American Pie (films), 95
amorality, 157
anger, narcissism and, 156
animals, 113–114
anterior cingulate, 121–122
antisocial behavior, 145
antisocial personalities, 152
anxiety, 121
anxious-ambivalent attachment, 38
anxious attachment, 8, 21–22, 48–50,
    74, 119, 121, 187–188
  breaking up and, 61–62
  jealousy and, 41
  needs based traits and, 37–38
Arizona, 176–177
aromanticism, 197
Aron, Arthur, 151, 188
Aronson, E., 144
artificial dopamine, 120–121
asexuality, 197
Ashley Madison (website), 78, 90
"As Long as You Love Me," 70, 74–75

Aspendorpf, Jens, 43
attachment, 37, 128, 132–133. *See also* anxious attachment
   anxious-ambivalent, 38
   avoidant, 21, 41–42, 61, 74
   breaking up and, 60–64
   insecure, 21, 38, 50–51, 64–65, 129–130
   primary figures, 39
   secure, 74
   severe issues in, 22–23
attention deficit hyperactivity disorder (ADHD), 121
attraction, 120, 122–123
   criminal, 168–170
avoidance, insecurity as, 41–42
avoidant attachment, 21, 41–42, 61, 74

Back, Mitja, 165
Backstreet Boys, 70, 74–75, 83
"bad apples," 153
badoo, 78
bad partners, 139–141
   criminal attraction and, 168–170
   Dark Triad and, 153–158
   Dark Triad and relationships, 158–165
   early investment in, 144–147
   egotism and, 165–167
   emotional intensity and, 151–153
   failing to acknowledge red flags of, 141–144
   manipulation and, 147–149
   truth not working for, 149–151
Barrett Impulsiveness Scale, 52–53
Barta, W. D., 90
basic personality, 49–50
Baumeister, Roy, 96
baya weaver bird, 198
BBPmeet, 78
Bed of Roses (film), 70, 184–185
Beethoven, Ludwig van, 82
behaviors, 43

antisocial, 145
   criminal, 23
   high-risk, 173–174
   human, 23, 37
   parasitic, 136–137
   sexual, 14
   in sociosexuality, 19–20
Benavidez, Theresa, 187–188
beta press, 78–80, 133
Bianchi, Ken, 169
bias
   cognitive, 10–11, 124, 138
   hindsight, 9–10, 28–29, 55
biased thinking, 6–7
"Big Five" personality traits, 49–50
biomarkers, of love, 14
bipolar disorder, 22–23, 121
birth control, 113
"body count," 93, 95
bonding task, 187–188
borderline personality disorder (BPD), 8, 22–23, 51–52, 64–65
Borgia, Ceaser, 104–105
Bowlby, John, 38
BPD. *See* borderline personality disorder
brain, love and sex as process in, 13–14
breaking up, 60–64
Brehm, Jack, 135
Brennan, K. A., 38–39
British Columbia, 30–31, 51–52, 69
broken promises, 106–107
Brunsvik, Anna, 82
bungee jumping, 53
Burton, Afton (Star), 170
Buss, David, 44–45, 67, 92, 102, 109–110, 113

calendar, of emotions, 206
callousness, 156
Campbell, W. K., 131
Canada, 14, 151
Capilano Suspension Bridge, 151
car analogy, for falling in love, 11

Carey, Jasmine, 72, 126
Castiglione, Baldassare, 105
casual sex, 21, 42–44, 79, 172
categorical thinking, 35
celebrities, 80–81
Chasing Amy (film), 12–13
ChatRoulette, 78
cheating, 85. *See also* infidelity
chemistry, love and, 1–2
chick-flicks, 72–73
children
  conceiving, 113
  family impact and, 192–195
  investing in, 113
  life history strategy and, 113–120
  media and, 66–67
  offspring diversification
    and, 116–118
  parent-child relationship, 134
  parenting dispositions and, 38
  rationalization for having, 111–112
China, 69
Christie, Richard, 157
Ciavera, Marylou, 149–150
Clark, C. L., 38–39
Clark, Douglas, 169
Cleckley, Hervey, 153–154
Clerks (film), 93
cliff jumping, 53, 152
cocaine, 120–121, 208
cognitive biases, 10–11, 124, 138
cognitive dissonance, 151
Cohen, Jacob, 40
Collins, W. Andrew, 13
commitment, 35–36, 130–133
  premature, 2, 26
commodity, women's sexuality as, 96
companionship, 17–18
Compton, Veronica, 169
condom use, 172
conscientiousness, 49–50, 105, 106
consummate love, 2–3, 35–36
contrast and exposure, theory of, 15
coolness, 68

Costa Rica, 68–69
costly signaling, 200–202
cougar, 78
craving, sexual, 122
criminal attraction, 168–170
criminal behavior, 23
criterion-related outcomes, 54
crushes, 18
cultural abandonment, 103–106
cultural norms, 66–67
  Beethoven and, 82
  celebrities and, 80–81
  current perceptions of love
    and, 75–76
  expressions of love and, 68–70
  historical figures and, 81–82
  life history strategy and, 115
  of passion, 68–69
  Rousseau and, 81
  summary, 83
  U.S. media and, 70–82
cultural scripts, 128–129, 134
culture, 109
  East Asian, 69
  infidelity and, 93
  popular, 71–72
  WEIRD, 67
  women's sexuality and, 96
Curtis, Shelby R., 40
cycles
  of emophilia, 6
  of violence, 143
cynical worldview, 157

"daddy issues," 8
The Dangerous Passion (Buss), 102
dangers of emophilia, 171–172
  domestic abuse and, 176–180
  drug initiation, 175–176
  love as not protection, 172–175
  selective attention to red flags
    and, 179–180
  summary, 180
Dark Tetrad, 166–167, 207

Dark Triad, 136–137, 153–158, 165–167, 175–178, 207. *See also* Machiavellianism; narcissism; psychopathy
  low targets of, 163–164
  relationships and, 158–165
Dasilva, Larry, 165
decision-making, irrational, 6–7
defense mechanisms, 142–143
depression, 22–23, 121, 198
desires, 43
developmental environment, 118–120
developmental plasticity, 115
devil's advocate, 151
diagnostic language, 35
Diamond, Lisa, 13–14, 17–18
disappearing act, for breaking up, 60–61
dispositional traits, 109
dissonance, 130–133
diversification, offspring, 116–118
divorce, 117
domestic abuse, 171–172, 176–180
dominance, 139
doomsday study, 146
The Doors (band), 70
dopamine, 120–122, 208
Drigotas, Stephen, 89
drugs, 174, 180
  abuse of, 40–41
  addiction, 6–7, 40–41, 112
  cocaine, 120–121, 208
  initiation, 171–172, 175–176
Dutton, Donald, 151
dysfunctional impulsivity, 52–53

early investment, 144–147
East Asian cultures, 69
ECR scale. *See* Experiences in Close Relationships
ego, infidelity and, 97–98
egotism, 139, 155, 165–167
eharmony, 78

elephants, 114
Elimidate (TV show), 96–97
Ellis, Bruce, 115, 117
emophilia. *See also specific topics*
  assessment of, 29
  basic personality and, 49–50
  byproducts of, 29
  cognitive biases and, 10–11
  cycles of, 6
  defined, 2–4
  defining as theoretical concept, 43–49
  developmental environment and, 118–120
  fading intent and, 110–112
  impulsivity and, 52–54
  as individual difference, 8–10
  infidelity and, 90–91
  jealousy and, 102–103
  life history strategy and, 113–120
  love experienced differently in, 35–36
  measuring, 30–35
  mental health, 8
  nature of, 9
  neurobiology of love and, 120–122
  as not borderline personality disorder, 51–52
  as not good or bad, 6–7
  as not "love at first sight," 11–12
  as not mental disorder, 35
  offspring diversification and, 116–118
  as "real" love happening faster, 12–15
  related concepts to, 37–41
  self-esteem and, 50–51
  sociosexuality combined with, 64
  spotting, 22–27
  summary, 64–65
  walking away from marital engagements, 59–60
emophilia research, 190
  conclusion, 208–209

emophilia research (*Continued*)
  costly signaling, 200–202
  future applications of, 203
  high school romance and, 191
  impact on family, 192–195
  joys, warnings, and risks, 204–208
  leaving someone and why, 199
  life stages and, 202–203
  low, 196–199
  partners as completing each
    other, 199–200
  risks and, 204–208
Emophilia Scale (EP Scale), 30–32,
    31*t*, 40, 46, 102, 203
  breaking up and, 61–62
  histogram and distribution curve
    of, 33*f*
  kurtosis of, 34
  scoring, 32
  self-deception and, 58–59
  skew of, 34
emotional disturbances, 50–51
"emotional flailing," BPD as, 51–52
emotional impulsivity, 24–25
emotional infidelity, 20–21, 86–87,
    92, 107
emotional intensity, 151–153
emotional intimacy, 14
emotional needs, 101
emotional penetration, 12–13, 17
emotional promiscuity, 3
emotional regulation, 121
emotional restriction, 20
emotional stability, 121
emotions
  calendar of, 206
  rush of, 10
empathy, 150, 153–154
ended relationships, moving past, 2
endocrine system changes, 202–203
endogenous dopamine, 120–121
"the ends justify the means," 156–157
EP Scale. *See* Emophilia Scale
equilibrium, 130

Eros, 35–36
Estrada, Roger, 187–189
evolutionary adaptations, 44–45
evolutionary biology, 93
evolutionary theory, 48–49, 108–109,
    111–112
excitement, 152–153
Experiences in Close Relationships
    (ECR scale), 38–39, 62
expressions of love, cultural, 68–70
external locus of control, 127
extradyadic involvement, 85
extraversion, 8–9, 19, 49–50, 54, 198
Eysenck, Hans, 19, 54

Facebook, 78
fading intent, 110–112
FAD-Plus, 126–127
false alibi testimony, 186–189
family, impact on, 192–195
fantasy, 43
  in sociosexuality, 19–20
fatalistic determinism, 126
fate, free will *versus*, 126–128
father absence, 118–119
fear, 152
  of abandonment, 48–49
  of rejection, 41–42
fear of being single (FoBS), 39, 48–49
fertilization, 92
Festinger, Leon, 144–145
fidelity, 85. *See also* infidelity
Figueredo, A. J., 102
film, 67
  American Pie, 95
  Bed of Roses, 70, 184–185
  Chasing Amy, 12–13
  chick-flicks, 72–73
  Clerks, 93
  Good Will Hunting, 2–3
  The Little Mermaid, 71–72
  The Matrix, 17
  Super Troopers, 185
first sexual intercourse, 118

Fisher, Helen, 117, 122
FoBS. *See* fear of being single
foodie calls, 136
forgiveness, 129–130
fragility, 155
free will, fate *versus*, 126–128
frequency
    in falling in love, 7, 11
    of sexual encounters, 19
    of sexual permissiveness, 45
Freud, Sigmund, 77–78, 82, 142–143,
    155
Frey, Dieter, 146
friends and friendship, 131
    concerns of, 5–6
    "just friends," 48–49
    platonic, 13–14
fulfillment, 2
functional impulsivity, 52–53

"Gainesville Ripper" (Danny
    Rolling), 168
Gallup, 90–91
Gangestad, Steve, 19–20, 42–43
Geis, Florence, 157
gender. *See also* men; women
    identities, 44–45
    of professors and students falling in
    love, 16
genuine conversation, for breaking
    up, 60–61
Gin Blossoms (band), 74
Gonzaga, Elizabetta, 104–105
Good Will Hunting (film), 2–3
grandiose individuals, 170
Greek society, 75
groupies, for serial killers, 168–169
guilt, 153–154

half-life, of love, 112
*Handbook of Sexuality-Related
    Measures*, 31
"Happy Philanderers," extraverts
    as, 54

"hard to get," playing, 185
Hare, Robert, 154–155
harming others, 181–186
    false alibi testimony and, 186–189
Harris, Christine, 87
Hazan, C., 39
Hendrick, Clyde, 19
Hendrick, Susan, 19
high-risk behaviors, 173–174
high school romance, 191
high sex drive, 14
hindsight bias, 9–10, 28–29, 55
Hippel, William von, 58
historical figures, 81–82
holding hands, 89
Holmes, J. G., 125
homelessness, 192
"hopeless romantic," 67
Horney, Karen, 38
Hosch, Harmon, 187
human behavior, 23, 37
Hunt, Morton, 75–76, 104–105
hypervigilance, 41

idealization, 167
identities, gender, 44–45
"if you were me" game, 150
"I Knew I Loved You," 74–75
illusions, positive, 125–126
impression management, 58–59
impulse control, 23, 53
impulsivity, 52–54
    dysfunctional, 52–53
    emotional, 24–25
    functional, 52–53
    motor, 52–53
inattention, 52–53
infatuation, 18
infidelity, 54–55, 84–86, 206–207
    broken promises and, 106–107
    defining, 87–92
    ego and, 97–98
    emotional, 20–21, 86–87, 92, 107
    emotional needs and, 101

infidelity (*Continued*)
  forgiveness and, 129–130
  jealousy and, 102–103
  knowing partner's past and, 95–97
  monogamish or cultural
    abandonment, 103–106
  partner's sexual and emotional
    history and, 93–95
  polyamory and, 98–100
  predicting, 85
  self-deception and, 88
  sexual, 86–87, 90–93
  sociosexuality *versus* emophilic
    tendencies toward, 92–93
information acquisition and
  distortion, 146
insecure attachment, 21, 38, 50–51,
  64–65, 129–130
insecurity, 136–137
  as avoidance, 41–42
Instagram, 78
intent, fading, 110–112
Intentions Toward Infidelity Scale
  (ITIS), 102
internal locus of control, 127
interpersonal locus of control, 127
intimacy, 35–36
  emotional, 14
  physical, 14
  sexual, 12
intimate secrets, sharing, 87–89
investment
  early, 144–147
  long-term, 111
  overinvestment, 26
  premature, 130–133
investment model
  perspective, 132–133
irrational decision-making, 6–7
irrational mindset, 109
ITIS. *See* Intentions Toward Infidelity
  Scale
"it's not you, it's me," 60–61

Jackson, Jenee, 42–43
Jdate, 78
jealousy, 5–6, 41, 102–103, 110
Jesperson, Keith, 168
jewelry, 200–201
Jonason, Peter, 158
Jones, Matthew, 73–74
Journal of Personality Assessment, 126
Judge Judy (TV show), 136
"just friends," 48–49

Kanazawa, 15
Karandikar, Sampada, 168
Karney, Benjamin, 125
Kendrick, 15
Kephart, William, 18
Kiene, S. M., 90
Kinsey, A. C., 42
Kirkpatrick, Lee, 42–43
Kunda, Ziva, 146
kurtosis, of EP Scale, 34

Lavalife, 78
Lechuga, Jacqueline, 159–160
Lester, David, 191
Leviev, Simon ("Tinder
  Swindler"), 4–5
Lewin, Kurt, 23, 202
lie detection, 58
life history strategy, 113–120
life narratives, 1–2
life outcomes, 2, 55–58
life satisfaction, 2
life stages, 202–203
likelihood, of falling in love, 47*f*, 47
limerence, 17–18
Lioy, Doreen, 169–170
The Little Mermaid (film), 71–72
locus of control, 127–128
Lombard, Matthew, 73–74
London, Sondra, 168–169
long-term investment, 111
long-term monogamy, 46–47
long-term orientation scale, 42–43

long-term relationships, 112, 122
lost love, 1–2
Louden, Jennifer Eno, 175–176
love. *See also specific topics*
  biomarkers of, 14
  as brain process, 13–14
  cultural expressions of, 68–70
  current perceptions of, 75–76
  defining, 2–3
  emophilia as experienced
    differently, 35–36
  half-life of, 112
  as human universal, 69
  knowing we are in, 17–19
  as lasting, 19–22
  limited understanding of
    nature, 16–17
  lost, 1–2
  neurobiology of, 120–122
  as not protection, 172–175
  premature, 166
  romantic, 17–18, 110
  serotonin and, 121–122
  true, 18
love at first sight, 9–12, 71
love bombing, 167
love drive, 122–123
love interests, multiple, 111
love letters, 181–182
low emophilia, 196–199
low self-esteem, 131–132, 136–137,
  155, 179
Ludus, 35–36, 91–92
Luvox, 121

Machiavellianism, 136–137, 156–160
Machiavelli, Niccolò, 156–157
Madsen, Stephanie, 13
Mania, 35–36
manipulation, 4–5, 60, 147–149, 157,
  158
manipulative individuals, 25–26,
  98–99
Manson, Charles, 170

marital engagements, walking away
  from, 59–60
marriage
  proposals, 96–97
  starter, 199
The Mask of Sanity
  (Cleckley), 153–154
masochism, 179
Massey, Ruth, 187–188
masturbation, 14
Match.com, 78
mate display, 152
The Matrix (film), 17
media, 66–67
  popular, 184–185
  U.S., 70–82
medium-term relationships, 122
men, 56
  infidelity and, 92
  more sexual partners desired by, 45
  partner's past and, 96
  Romantic Beliefs Scale and, 72
  sexual and emotional history of, 94
  younger women and, 67
mental associations, 124
mental disorder, emophilia as not, 35
mental health, 8, 150
"meso-limbic" region, 120–121
Messick, Samuel, 31
Meston, Cindy, 14
Metts, S., 72
Mexican Americans, 33
Mexican Nationals, 33
Mexico, 115
mid-adolescence, 13
Mills, J., 144
mistresses, 86
money loaning, 137
monogamish, 103–106
monogamy, 17
  long-term, 46–47
  serial, 117, 133
Montefeltro, Guidobaldo di (Duke of
  Urbino), 104–105

mother absence, 119
motivation, 146
motor impulsiveness, 52–53
MSOI. *See* Multi-Dimensional
    Sociosexuality Orientation
    Inventory
Mueller, Steven, 120
Multi-Dimensional Sociosexual-
    ity Orientation Inventory
    (MSOI), 42–43
Murray, S. L., 125
music, 67

narcissism, 131, 136–137, 155–156,
    158, 165–166, 170, 205, 208
    abuse and, 177–178
    self-deception and, 156
    targets, 161
Narcissus (Greek character), 155
The Natural History of Love
    (Hunt), 75
Nebraska, 29
"need for mystery," 72
need process, want processes *versus*, 40
Neff, Lisa, 125
Neria, Adon, 187
neurobiology, of love, 120–122
neuroticism, 49–50
Nevada, 203
nicotine addiction, 100
nonplanfulness, 52–53

obsessive-compulsive disorder
    (OCD), 121–122
offspring diversification, 116–118
OKCupid, 78
Olderbak, Sally, 102
one-night stands, 19–20, 172
online temptations, 133
openness to experience, 49–50
optimism, unrealistic, 24–25
oral sex, 93
over-benefiting, 131
overconfidence, 155

overconfident individuals, 25–26
overinvestment, 26
oysters, 113–114

parasitic behaviors, 136–137
parenting dispositions, 38
parents
    parent-child relationship, 134
    stepparents, 193
partners. *See also* bad partners
    affair, 86
    as completing each other, 199–200
    mistreatment of, 176–180
    past of, 95–97
    struggling to find, 196–199
passion, 17–18, 35–36
    cultural norms of, 68–69
    fading, 26
Paulhus, Del, 30–31, 58–59, 116, 126,
    153, 165–166, 173–174
    on locus of control, 127
    SD3 and, 159–160
PCL-R. *See* Psychopathy
    Checklist-Revised
Penke, Lars, 43
permanent abandonment, 48–49
persistence, 185
personality
    assessment, 44–45
    basic, 49–50
    "Big Five" traits, 49–50
    frequent sexual encounters, 19
    heritable traits of, 108–109
    psychology, 30–31
    subclinical, 153
Personality and Individual Differences
    (journal), 50
personality types, 6–7
perspective-taking, 150
physical intimacy, 14
physical penetration, 12–13
physiological reactions, to love, 14
Pinsky, D., 155
platonic friendships, 13–14

players, 98–99
Plentyoffish, 78
polyamory, 12, 98–100
Ponzi scheme, 4–5
popular culture, 71–72
popular media, 184–185
positive illusions, 125–126
possession, 167
power dynamics, 15–17
Pragma, 35–36
predatory individuals, 194
pregnancy, unwanted, 171–172
premature commitments, 2, 26
premature investment, 130–133
premature love, 166
premature promises, 26
premature trust, 103, 143, 171–172, 203
presence, 73–74
Presley, Elvis, 126
press
    alpha, 78–81
    beta, 78–80, 133
primary attachment figures, 39
Princeton University, 146
professors, falling in love with students, 15–16
promises
    broken, 106–107
    premature, 26
protection
    love as not, 172–175
    sexual, 171–172
    unprotected sex, 172–173
Prozac, 121
psychological reactance, 134–136
psychological trauma, 171–172
psychological validation, 50–51
psychology, 37
    personality, 30–31
    WEIRD cultures and, 67
Psychology & Health (journal), 173–174
psychometric scales, 31

psychopathology, 23–24, 153–155, 162–163
psychopathy, 23, 136–137
Psychopathy Checklist-Revised (PCL-R), 154
psychoticism, 19, 54
puppy love, 18

rabbits, 113–114
Ramirez, Richard, 169–170
rationalization, 77–78
reactance, psychological, 134–136
recklessness, 139
red flags, 2, 179, 207
    failing to acknowledge, 141–144
    ignoring, 25
    selective attention to, 179–180
red, orange, yellow, green, blue, indigo, and violet (ROY G BIV) analogy, 49–50
rejection, fear of, 41–42
relationships, 2
repression, 77–78
reproduction. *See* children
retrograde cravings, 100
reward-based processes, 40
Rimes, LeAnn, 74
risk, 204–208
    of abuse, 178–180
    high-risk behaviors, 173–174
rock climbing, 53
Rogers, Kate, 165
Rolling, Danny ("Gainesville Ripper"), 168
Romantic Beliefs Scale, 67, 72
romantic fidelity, 85
romantic film market, 73
romantic love, 17–18, 110
romantic motives, 15–17
romantic relapse, 100
Romeo and Juliet (Shakespeare), 71, 83
rose-colored glasses, 125
Rousseau, Jean-Jacques, 81

ROY G BIV (red, orange, yellow, green, blue, indigo, and violet) analogy, 49–50
"Rule of 3," 95
Rusbult, Caryl, 132
rush, of emotions, 10
Rutgers University, 142

sadism, 168
satisfaction, 132–133
Savage, Dan, 10, 75
Savage Garden, 74–75
scams, 204
Schaefer, Gerard, 168
Schmitt, David, 44–45, 50–51, 113
scientific causation, 126
scientific truth, 72
SD3. See Short Dark Triad
secrets, sharing intimate, 87–89
secure attachment, 74
security, sense of, 37–38
selective attention, to red flags, 179–180
selective serotonin reuptake inhibitors (SSRIs), 121–123
self-aggrandizement, 155
self-beliefs, 131–132
self-centered thinking, 150
self-deception, 65, 107, 110–111, 129, 166, 193
    costly signaling and, 201
    EP Scale and, 58–59
    infidelity and, 88
    narcissism and, 156
    red flags and, 142–143
self-enhancement, 58–59
self-esteem, 50–51
    low, 131–132, 136–137, 155, 179
    sociosexuality and, 50–51
self-interest, 186–187
selfishness, 91–92
self-reflection, 10
self-reporting, 31
Selterman, D., 90

sensation seeking, 8–9, 53
serial killers, 168–170
serial monogamy, 117, 133
serotonin, 121–122. See also selective serotonin reuptake inhibitors
seven-year itch, 117
sex. See also sociosexuality
    as brain process, 13–14
    casual, 21, 42–44, 79, 172
    frequent encounters, 19
    oral, 93
    physical intimacy and, 14
    psychological validation and, 50–51
    unprotected, 172–173
sex drive, 120, 122–123
    high, 14
sexism, 97
sexual behavior, 14
sexual craving, 122
sexual dissatisfaction, 104
sexual energy, 82
sexual fidelity, 85
sexual harassment, 15, 185–186
sexual infidelity, 86–87, 90–93
sexual intercourse, first, 118
sexual intimacy, 12
Sexuality and Culture (journal), 96
sexually transmitted infections (STIs), 96, 171–174, 179
sexual motives, 15–17
sexual permissiveness, 20–21, 44–45, 79, 90. See also sociosexuality
sexual protection, 171–172
sexual shame, 76
sexual strategies theory (SST), 44–45
Shakespeare, William, 71, 83, 188
shame, 76
    sexual, 76
Shaver, P. R., 38–39
Shinelan, Judy, 136
Short Dark Triad (SD3), 159–160
short-term relationships, 112
short-term thinking, 54

Simon, Carly, 74
Simpson, Jeffrey, 19–20, 42–43
sincerity, costly signaling and, 201
singleness. *See* fear of being single
skew, of EP Scale, 34
skydiving, 53
Smith, Kevin, 12–13, 93, 94
smoking, 100, 175–176
Snapchat, 78
social exchange theory, 130
social interaction, 50
socialization, infidelity and, 93
social role expectations, 136
Society for Personality and Social
    Psychology, 108–109
sociopolitical locus of control, 127
sociosexuality, 21, 37, 42–43, 90–91,
    118–119, 159–160
    emophilia combined with, 64
    emophilic tendencies toward
        infidelity *versus*, 92–93
    Ludus and, 35–36
    self-esteem and, 50–51
    unrestricted, 19–20, 63, 64, 194
Sociosexual Orientation Inventory
    (SOI), 19–20, 42–43
SOI. *See* Sociosexual Orientation
    Inventory
South Korea, 69
speed
    in falling in love, 7, 11
    of sexual permissiveness, 45
Sprecher, Susan, 72, 95
SSRIs. *See* selective serotonin reuptake
    inhibitors
SST. *See* sexual strategies theory
stalking, 181–182
standard deviations, 34
starter marriage, 199
stealing, 140
stepparents, 193
sterilization techniques, 113
Sternberg, Robert, 2–3, 35–36
Still, 15

STIs. *See* sexually transmitted
    infections
Stockton University, 133, 191
Storge, 35–36
students, professors falling in love
    with, 15–16
subclinical personality, 153
sublimation, 82
suicidal thoughts, 198
suicide, 191
Super Troopers (film), 185
Swann, Bill, 131–132

Taiwan, 67, 69, 115
"talk is cheap," 59–60
"tanking," 76
teenage dating, 191
teeth, 200–201
temptations, online, 133
Texas, 29–30, 175–176
"That's the Way I've Always Heard It
    Should Be," 74
theft, 140
A Theory of Cognitive Dissonance
    (Festinger), 144
therapy, 150
thinking
    biased, 6–7
    categorical, 35
    self-centered, 150
    short-term, 54
Thomson, J. A., 122
threats, vigilance to, 40
thrill-seeking, 151
"Till I Hear It from You," 74
Tinder, 78–79, 133, 136
"Tinder Swindler" (Simon
    Leviev), 4–5
Tonic (band), 133
Tracy, Jessica, 39
trauma
    bonding, 151–152
    psychological, 171–172
Treating Infidelity (Weeks), 88

Trivers, Robert, 58, 142
true love, 18
"Truly, Madly, Deeply," 75
trust, 6–7
    premature, 103, 143, 171–172, 203
    trustworthiness, 164
tunnel vision, 24–25
Twitter, 78

UBC. *See* University of British
    Columbia
under-benefiting, 131
unfaithfulness, 85, 87–88
United States (U.S.)
    life history strategy and, 115
    media in, 70–82
University of Arizona, 176–177
University of British Columbia
    (UBC), 30–31, 51–52, 69
University of Nebraska, Lincoln, 29
University of Nevada, Reno, 203
University of Texas, El Paso, 29–30,
    175–176
University of Utah, 115
unprotected sex, 172–173
unrealistic optimism, 24–25
unrestricted sociosexuality, 19–20,
    63, 64, 194
unwanted pregnancy, 171–172
Urberg, Katherine, 175–176
Urbino, Duke of. *See* Montefeltro,
    Guidobaldo di
Utah, 115

violence, cycle of, 143
virginity, 12–13, 76

Vohs, Kathleen, 96
vulnerability, 6–7, 155, 197

want processes, need processes
    versus, 40
warning signs. *See also* red flags
    ignoring, 25
wedding planning, 60
Weeks, G. R., 88
WEIRD (Western, educated, indus-
    trialized, rich, and democratic)
    cultures, 67
Weiser, Dana, 3, 87–88
Western, educated, industrialized,
    rich, and democratic (WEIRD)
    cultures, 67
White Americans, 33
A Winter's Tale (Shakespeare), 188
Without Conscience (Hare), 154
women, 56–58
    divorce for, 117
    infidelity and, 92
    partner's past and, 96
    Romantic Beliefs Scale and, 72
    sexual and emotional history of, 94
    sexuality of, 96
    younger, 67
Wood, James, 175–176
"wrong number" scams, 204

Yahoo personals, 78
younger women, 67
Young, S. M., 155

Zoloft, 121
Zoosk, 78